CAN A
'HISTORY OF ISRAEL'
BE WRITTEN?

CAN A 'HISTORY OF ISRAEL' BE WRITTEN?

edited by

LESTER L. GRABBE

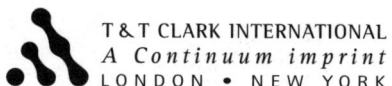

T & T CLARK INTERNATIONAL
A Continuum imprint
LONDON • NEW YORK

Published by T&T Clark International
A Continuum imprint
The Tower Building, 11 York Road, London SE1 7NX
15 East 26th Street, Suite 1703, New York, NY 10010

www.tandtclark.com

Copyright © 1997 Sheffield Academic Press
First published as JSOTS 245/European Seminar in Historical Methodology 1
by Sheffield Academic Press
This edition published 2004

British Library Cataloguing-in-Publication Data
A catalogue record for this book is available from the British Library

ISBN 0567043207 (paperback)

Typeset by Sheffield Academic Press
Printed on acid-free paper in Great Britain by Cromwell Press Ltd, Trowbridge,
Wilts

CONTENTS

ABBREVIATIONS

AB	Anchor Bible
ABD	D.N. Freedman (ed.), *Anchor Bible Dictionary*
ANET	J.B. Pritchard (ed.), *Ancient Near Eastern Texts*
AOAT	Alter Orient und Altes Testament
ATD	Das Alte Testament Deutsch
AUSS	*Andrews University Seminary Studies*
BA	*Biblical Archaeologist*
BARev	*Biblical Archaeology Review*
BASOR	*Bulletin of the American Schools of Oriental Research*
BETL	Bibliotheca ephemeridum theologicarum lovaniensium
BHT	Beiträge zur historischen Theologie
BibOr	Biblica et orientalia
BZAW	Beihefte zur *ZAW*
CBQ	*Catholic Biblical Quarterly*
FRLANT	Forschungen zur Religion und Literatur des Alten und Neuen Testaments
HALAT	W. Baumgartner *et al.*, *Hebräisches und aramäisches Lexikon zum Alten Testament*
HAT	Handbuch zum Alten Testament
HSM	Harvard semitic Monographs
HTR	*Harvard Theological Review*
IEJ	*Israel Exploration Journal*
JBL	*Journal of Biblical Literature*
JJS	*Journal of Jewish Studies*
JNES	*Journal of Near Eastern Studies*
JNSL	*Journal of Northwest Semitic Languages*
JSJ	*Journal for the Study of Judaism*
JSOT	*Journal for the Study of the Old Testament*
JSOTSup	*Journal for the Study of the Old Testament*, Supplement Series
JSS	*Journal of Semitic Studies*
LCL	Leob Classical Library
OBO	Orbis biblicus et orientalis
OrAnt	*Oriens antiquus*
OBT	Overtures to Biblical Theology
OTL	Old Testament Library
PEQ	*Palestine Exploration Quarterly*

SBL	Society of Biblical Literature
Sem	*Semitica*
SJOT	*Scandinavian Journal of the Old Testament*
SPB	Studia postbiblica
ST	*Studia theologica*
SWBA	The Social World of Biblical Antiquity
TRu	*Theologische Rundschau*
TZ	*Theologische Zeitschrift*
UF	*Ugarit-Forschungen*
VT	*Vetus Testamentun*
VTSup	*Vetus Testamentum*, Supplements
WBC	Word Biblical Commentary
WMANT	Wissenschaftliche Monographien zum Alten und Neuen Testament
ZAW	*Zeitschrift für die alttestamentliche Wissenschaft*

LIST OF CONTRIBUTORS

Hans M. Barstad is Professor of Biblical Studies at the University of Oslo, Norway

Bob Becking is Professor of Old Testament Studies at the University of Utrecht, The Netherlands

Robert P. Carroll is Professor of Old Testament at the University of Glasgow, UK

Philip R. Davies is Professor of Biblical Studies at the University of Sheffield, UK

Lester L. Grabbe is Professor of Hebrew Bible and Early Judaism at the University of Hull, UK

Niels Peter Lemche is Professor of Theology at the University of Copenhagen, Denmark

Herbert Niehr is Professor of Biblical Introduction and History of the Biblical Period at the University of Tübingen, Germany

Thomas L. Thompson is Professor of Theology at the University of Copenhagen, Denmark

INTRODUCTION

Lester L. Grabbe

In July 1996 the European Seminar on Methodology in Israel's History had its inaugural meeting in Dublin. Although it met under the aegis of the Society of Biblical Literature International Meeting, it is an independent working group made up of members from a variety of European countries. The group originates from the frustrations that I, for one, have felt over the current state of the debate about how to write the history of ancient Israel and Judah in the second and first millennia BCE and into the first century or so of the Common Era.

In the past several years, a number of scholars—most of them European by origin or adoption—have been making a radical attack on the way the history of 'Israel' has been written. Even those once regarded as radical have not escaped the critique. This has been a minority movement and at first made only a measured impact on the debate. Recently, however, it has come into its own, but one reponse has been the raising of voices in protest, including the suggestion that such trends are dangerous or can be safely ignored or—rather curiously—even both of these at once.

Unfortunately, in such a heated atmosphere a genuine debate is often replaced by polemics, apologetics and the building of academic bunkers. This is not necessarily all bad—it can even be a lot of fun—but it struck me that we had reached the point where more heat than light was being generated. This suggested that the time was ripe for something more organized to address the central issues in a systematic manner and to determine what the real positions and problems are. Agreement is not necessary, but it is important to understand one another. Assaults on straw soldiers does not win any battles in the end. The type of organization to tackle this task seemed crucial. It needed several elements if it hoped to succeed and have the desired impact in international biblical scholarship.

Since much of the work was being done in Europe, it seemed best to begin here. Therefore, the initial task was to bring together European specialists who are broadly in agreement that a problem actually exists. In other words, what was important was not a particular position on the subject but an ability to talk to one another. It would not help to bring together a group of people who thought there was no problem or whose views were so different that dialogue was impossible. Therefore, although no attempt was made to seek to impose a particular view-point on the group, participating scholars would need to share a common view about some of the main problems with past approaches and sufficient sympathy toward the radical questioning currently going on to engage in serious debate on the subject. Membership was by invitation and currently includes the following:

Rainer Albertz (Germany)
Hans Barstad (Norway)
Bob Becking (Netherlands)
Robert Carroll (UK)
Philip Davies (UK)
Josette Elayi (France)
Lester Grabbe (UK)
Ulrich Hübner (Germany)
Knud Jeppesen (Denmark)
Axel Knauf-Belleri (Switzerland)
Niels Peter Lemche (Denmark)
Mario Liverani (Italy)
Andrew Mayes (Ireland)
Hans-Peter Müller (Germany)
Herbert Niehr (Germany)
Michael Niemann (Germany)
Ed Noort (Netherlands)
Thomas Thompson (Denmark)
Helga Weippert (Germany)
Manfred Weippert (Germany)
Keith Whitelam (UK)

Even defining the subject of the Seminar has not been a simple task. The general area is the one traditionally going under the name 'history of ancient Israel', but even the use of this term already raises many problems. The charged atmosphere of current Middle Eastern politics unfortunately makes many terms offensive to some section or other, even of the scholarly community. This includes terms such as 'Palestine', 'Israel', 'land of Israel' and even 'Judah'. To speak of 'history of Israel' already begs some questions, in the opinion of some. On the other hand, avoidance of the traditional phrase is already taken as a slogan by others.

In the interests of discussion, the term 'Israel's history' is used in relation to the Seminar's work simply to define the subject of discussion as having at its core a long-standing and widely familiar academic discipline. Indeed, the phrase can be understood as being in quotation marks. In formal terms, the Seminar is concerned with the history of the peoples in Syria, Lebanon, Palestine (a purely geographical term, with no implications whatsoever for modern politics of the Middle East) and Transjordan. Thomas Thompson's term is the South Levant; Niels Peter Lemche prefers 'Greater Syria', to include even a portion of southern Anatolia. This scope naturally includes the ancient kingdoms of Israel and Judah but is not confined to them. In chronological terms it covers the period from approximately 2000 BCE to about 150 CE, including what are traditionally referred to as the First and Second Temple periods of Israelite and Judaean history.

The Seminar is intended to be a serious working group, not just a loose SBL-type section for all and sundry to read papers. On the other hand, it differs from some of the tightly structured seminars also known in SBL, such as the Jesus or Q seminars that attempt to produce a single and agreed output (if perhaps a composite one). We could not and should not hope to speak with one voice. A genuine dialogue needs to be carried on. Therefore, our initial format is to read, respond to and critique papers focused on particular issues or themes. This first meeting, however, was devoted to position papers. All papers addressed in some fashion or other the two following questions: Can a 'history of Israel' be written and if so, how? What place does the text of the Old Testament/Hebrew Bible have in the matter?

In preparation for the first meeting, I circulated a copy of my paper to members of the Seminar. They were free to react to it or ignore it as they saw fit. In it I was drawing on my own experience in trying to write history. My experience has been mainly with the Second Temple period, but there are some who would argue that when we use the Old Testament as a source, we are dealing with the Second Temple anyway.

My basic conclusions are the following: (1) on the question of whether we can write a history of ancient Syria-Palestine-Israel, my answer is yes—in the sense that we can write a history of any society for which we have some information, including prehistoric societies. Also, the basic task of historians of ancient Palestine and/or of ancient Israel is not different from that of historians of other periods. (2) In writing such a history, the biblical text can and must be used. (3) The difficulties of using the biblical text should not, however, be under-estimated. The use of the text needs to be argued for in each case, not just accepted without further comment. (4) The various types of sources need to be evaluated each in its own right before attempting a synthesis. Far too often we have seen supposed accounts of the archaeo-logy that mixed textual and other data so promiscuously that it was impossible to tell what had actually been found in the ground. Synthesis and reconstruction should come about only after a careful analysis of each source in its own right. (5) An effort should be made to indicate the probabilities of any reconstruction. There is nothing wrong with speculation and imaginative reconstruction, but this should be admitted and clearly labelled.

I argued in my paper that our goal as historians is to find out 'what actually happened'. I emphasize that this is our *goal*—that does not mean that we are necessarily able to reach that goal. In many periods of history, we do not have enough information to come to many certain conclusions. Our reconstructions may be tentative at best; our actual work will be relativistic (though we would not be doing reconstructions in the first place if we did not have a positivistic goal). In that case, the historian is probably best described as a juggler. The secret is to keep as many balls as possible in the air at once but without dropping any.

Only one participant took up the offer to respond directly to my paper, though this was only in a verbal statement not published here; however, several others seem to make reference to it indirectly. A number of the contributors addressed the basic questions asked by dealing with specific examples or topics that served as a vehicle to make comments on the questions. The following summaries can only be a rough guide for the convenience of readers and in no way deal ade-quately with the careful and often subtlely nuanced arguments of the papers themselves. More details, including the interaction of the parti-cipants in the discussion, are found in the concluding essay, 'Reflections on the Discussion'.

Hans M. Barstad tackled the vital question of developments in the field of historiographical study in general, and many will find his survey and bibliography immensely useful. It is now widely recognized among many historians that new thinking from a variety of viewpoints makes a fundamental attack on the old ways of doing history. Some would even see an end to history, but most historians have not taken that route. Nevertheless, the crisis is even more dramatic in Israelite historiography. There are dangers in biblical scholars embracing too quickly some recent trends in history writing (e.g., the *Annales* school). In the end, even 'the minimalists' have not achieved a paradigm shift but are still in the tradition of nineteenth-century historiography. On the specific questions asked, Professor Barstad argues that a history of Israel can be written in some sense, and that the biblical text has a place in that writing. But he comes to this conclusion in large part by pointing to a new view of historical truth that replaces traditional analytical history with narrative history.

Bob Becking tackles three questions: (1) What is meant by 'Israel'? (2) What is meant by 'history writing'? (3) How is the Old Testament text to be used as a historical source? On the first question, confusion arises when Israel is treated as a political or ethnic term; however, if Israel is taken as a geographical entity, it is possible to deal with the question of writing its history. The second question is more difficult. Huizinga's famous dictum is not as helpful as might appear on the surface. Collingwood provides a more solid foundation on which to build. The rest of the paper is devoted to the third question, using the Gedaliah incident (2 Kgs 25.22-26; Jer. 40.7–41.15) to illustrate the problem. A number of seals with names on them have been used to discuss historicity of this account, and these arguments are examined in detail. A scale of one to ten is used to suggest degrees of probability with various aspects of the story. The question of whether it is possible to write a history of Israel is given a positive answer, though discussion of evidence in great detail and a balanced philosophy of history are essential to the task.

To approach the questions asked, Robert Carroll uses the analogy of Ossian, a supposed third-century Celtic poet, who was in fact invented by an eighteenth-century Scot. He then considers the three examples of Balaam, Omri and Baruch to demonstrate the ideological nature of the Bible. All three of the figures were, or may have been, historical figures, but they have been recontextualized in the biblical literature, and the external data for these figures have often been interpreted in the light of the biblical data. Professor Carroll is especially concerned by the tendency for some to pronounce biblical tales as 'historical' just because an authentic name occurs in them. On the question of whether a history of Israel can be written, he answers that such a history will be only a 'bogus history' because it will be based on the Bible.

Those who have read Philip Davies's *In Search of 'Ancient Israel'*[1] will recognize that his paper builds on this foundation. He accepts that *a* history of *an* ancient Israel can be written. The Bible can be used, but how it is used is the important consideration. Here the problematic nature of the biblical text comes to the fore. The non-biblical data should set the agenda and provide the framework, not vice versa. The question of historical knowledge and the methods and techniques used to attain it need to be seriously addressed. The historian also needs to make clear the sort of history being written (whose history? whose Israel?). He goes on to clarify three possible meanings of 'history', arguing that we should retain this term for the past and seek other terms for a story about the past and about the scholarly discipline of history. What we write is not the past but a more or less arbitrary narrative about the past, which should be designated 'historiography'. All stories about the past are historiography, but different historiographies can be judged as to their quality on the basis of their adherence to critical criteria. The job of the critical historian is to encourage the production of historiographies from different perspectives, to expose deceits practised in the name of history, and to remain sceptical and critical at all times.

The first part of Niels Peter Lemche's paper has already been published and is reprinted here (with minor revisions and corrections) by permission.[2] Much of this article is a review of Keith Whitelam's book.[3] A short paper read at Dublin has been added as an appendix. A good deal of the article takes the form of an appreciation of Whitelam's book but there are also some areas of criticism, both in the original article and in the appendix. For our purposes, one of the most important areas concerns the entity of 'ancient Israel'. Professor Whitelam argues that Israel has dominated the study of the region, denying the Palestinians their history. Professor Lemche points out that Palestine, until very recently, was seen simply as the designation of a region of

1.   JSOTSup, 148; Sheffield: Sheffield Academic Press, 1992.
2.   Originally published in *SJOT* 10 (1996), pp. 88-114.
3.   K.W. Whitelam, *The Invention of Ancient Israel: The Silencing of Palestinian History* (London: Routledge, 1996).

Syria, so that the focus should be 'history of Syria' and not 'history of Palestine' or 'history of the Palestinians'. Otherwise, there is a danger of inventing a new ethnic group of 'Palestinians', at the same time as getting rid of an ethnic concept of 'Israelites'. This does not mean that a 'kingdom of Israel' (alongside a kingdom of Judah) did not exist, but it was only one of the minor states in Syria; the concept of an 'Israelite empire' has to be abandoned. It should be noted that Professor Lemche himself has recently published a book on the 'pre-history of Israel'.[4]

Herbert Niehr looks at the question of the various types of sources and the methodological problems with using each of them. The basic level of study is 'historical anthropology', which makes use of non-written sources including climatology, geography, archaeology, agriculture, sociology and economics. Primary sources, those written close to the event, are the second level of investigation. Secondary sources are copies, interpretations, rewritings and re-editings of the original. The biblical text is clearly a secondary source in most cases, because it is removed in time from the events it purports to describe. In some cases (e.g., the books of Chronicles) the biblical text is only a tertiary source. Yet it still has a function in the task of writing a history and cannot just be dismissed, for it serves to integrate primary written and unwritten data. Also, the text is a primary source for the mentality of the (re)writers or editors. A critical history of ancient Israel can begin with the time of Jeroboam and Omri. History is not what is in the sources; history is what historians write, though it is based on a critical evaluation of all sources.

Thomas Thompson divides his paper into three parts. The first is a critique of some of William Dever's recent writings relating archaeology to the question of ethnicity. This is regarded as completely illegitimate and, depite his disavowel of 'biblical archaeology', Dever in fact uses assumptions based on the biblical picture to answer his questions rather than strict archaeological data. Markers of ethnicity are simply not present in the artifactual finds, and there is nothing in the archaeology of the highlands to distinguish it from other regions. In the second part of his article, Professor Thompson builds on the insights of Keith Whitelam's recent book and its implications for writing a history of this region. In the last part of his paper, he deals with the

---

4. N.P. Lemche, *Die Vorgeschichte Israels: Von den Anfängen bis zum Ausgang des 13. Jahrhunderts v. Chr.* (Biblische Enzyklopädie, 1; Stuttgart: Kohlhammer, 1996).

question asked about trying to write a history of the region. He (along with Cryer and Lemche) is trying to develop a more archaeological and geographically based historiography, making use of a 'spectrum method'.[5] The biblical texts have their contexts in the Graeco-Roman period (165 BCE to 135 CE), since Qumran shows them still in formation. Thus they do not reflect the voice of 'ancient Israel' but of a later or 'new Israel'.

5. See especially T.L. Thompson, *The Settlement of Palestine in the Bronze Age* (Beihefte zum Tübingen Atlas des Vorderen Orients, 34; Wiesbaden: Dr Reichert Verlag, 1979), pp. 7-67; N.P. Lemche, *Early Israel* (VTSup, 37; Leiden: Brill, 1985), pp. 152-63, 245-90.

ARE HISTORIANS OF ANCIENT PALESTINE FELLOW CREATURES—OR DIFFERENT ANIMALS?

Lester L. Grabbe

1. *What Is the Historian's Task?*

I think of myself as a historian, among other things. This illusion comes from having written a couple of tomes which proclaim themselves as historical studies.[1] I mention this to deflect criticism in case someone wishes to accuse me of not being completely up to date with the current debate. I freely admit that I have not read everything I should have on the subject, but I plead a demanding spouse: I have been married to university administration for a number of years.[2] So I want to make it clear that the comments which follow come not from ivory-tower, armchair, arms-length theorizing but from the bleary-eyed, battle-weary perspective of having wrestled with the problems of actually trying to write history.

In universities across the world are departments of history in the hundreds, if not the thousands. Academics within these academic departments may conduct their work on a variety of individual tasks and specialties. Most of them will, however, be attempting to reconstruct the past in one form or other. This may take the form of biography, of political history, of an investigation of the economic forces or how society functioned. Methods of all sorts may be used, depending on the period and the sources available. But when all is said and done, most

---

1. *Judaism from Cyrus to Hadrian.* I. *Persian and Greek Periods;* II. *Roman Period* (Minneapolis: Fortress Press, 1992; British edition in one-volume paperback, London: SCM Press, 1994); *Priests, Prophets, Diviners, Sages: A Socio-historical Study of Religious Specialists in Ancient Israel* (Valley Forge, PA: Trinity Press International, 1995).

2. Having become Dean of Humanities in 1990, I have not been able to effect a divorce, apart from an all too brief separation for about ten months after the first three years. I shall spare the gentle reader further sordid details.

historians have a positivistic goal: they are trying to get at the question of 'what actually happened' and do not regard that as an absurd goal. They are trying to reconstruct a particular historical entity, whether of the recent or the remote past. For most historians, this is what 'doing history' is about.[3]

Ranke's 'wie es eigentlich gewesen ist' still continues to be a desirable goal to most working historians. As Raymond Martin recently put it, the historian wants to know 'what happened' and 'what it means that it happened'. Also, 'an essential part of our task, as historians, is to figure out which among these alternative interpretations [which may fit the data] is best, which involves, among other things, determining which among them is most likely to be true... For the fundamental point of the historical quest, from the start, has been to discover the truth.'[4]

Naturally, this task varies greatly in complexity and the problems faced. A historian of recent events may be so overwhelmed with data that organizing and finding a coherent path through the sources is the main concern. For the ancient historian, the opposite is the case: the maximum information must be extracted from bits and scraps, from debris and dustbin contents, from midden piles and trash heaps—from those few fragments preserved by chance from the past. The nature of the data makes the approaches and methods of working different. The historian of recent times may be able to construct comparative graphs and do statistical analyses because there is enough quantifiable information to make this legitimate. This applies even to the mediaeval historian. The ancient historian, on the other hand, can only sit in envy at

---

3. Cf. the comments of P. Novick, *That Noble Dream: The 'Objectivity Question' and the American Historical Profession* (Cambridge: Cambridge University Press, 1988), pp. 593-95. Although his comments are on the American situation, my impression is that the position is similar in the UK. Of course, what Novick is doing is tracing the currents which led to a challenge to the question of objectivity. In the decade since his book appeared, however, the concept of objectivity in historical study has by no means been given up. See the articles listed in the next note.

4. R. Martin, 'Objectivity and Meaning in Historical Studies: Toward a Post-Analytic View', *History and Theory* 32 (1993), pp. 25-50, especially pp. 28-29. Some other recent studies which appear to voice similar views include C. Behan McCullagh, 'Can Our Understanding of Old Texts Be Objective?' *History and Theory* 30 (1991), pp. 302-23; M. Bevir, 'Objectivity in History', *History and Theory* 33 (1994), pp. 328-44; A.P. Norman, 'Telling it Like it Was: Historical Narratives on their own Terms', *History and Theory* 30 (1991), pp. 119-35.

this abundance of data, for to have enough information to quantify data and produce statistics is a luxury much desired but seldom fulfilled.

Yet the basic goal of each historian is the same. They want to gain as detailed a reliable picture of a particular part of the past as possible. The problem that the 'past is a foreign country' is true for the contemporary historian as well as for the ancient.[5] Everything in the past is no longer directly accessible—not just the distant past but anything older than the past fraction of a second. We can debate the nature of the sources and their reliability, but we are ultimately trying to get at something which no longer exists. Whatever we do, we are engaging in historical reconstruction. We are making guesses (preferably intelligent ones) about a lost world, whatever our sources—whether 'eyewitness' memory, documents, literary texts, or artefacts.

It follows that we can never be sure whether we are right, so scholarship has developed the historical method. This is a procedure by which some discipline can be introduced into the guesswork. It is a means of trying to make the choice of possible alternatives more than just a subjective decision by establishing conventions of evidence and argument. It attempts to introduce probability into the debate so that some scenarios can be considered more likely than others, so that some can be ruled out as very improbable but others considered reasonable and even likely.[6] If we cannot agree on these basic ground rules, we cannot carry on a conversation. Biblical fundamentalists cannot engage in any debate about the history of ancient Israel because they do not accept the historical method in that particular arena.[7]

But despite the developments in historical method, history is far from an exact science. There is no magical key to know what is historical

5.   Cf. D. Lowenthal, *The Past Is a Foreign Country* (Cambridge: Cambridge University Press, 1985).

6.   This basic principle seems to have escaped I. Provan in his criticisms of Davies and Knauf ('Ideologies, Literary and Critical: Reflections on Recent Writing on the History of Israel', *JBL* 114 [1995], pp. 585-606, especially pp. 600-601). It is not just 'positivistic' historians who are sceptical of texts whose primary aim is to deliver a religious message; on the contrary, it has been a basic presupposition of critical historical study at least since the Enlightenment. See further at n. 25 below.

7.   Cf. my article 'Fundamentalism and Scholarship: The Case of Daniel', in B.P. Thompson (ed.), *Scripture: Method and Meaning: Essays Presented to Anthony Tyrrell Hanson for his Seventieth Birthday* (Hull: Hull University Press, 1987), pp. 133-52.

and what is not. Writing history is a messy business. It is very akin to mud-wrestling or muck-spreading. If you actually get down to trying to be a historian, you are going to get dirty. You will have to make judgments, weigh evidence, and deal with problematic data. Many of your reconstructions are likely to be fragile and open to criticism. You will not be able to sit on the fence.

2. *What to Do with the Text?*

Much of the recent debate between 'the sceptics' and others concerns the use of the text in writing a history of Israel. Is it possible to write a history from archaeology alone? Yes, it is—prehistorians have been doing so for decades. But the resulting history is no more than a skeleton or even just a backbone. This is not denigration of the enormous efforts made by prehistorians using some of the most intractable of material. Prehistorians write history from such material because that is all they have.[8] If they had reliable texts, they would also use them.

In those cases where written material has been discovered, it has been used with alacrity as, for instance, in the case of the Linear B texts which provided written material for ancient Crete where none had previously existed.[9] Prehistorians are prehistorians by necessity, not by choice. So would it not seem strange to most if some historians decided that they would act only as prehistorians even though written material was available?

It seems to me that the problem we have with the biblical text is very similar to the one we have with the Homeric poems.[10] It is generally accepted now that there was a Troy and that some historical reality lies behind the account of the Trojan War. Yet the matter is a complex one. Some of the names of Greek cities which supposedly

---

8.   For example, the homeland of the original Indo-Europeans has been deduced by reconstructing the name of trees in the original language.

9.   See J. Chadwick, *Corpus of Mycenaean Inscriptions from Knossos* (3 vols.; Cambridge: Cambridge University Press, 1987–93).

10.   This analogy was dealt with at some length by R. de Vaux, 'On Right and Wrong Uses of Archaeology', in J.A. Sanders (ed.), *Near Eastern Archaeology in the Twentieth Century* (Garden City, NY: Doubleday, 1970), pp. 64-80. It seems to me that de Vaux's sentiments in this article are correct, however much he may be faulted on some of his specific attempts to relate archaeology to the biblical text.

contributed troop contingents were cities thriving in the Mycenaean period but which had long been abandoned by the time the Homeric poems reached their final form about the eighth century BCE. Customs and realia from different ages jostle each other in the text, with historical elements from the Bronze Age next to those from the Dark Age or the Iron Age of Greek history.[11]

Some of the individuals in the text may represent actual historical figures. Among the Greek heroes, this is most likely the case with Agammenon. Someone like Odysseus seems a suitable fictional hero and is less likely to have an actual figure behind him. Some of the names of Trojans are simply Greek names and unlikely to be historical; others are known from the Linear B texts and may be authentic. In this case, the text is problematic. Historical elements within the text have been demonstrated, but much of the elucidation has not come from a study of the text itself but from archaeology and other sources.

Similarly, the past century has brought an enormous amount of native Egyptian material to light. The study of ancient Egyptian culture is now completely different from that before 1800 when practically the only sources were those of Greek and Roman writers. Before then one of the most important sources were the remains of Manetho, an Egyptian priest writing in Greek in the early Ptolemaic period. Our knowledge of his work, which has been only partially preserved, comes entirely from much later sources, primarily Josephus and the Christian writers Eusebius and Syncellus.[12] Eusebius and Syncellus in turn took their information from the Christian writer Julius Africanus. Despite the much improved knowlege from hieroglyphic writings, however, Manetho is still an important source in the reconstruction of Egyptian history.[13] Whatever the difficulties with using his work—

---

11. Studies on the relationship between the Homeric poems and history include M.P. Nilsson, *Homer and Mycenae* (repr.; Philadelphia: University of Pennsylvania, 1972 [1933]); D.L. Page, *History and the Homeric Iliad* (Berkeley: University of California Press, 1959); C.M. Bowra, *Homer* (Classical Life and Letters; New York: Scribner; London: Routledge, 1972); M. Wood, *In Search of the Trojan War* (London: Guild Publishing, 1985).

12. The text and a translation are conveniently available in W.G. Waddell (ed.), *Manetho* (LCL; Cambridge, MA: Harvard; London: Heinemann, 1940).

13. For example, D.B. Redford notes, 'When one wishes to examine the kinglist tradition in the years that follow the Ramesside Age in Egypt, one is thrown back on to Manetho; for we lack any reliable evidence on how the official king-list was

whatever the lateness and textual corruption of the surviving manu-
scripts—Egyptologists would regard it as rather foolish to allow these
to prevent the use of Manetho.

We do not normally have a choice in our sources. We have to make
do with whatever the vicissitudes of history have thrown up. Naturally,
we might prefer to have this or that source, but beggars cannot be
choosers. We use the biblical text because we have it and do not have a
lot of other sources which we would definitely prefer. The fact is that
a great deal of interpretation of artifactual and other evidence has
directly or indirectly depended on information found in the biblical
text.[14]

In order to grapple properly with the text, it may be helpful to
examine some examples where the text can be judged by extra-biblical
information.

3. *Comparative Examples*

A useful exercise would be to compare statements or representations
in the Old Testament with those in the ancient Near Eastern literature
or inscriptions approximately contemporary with the events purported
to be described. This can only be a rough-and-ready exercise at this
point since any comparison would need detailed discussion, but it
might suggest something about how we are to proceed when considering
whether or how to use the text.[15]

---

faring from the end of the reign of Ramesses II to the 3rd Century BC, a span of
1000 years.' (*Pharaonic King-Lists, Annals and Day-Books: A Contribution to the
Study of the Egyptian Sense of History* [Society for the Study of Egyptian Antiquities,
Publication 4; Mississauga, Ontario: Benben, 1986])

14. This point is very well made by both J.M. Miller ('Is it Possible to Write a
History of Israel without Relying on the Hebrew Bible?') and G.W. Ahlström ('The
Role of Archaeological and the Literary Remains in Reconstructing Israel's History')
in D.V. Edelman (ed.), *The Fabric of History: Text, Artifact and Israel's Past*
(JSOTSup, 127; Sheffield Academic Press, 1991), pp. 93-102, 116-41.

15. *ANET* is the main source for what follows, unless otherwise indicated. For
the broad aims of this quick perusal, it is adequate.

Old Testament Picture	Ancient Near Eastern Texts
Ahab	*Ahab*
Ahab fights the Arameans	Ahab allied with Arameans
Assyrians not mentioned	Enemies are the Assyrians
Ahab weak	Ahab strong
Mesha	*Mesha*
King of Moab and vassal of Ahab	King of Moab and vassal of Omri and Ahab
Mesha rebelled after Ahab's death	Mesha rebelled during Ahab's lifetime
Jehu	*Jehu*
Nothing about the Assyrians	Jehu submits to Shalmaneser III
Jehoash/Joash (of Israel)	*Jehoash/Joash (of Israel)*
No reference to the Assyrians	Pays tribute to Adad-nirari III
Azariah/Uzziah	*Azariah/Uzziah*
No reference to the Assyrians	Pays tribute to Tiglath-pileser III?[16]
Jehoahaz/Ahaz (of Judah)	*Jehoahaz/Ahaz (of Judah)*
Becomes Assyrian vassal to gain aid against Israel and Damascus	Pays tribute to Tiglath-pileser III
Menahem	*Menahem*
Pays tribute to Pul (Tiglath-pileser III)	Pays tribute to Tiglath-pileser III
Pekah	*Pekah*
Overthrown by Hoshea	Overthrown by internal revolt
Hosea	*Hosea*
Takes throne in internal coup	Tiglath-pileser III puts Hosea on throne
Conquered by Shalmaneser (V)	Conquered by Sargon II according to Sargon's inscriptions; conquered by Shalmaneser V according to the Babylonian Chronicle which is more likely to be correct.[17]

16. The standard edition of Tiglath-Pileser's inscriptions is now Hayyim Tadmor, *The Inscriptions of Tiglath-Pileser III King of Assyria: Critical Edition, with Introductions, Translations and Commentary* (Jerusalem: Israel Academy of Sciences and Humanities, 1994). It is still debated as to whether the Azriyau is Azariah/Uzziah or an otherwise unknown king in Syria. See Tadmor, pp. 273-74.

17. See A.K. Grayson, *The Assyrian and Babylonian Chronicles* (Texts from

Hezekiah	*Hezekiah*
Pays tribute; Jerusalem delivered miraculously.	Submits to Sennacherib and pays tribute, but despite a large siege Jerusalem does not fall
Sennacherib killed (by two sons).	Sennacherib killed (by one son).
Manasseh No reference to Assyrians (2 Kgs 21)/ Taken captive to Babylon by Assyrians (2 Chron. 33)	*Manasseh* Required to send tribute to Esarhaddon and Ashurbanipal
Jehoiachin Taken captive by Nebuchanezzar	*Jehoiachin* Taken captive by Nebuchadnezzar
Zedekiah Jerusalem conquered by Nebuchadnezzar.	*Zedekiah* No information after 594 BCE.[18]

This hasty overview tells us two things. First, the text is reasonably accurate about the framework. From the mid-ninth century all kings attested in external sources are not only found in the biblical text but they are found in the same sequence and even the approximate chronological period. Secondly, we can have little *prima facie* confidence in the details. Sometimes they seem accurate, but at other times they are demonstrably misleading or wholly inaccurate and perhaps even completely invented.

4. *Lies, Damned Lies and Statistics—*
Or Historical Fiction, Naive History and Critical History

A study of historical fiction can be a salutary exercise. Historical fiction as it is understood in the modern context is admittedly fiction but with a historical context and (supposedly) authentic historical detail. Some examples from modern historical fiction might tell us something.

James Joyce's *Ulysses* is a prime example of historical fiction. It describes a day in the life of a fictional character (Leopold Bloom)

Cuneiform Sources, 5; Locust Valley, NY: J.J. Augustin, 1975), p. 73.
   18.   There is an inscription about a tour of Palestine by Psammetichus II about the year 589; see F.L. Griffith, *Catalogue of the Demotic Papyri in the John Rylands Library, Manchester with Facsimiles and Complete Translations* (3 vols.; Manchester: Manchester University Press, 1909), II, pp. 64-65. It does not mention Zedekiah or the situation in Jerusalem, however.

and other characters who form a part of his life (e.g., Molly Bloom) or come across his path. Although the characters are made up, the setting is supposed to be authentic—Dublin, 16 June 1904. In the year 3996, if *Ulysses* was the only source preserved for the twentieth century, there would be a lot we would not know. World War I, World War II, the Cold War, and other global events of history would be unknown. But a city and the daily lives of many people in the early twentieth century would be accessible.

I may be a sceptic, but I do not believe there was a Leopold Bloom. I do not believe that an actual Molly Bloom ever uttered a stream-of-conscious soliloquy about love, sex and life in general. Verisimilitude does not prove that these individuals were historical. There may have been people like them, and from my present knowledge I am happy to accept that the society, general events, and to some extent even the thoughts and actions of the fictitious individuals can be used as historical evidence.

Historical fiction of this sort does not seem to be attested in the ancient Near East. The attempt to write a work with fictional characters and plot but with attention to authenticity of historical context appears to be unknown in antiquity. On the other hand, we may have something analogous to historical fiction at that time. These are stories about historical figures which have a historical core to them but have submerged the history under a fictional layer. For example, Diodorus Siculus (probably borrowing from Ctesias of Cnidus) lists in detail the doings of Ninus and Semiramus in Mesopotamia.[19]

Like the Homeric poems, these fictional narratives with a historical core are often hard to judge without some sort of corroborating evidence. From Diodorus/Ctesius alone, it would be hard to know what to make of Ninus and Semiramus. Some judgments can be made because of native cuneiform sources which give a more authentic picture of the historical rulers. But once we have a general idea of the historical basis of the figures, it may still be possible to extract some sort of information from the fictionalized accounts. It is now believed that behind the figures of the Greek account lie the Assyrian king Šarrukīnu II and his wife Sammuramat.[20]

---

19. See F.W. König, *Die Persika des Ktesias von Knidos* (Archiv für Orientforschung Beiheft, 18; Graz: Archiv für Orientforschung, 1972), especially pp. 34-40.

20. König, *Die Persika*; W. Eilers, *Semiramis: Entstehung und Nachhall einer*

Naive history is history which takes the sources at face value. There are all sorts of naive history, including ideological writings which take sources at face value because they can be exploited in support of their ideology. A good example is the nineteenth-century anti-Catholic work of Alexander Hislop, *The Two Babylons*. Hislop attempted to demonstrate that the Catholic religion was the result of a millennia-old conspiracy, dating from the time of the Nimrod of Genesis 9. Hislop equated Nimrod with the Ninus of legend. This allowed him to introduce Semiramis, although no woman is associated with Nimrod in the biblical text, and make her 'mother of all harlots'—a role that he also assigns to the Roman Catholic Church. Despite the fact that Assyriology has long since shown this picture to be absurd, Hislop's book is still being reprinted and widely circulated among fundamentalist Protestant Christians.[21]

Thus, one sort of naive history is really apologetic history. Most of us can spot the apologetic history writing of biblical fundamentalists without much difficulty. Where there are data which can be used to support the biblical text, they are quickly brought forward, and no alternative explanations of the data are allowed, however much better they explain the data. If there are no empirical data, it is asserted that 'arguments from silence' are dangerous, that there are discoveries yet to be made which will support the biblical text, that 'there is no reason to doubt' that the biblical picture is correct, etc. And, most of all, there is a really healthy scepticism; unfortunately, it is always directed against any argument or information which seems to compromise the biblical text and never at the biblical account.[22]

What is harder to spot, or at least harder to deal with, is the apologetic history which defends the biblical text but is clearly not fundamentalist. It tends to come from those who are not fundamentalists but have a deep-felt religious belief and whose attachment to the 'truth of the text' is strong. There is a strong tendency to take a position of

altorientalischen Sage (Sitzungsberichte der Österreichische Akademie der Wissenschaften, Phil.-hist. Klasse 274, 2. Abhandlung; Vienna: Kommissionsverlag der Österreichischen Akademie der Wissenschaften, 1971); W. Schramm, 'War Semiramis assyrische Regentin?' *Historia* 21 (1972), pp. 513-21.

21. A 'second edition' of his work was printed in London in 1862. I have not been able to ascertain when the original edition was published.

22. Much of this is discussed at length in Grabbe, 'Fundamentalism and Scholarship'.

'maximal conservatism',[23] to defend the text as far as possible and place the best picture on contrary facts. The stance is within the general bounds of critical scholarship but refuses to go down the critical road any further than absolutely necessary. This seems to be the position which John Bright encapsulated in his assertion that 'the Hebrew even lacks a word for "goddess"'.[24] This sort of history writing can be in some ways more insidious than blatant fundamentalism. It is at this sort of history writing which 'the sceptics' have taken aim and which has so annoyed those who oppose them.[25]

Critical history is a matter of weighing the arguments and the probabilities. No-one can be absolutely sure about what happened; one can only make intelligent guesses. If any sort of historical reconstruction— if any sort of historical *writing*—is to take place, an attempt to sort out the more probable from the less probable must be made. In doing that, all resources have to be considered. If we accept only what we

23. This term comes from J. Barr, *Fundamentalism* (London: SCM Press, 1977), pp. 85-89. Although Barr is discussing the idea in a fundamentalist context, it seems to me to apply very well to what quite a few mainstream Old Testament scholars have done.

24. J. Bright, *A History of Israel* (London: SCM Press, 3rd edn, 1981), p. 158. The statement remained unchanged from the first edition of 1959 (p. 138).

25. This is the only way I can interpret Provan, 'Ideologies, Literary and Critical'. My criticisms of Provan are the following: (1) He speaks of the epistemological problems of writing history as if those he criticizes are unaware of them, which is clearly untrue. He can maintain his criticism only because (2) he distorts and unfairly represents the positions of those he criticizes (see the replies by T.L. Thompson and P.R. Davies in the same *JBL* issue, pp. 683-705). For example, his representation of G.W. Ahlström's position seems a wilful misreading by selective quotation, as anyone who reads the whole context will see (Provan, p. 594). (3) He asserts that there is no such thing as objectivity in history writing, completing ignoring the reasoned comments about objectivity by E.A. Knauf in an article Provan himself cites but apparently has not read thoroughly (see Knauf, 'From History to Interpretation', in Edelman [ed.], *The Fabric of History*, pp. 26-64, especially pp. 27-34). (4) He leaves the impression that since subjective judgments must be made in any reconstruction, one is as good as another; however, I do not think for one moment that Provan actually believes that. (5) He also leaves the impression that the biblical text is unproblematic. Again, I do not think that this is really Provan's position, but because he deals only on the level of generalities, he does not have to grapple with the genuine problems of using the biblical text for history. I would challenge him to show how he would actually deal with Joshua 1–15, for example, and still maintain there is no considerable distance between story and history.

can be absolutely certain about, we might as well give up the historical task *ab initio* because extremely little falls in that category. Furthermore, if we are to write about the society at all, we must use the text. Very little about matters of society and religion can be gleaned from artifactual evidence alone. Without the text, we could hardly expect to say anything.

5. *The Biblical Text and the History of Israel*

I have argued for the general principle that the biblical text must be used for writing a history of the ancient geographical area of Palestine. Accepting that principle does not, of course, suddenly make the task easy. The biblical text is very problematic. The 'sceptics' have not exaggerated the difficulties in trying to extract historical data from the text. For example, I have already argued that the text can be used—with due caution and critical care—for social history and have suggested some principles which help us to evaluate it. Without repeating the arguments used, the following principles were advanced.[26]

1. Hints in the text which go contrary to its overall bias suggest some authentic information has survived the editorial process.

2. Cross-cultural comparisons may help to confirm or deny whether the textual picture is credible.

3. There are some authentic texts, by wide consensus.

In light of further reflection, including some of the discussion above, I believe some more ideas about the text can now be advanced:

4. The text seems to have relatively accurate knowledge about the order and rough chronological order of the kings. This is demonstrated from the middle of the ninth century where external data allow some sort of check on the biblical picture. Thus, where it cannot be checked, it is reasonable to assume that this also pertains. It is not a great leap of rashness to accept that David and Solomon and even Saul existed at a time only a century or so removed from Omri. On the other hand, this same survey gives no confidence in the details of the biblical text. Sometimes they seem to be accurate, but at other times the biblical text is evidently untrustworthy. The biblical text is thus more likely to be trustworthy for some data than others: the main

26. Grabbe, *Priests, Prophets, Diviners, Sages*, pp. 8-12.

characters, important events and the functioning of society.

5. Attention has to be paid to the probabilities of a particular reconstruction. We can all speculate; it is interesting, and it can be valuable, but it is still speculation. Too often the speculation of one passage has become the foundation for further work in a later passage. Too often what is 'possible' at one point has become 'fact' at another. It is difficult to maintain provisionality, but that is precisely what we must do. The fact that no one has come up with a better explanation is not the same as demonstration and should be recognized.

6. Historical questions must be asked. This does not rule out questions of intertextuality, tradition history, form criticism, and the like; indeed, these may be a part of putting the historical question. Nevertheless, there is a danger in confusing such questions with asking about historicity. The assumption is that once questions of tradition history have been answered, we have the answer to the historical questions. This is not necessarily the case, not least because of the subjective nature of tradition history. There is also the possibility that traditions may continue to preserve historical data despite the alterations brought about by the transmission process. This is why test cases where it is possible to obtain clear answers need to be used as some sort of control.

7. Similarly, the question of genre of the biblical texts should not deflect us from asking proper historical questions. The recent debate about historiography in the biblical and ancient Near Eastern worlds is an example of where genre questions start to miss the point about trying to do history. This needs discussion at some length.

Much energy has been expended into whether the Israelites wrote history or not. A lot naturally depends on how one defines history, and part of the differences in the debate arises from differences on how to define history writing in the first place. Whatever the ultimate judgment about whether Israel wrote what can be called history or not, it seems to me that history in the modern sense of critical history is first attested among the Greeks. It evidently owes much to the pre-Socratic philosophers who began to ask questions about the world and did not take surface appearances for granted. But already in Herodotus, 'the father of history', we see the critical questioning, the weighing of evidence, the healthy scepticism necessary for doing critical history.

For example, Herodotus raises some serious questions about the Trojan War (2.118-20). He points to a tradition (obtained from the Egyptian priests) at some variance with that found in the Homeric poems, a rather bold criticism since the Homeric poems had a quasi-canonical status in the Greek world. This version says that when the Greeks came, the Trojans swore to them that Helen was no longer there but had already absconded to North Africa. With wonderful critical acumen Herodotus notes that this was likely to be true since no nation would allow itself to be besieged for ten years for the sake of a mere woman, queen though she might be.

There were no doubt individuals who sniffed at Herodotus's account with the comment that there was 'no reason to disbelieve' the account in the Homeric poems. We do not know what happened at Troy, of course, but what Herodotus did was to cast considerable doubt on the standard explanation. He placed the burden of proof on those who would continue to accept it at face value.

However, the discussion about what can be called history can divert the proper evaluation of the biblical text. Too much has been made of the aim or purpose of the texts. It has sometimes been noted that particular texts are or are not 'historigraphic' in nature. This suggests that only texts which were intended to be history have value for historical writing. Granted that some sorts of text are very dubious for writing history, it is still the case that historians may draw on all kinds of material as sources. The intent of the text may be irrelevant for its value to the historian. Conversely, narratives intended as history by the author may be very problematic to the historian for all sorts of reasons. And those who argue about the 'intent' of the author seem to assume that it would be the same as that of a modern historian. It assumes that they would have understood the concept of history in the same way as we do today. The question of whether it was intended to be history or intended to be theology is a question that few, if any, writers would have understood, it seems to me. Certainly the biblical writer would have made no distinction between the account of creation in Genesis 1, the narrative of the exodus, or the story of Solomon's accession.[27] For modern scholars to make a distinction between one and the other as a way of determining the intent of the writer is illegitimate.

Another reason why intent is problematic is that the biblical text does not clearly state a historical intent. A theological or religious intent seems clear from the focus on obedience, the judging of kings by

---

27. This point was well made by Dr C. Bultmann in the question-and-answer session following the address by Provan which has recently been published (see n. 6 above).

religious criteria, and the emphasis on divine activity. An intent to write history is not so clearly a part of the content. On the other hand, with the Greek and Roman historians such as Thucydides, Polybius, and many others, they discuss what they are going to do. But even when they tell us what they are going to do, they do not necessarily live up to their stated aims. Someone like Josephus, for example, begins both the *War* and the *Antiquities* with statements about the insufficiencies of others who have written on the subject and his commitment to truth. A careful examination of his accounts shows, however, that he often fails to live up to these high intentions.[28] Thus, whether or not a writing should be called 'history' or even 'historiographical' may be quite irrelevant for its value as a history source to the modern historian.

Xenophon produced valuable accounts of the Persian expedition in the rebellion of Cyrus the Younger in 401 BCE (*Anabasis*) and also the progress of the Peloponnesian War (*Hellenica*, picking up where Thucydides' account ended). Although he was no Thucydides, Xenophon was certainly a historian. He also wrote another work which most scholars consider a historical novel at best, the *Cyropaedia*.[29] What was his intent? Was it different from his history of the Peloponnesian War? If it was, he does not tell us. In this case, a debate about intent seems somewhat pointless. The important issue is that the *Cyropaedia* does not measure up to the critical criteria for authentic history but his others writings do. Once we know that, the question about intent is academic.

It seems to me perverse to label the Deuteronomistic History as 'history', when it is manifestly very wrong or misleading in places, but to exempt the Babylonian Chronicles from the category of history

28. See especially S.D.J. Cohen, *Josephus in Galilee and Rome: His Vita and Development as a Historian* (Columbia Studies in Classical Texts, 8; Leiden: Brill, 1979), and Grabbe, *Judaism from Cyrus to Hadrian*, which devotes a good deal of space to Josephus in most chapters. My quarrel with Steve Mason, *Flavius Josephus on the Pharisees: A Composition-Critical Study* (SPB, 39: Leiden: Brill, 1991) is that he appears to take Josephus's stated aims at face value; see my review in *JJS* 45 (1994), pp. 134-36.

29. Some recent studies include Deborah Levine Gera, *Xenophon's Cyropaedia: Style, Genre, and Literary Technique* (Oxford Classical Monographs; Oxford: Clarendon Press, 1993); J. Tatum, *Xenophon's Imperial Fiction: On The Education of Cyrus* (Princeton, NJ: Princeton University Press, 1989); B. Due, *The Cyropaedia: Xenophon's Aims and Methods* (Aarhus: Aarhus University Press, 1989).

even though where they can be tested, they are remarkably accurate and unbiased. Whether we use the term 'history' or not with either, the Babylonian Chronicles are primary sources with fewer problems and greater *prima facie* weight than the Deuteronomistic History.[30]

Some texts may indeed have more reliable data for historical purposes than others, but this is not necessarily because of their intent or even their genre. It is merely what has survived, perhaps in spite of the authorial or editorial process.[31] I accept that genre may be a clue to reliability. For example, I do not find it difficult to believe that there was an Israelite leader named Saul whose career was not completely different from that described in 1 Samuel. On the other hand, the story of Samson has so many novelistic features, I would be sceptical about any historical figure lying behind it. That possibility cannot be ruled out, but it seems to me difficult to believe without more information. Yet even quite legendary accounts may contain a historical core of some sort. Even something so unhistorical in genre as the *Niebelungenlied* is believed to reflect some known historical events: the context of the 'barbaric' invasions of the fifth century, in particular the destruction of the kingdom of Burgundy by the Huns.[32]

I find little which compels me to see a different intent or a different genre between the story of Ezra and the story of Nehemiah. Very unusually, there is a strong consensus in scholarship that a personal

30. J. Van Seters (*In Search of History: Historiography in the Ancient World and the Origins of Biblical History* [New Haven: Yale University Press, 1983], pp. 179-92, 357-59) and apparently also B. Halpern (*The First Historians: the Hebrew Bible and History* [San Francisco: Harper & Row, 1988], p. 6) reject the Babylonian Chronicles as history. On the contrary, it seems to me that the Babylonian Chronicles fulfil all the criteria for being labelled 'history', especially if one wishes to include the Deuteronomistic History in that category. See A.K. Grayson, 'Assyria and Babylon', *Orientalia* 49 (1980), pp. 137-94, and Z. Zevit, 'Clio, I Presume', *BASOR* 260 (1985), pp. 71-82.

31. B. Halpern, *The First Historians*, pp. 3-15. I found this discussion confusing, and having read it several times I still do not know how he thinks history is to be distinguished from fiction. But he does seem to place a good deal of emphasis on the intent of the author. Provan, 'Ideologies, Literary and Critical', also places a good deal of weight on the supposed intent of the biblical writer.

32. See H. de Boor (ed.), *Das Nibelungenlied, Zweisprachig* (Sammlung Dieterich 250; Leipzig: Sammlung Dieterich, 1959); A.T. Hatto (trans.), *The Niebelungen Lied* (Penguin Classics; London: Penguin, 2nd edn, 1969). One should be aware that Wagner's *Ring* is based not so much on the classical German *Niebelungenlied* as on the Scandinavian version in the *Völsungasaga*.

account of Nehemiah himself lies at the core of the book in his name. This original account has clearly been edited, and where the boundaries of the 'Nehemiah Memorial' are to be found is debated. But I find it easier to get at Nehemiah's own thoughts than those of Ezra. Some have argued that an 'Ezra Memoir' lies behind Ezra 7–10.[33] Whether this is the case or not is beside the point because the historical Ezra (if there was one) lies so submerged under the layers of legend as to be accessible (if at all) with difficulty.[34]

6. *Conclusions*

The following conclusions appear to me to follow from the preceding discussion:

1. The task of historians of ancient Palestine and/or of ancient Israel is not different from that of historians of other periods. Methods and approaches of a particular time, place and subject have to be adapted to the particular circumstances, especially the available sources, but the general goals remain the same.

2. In writing the history of ancient Palestine and/or Israel, the biblical text can and must be used. A great deal about the ancient society—including much about the religion—leaves little or nothing in the archaeological record. A good deal of the interpretation of archaeology depends directly or indirectly on the text. Although it would in theory be possible to put aside all knowledge gleaned from the text and interpret the archaeological and other data in isolation, that would only be a foolish conceit. We should accept all the help we can get, and the text can give us information we cannot get elsewhere.

3. The difficulties of using the biblical text should not, however, be underestimated. The use of the text needs to be argued for in each case, not just accepted without further comment.

4. The various types of sources need to be evaluated each in its own right before attempting a synthesis. Far too often we have seen supposed

---

33. This has recently been argued by H.G.M. Williamson, *Ezra, Nehemiah* (WBC, 16; Waco, TX: Word Books, 1985), pp. xxviii-xxxii.

34. See my studies, 'Reconstructing History from the Book of Ezra', in P.R. Davies (ed.), *Second Temple Studies, 1. The Persian Period* (JSOTSup, 117; Sheffield: JSOT Press, 1991), pp. 98-107; T.C. Eskenazi and H.K. Richards (eds.), 'What Was Ezra's Mission?' *Second Temple Studies, 2. Temple and Community in the Persian Period* (JSOTSup 175, Sheffield: JSOT Press, 1994), pp. 286-99.

accounts of the archaeology in which textual and other data were mixed so promiscuously that it was impossible to tell what had actually been found in the ground.[35] Synthesis and reconstruction should come about only after a careful analysis of each source in its own right.

5. An effort should be made to indicate the probabilities of any reconstruction. There is nothing wrong with speculation and imaginative reconstruction, but this should be admitted and clearly labelled. What we cannot show, we do not know.[36]

I have argued above that our goal as historians is positivistic. That does not mean that we are necessarily able to reach that goal. In many periods of history, we often do not have enough information to come to certain conclusions. Our reconstructions may be tentative at best; our actual work will be relativistic (though we would not be doing reconstructions in the first place if we did not have a positivistic goal). In that case, the historian is probably best described as a juggler. The secret is to keep as many balls as possible in the air at once without dropping any.

35. A good bad example is G.E. Wright's discussion of the later archaeology of Shechem in *Shechem: The Biography of a Biblical City* (New York: McGraw-Hill, 1964), pp. 170-84, and in *Archaeological Encyclopedia of the Holy Land* (ed. M. Avi-Yonah and E. Stern; Jerusalem: Israel Exploration Society; Oxford: Oxford University Press, 1978), pp. 1093-94. The *New Archaeological Encyclopaedia of the Holy Land* (ed. E. Stern; Jerusalem: Israel Exploration Society; New York: Simon & Schuster, 1993) is generally much better, but there are still articles which are too interpretative and not sufficiently descriptive in the presentation of the data.

36. This is a point forcibly made by J. Neusner in many writings. See most recently his *Rabbinic Literature and the New Testament: What We Cannot Show, We Do Not Know* (Valley Forge, PA: Trinity Press International, 1994).

HISTORY AND THE HEBREW BIBLE

Hans M. Barstad

I

The much debated crisis in history appears, finally, to have reached even biblical studies. The most important question seems to be whether or not it is possible to write a history of ancient Israel on the basis of Old Testament historiography. The matter may, in brief, be illustrated through the following development.

In the article on 'History' in the second edition of the *Encyclopaedia Britannica*, which appeared during the years 1777–83, the biblical Book of Genesis may still be regarded as the historians' most important source for how the world came into existence. Here the following arguments for the dating of the earth (which is exactly 6096 years old) are typical:

> the whole account of the creation rests on the truth of the Mosaic history; and which we must of necessity accept, because we can find no other which does not abound with the grossest absurdities, or lead us into absolute darkness. The Chinese and Egyptian pretensions to antiquity are so absurd and ridiculous, that the bare reading must be a sufficient confutation of them to every reasonable person. Some historians and philosophers are inclined to discredit the Mosaic accounts, from the appearances of volcanoes, and other natural phaenomena: but their objections are by no means sufficient to invalidate the authority of the sacred writings.. .

Since then, not only have historians stopped using the Bible as a major historical source,[1] but we have also been witnessing a development where every new generation of authors of that particular scholarly genre most commonly referred to as 'The History of Ancient Israel'

---

1. For a survey of the development of the study of history in the West, see E. Breisach, *Historiography: Ancient, Medieval, and Modern* (Chicago: University of Chicago Press, 1983). See in particular the chapter on 'The Eighteenth-Century Quest for a New Historiography', pp. 199-227.

have had their sources drastically curtailed. First, biblical cosmogony, then Moses,[2] then Abraham,[3] and finally the Exodus event and the conquest of Palestine[4] all took leave of history. Typically, in the recent history of Ancient Israel by Miller and Hayes, both of whom must be regarded as belonging to the 'conservative wing' of biblical scholarship, the authors take the view that, following the nature of the biblical sources, one cannot write a history of ancient Israel before the time of the monarchy.[5]

Obviously the matter could not stop here, and what we are witnessing at present is the beginning of the end of a history project which over the years has become more and more problematic. Elucidating symptoms of this is clearly seen in recent books by Davies[6] and Thompson,[7] the former claiming, among other things, that there was no united kingdom in ancient Israel in the eleventh century BC, and that this is a creation of late Persian times, wheras the latter attempts to write about ancient Israel without using the Bible as an historical source at all. Thompson, too, argues that the idea 'Israel' was created in late Persian times.

2.   See typically H. Gressmann, *Mose und seine Zeit. Ein Kommentar zu den Mose–Sagen* (FRLANT, 18; Göttingen: Vandenhoeck & Ruprecht, 1913). Cf. also the recent books by G.W. Coats, *Moses: Heroic Man, Man of God* (JSOTSup, 57; Sheffield: Sheffield Academic Press, 1988), and J. Van Seters, *The Life of Moses. The Yahwist as Historian in Exodus–Numbers* (Contributions to Biblical Exegesis and Theology, 10; Kampen: Kok Pharos, 1994). On the history of research of the Pentateuch, see most recently C. Houtman, *Der Pentateuch. Die Geschichte seiner Erforschung neben einer Auswertung* (Contributions to Biblical Exegesis and Theology, 9; Kampen: Kok Pharos, 1994).

3.   Well known studies are T.L. Thompson, *The Historicity of the Patriarchal Narratives: The Quest for the Historical Abraham* (BZAW, 133; Berlin: de Gruyter, 1974), and J. Van Seters, *Abraham in History and Tradition* (New Haven: Yale University Press, 1975).

4.   Covered most thoroughly by N.P. Lemche, *Early Israel: Anthropological and Historical Studies on the Israelite Society before the Monarchy* (VTSup, 37; Leiden: Brill, 1985).

5.   J.M. Miller and J.H. Hayes, *A History of Ancient Israel and Judah* (London: SCM Press, 1986), pp. 77-79.

6.   P.R. Davies, *In Search of 'Ancient Israel'* (JSOTSup, 148; Sheffield: Sheffield Academic Press, 1992).

7.   T.L. Thompson, *Early History of the Israelite People From the Written and Archaeological Sources* (Studies in the History and Culture of the Ancient Near East, 4; Leiden: Brill, 1992).

Against the background of the development which I have very briefly outlined above, it appears that it is now time to ponder a little on what it is that is going on in biblical studies. Before we do this, however, some consideration should be given to recent developments in the academic history debate in general.

II

What, above all, characterizes the *present* 'state of the art' is that the old models of historical science, which have dominated historical scholarship from the nineteenth, and at least through the first half of the twentieth century, and which were, basically, determined by the culmination of the critical historiography of Renaissance humanism in Germany from the end of the eighteenth century, by most theoreticians today are regarded as inadequate.[8] Quite contrary to what some scholars appear to believe, this is far from being only to do with the impact of the modern social sciences and changes in political and social realities. *Rather, the new situation should be regarded as a fundamental attack on the ways in which we think about history.*

It is, of course, nothing new in itself to raise doubts about such 'positivistic' notions as objectivity, historians' value freedom, primary and secondary sources, the existence of a continuous history, historical truth, or history as a science. Thus, it has for a long time sporadically been claimed that there is a 'crisis' in history. What is new, however, may be summarized in the following way: (1) The view that there is a crisis in conventional historiography has become 'commonplace'. (2) The whole question of history, historicity, historical consciousness, historical understanding, historicism, and historiography has been

---

8. The bibliography in this field is already vast, and it is possible throughout this study to refer to only a small part of it. Easily accessible surveys of recent developments in history theory are found in G.G. Iggers, *Geschichtswissenschaft im 20. Jahrhundert. Ein kritischer Überblick im internationalen Zusammenhang* (Kleine Vandenhoeck-Reihe, 1565; Göttingen: Vandenhoeck & Ruprecht, 1993)—a short, but useful introduction (unfortunately there are some errors in the bibliographic references), and J. Appleby, L. Hunt and M. Jacob, *Telling the Truth about History* (New York: Norton, 1994), pp. 198-237 and *passim* (on the whole, I find this study to be an excellent introduction to the topic). A very important book, theoretically advanced and most instructive, is R.F. Berkhofer, *Beyond the Great Story: History as Text and Discourse* (Cambridge, MA: The Belknap Press of Harvard University Press, 1995).

radicalized through the work of so-called 'postmodernist' theorists.

Whether your name was Leopold von Ranke or Fernand Braudel it was always a hermeneutical presupposition, shared by 'all' historians to the present day, that the historian can *understand* the past. Thinkers like I. Kant,[9] F. Nietzsche, M. Heidegger, H.-G. Gadamer, P. Ricoeur, J. Derrida, R. Barthes, M. Foucault, J.-F. Lyotard and J. Baudrillard, have made the very nature of such an understanding problematic, or even denied its possibility.[10]

Whereas Heidegger and Gadamer still stressed the relationship between the concrete interpretation of a part of something and the meaning universe within which the actual interpretation takes place, 'postmodernist' thinkers have gone much further in their critique. French theorists especially have attacked 'The Great Story' altogether and denied the existence of a 'metastory' which allegedly constitutes our horizon for understanding and which brings subject and object, the understander and the understood, together. In its most radical form the postmodernist critique has given a new meaning to the old discussion about objectivity. There can be no objectivity because there is no object 'the past' against which one can judge the different interpretations. And even if we do not have to deny altogether the existence of a given past, we must realise that we have no access to it. History writing, in other words, is impossible.

The consequences of the crisis in hermeneutics for the historian is obvious.[11] We do not always have to agree with the philosophers, but we cannot pretend that there is not a problem here. This is particularly true in the case of students of the Hebrew Bible who are, after all,

9.   The role of Kant as one of the 'founding fathers' of postmodernism is sometimes overlooked. For Kant's views on history, see the survey in H. White, *Metahistory: The Historical Imagination in Nineteenth-Century Europe* (Baltimore: The Johns Hopkins University Press, 8th edn, 1993 [1973]), pp. 55-58. On the relevance of Kant for the view of history in French postmodernism, see also J.-F. Lyotard, 'The Sign of History', in D. Attridge, G. Bennington and R. Young (eds.), *Post-Structuralism and the Question of History* (repr.; Cambridge: Cambridge University Press, 1993 [1987]), pp. 162-80.

10.   Thus, the post-modernist attack on history, in its most radical form a rejection of history altogether, also comprises the so-called 'new historians' (for various forms of the 'new history', see P. Burke (ed.), *New Perspectives on Historical Writing* (repr., Cambridge: Polity Press, 1993 [1991]).

11.   An excellent survey of the new situation, written by a historian, is Berkhofer, *Beyond The Great Story*.

dealing with texts which are more than two thousand years old!

Closely associated with the crisis in hermeneutics is the impact of linguistics and literary theory on modern historiography ('the linguistic turn').[12] In particular, thinkers like Derrida, Ricoeur and Barthes have stressed the autonomous character of the text and claimed that texts do not refer to any reality outside themselves.

Historians are text *readers* and have to deal with the hermeneutic problem that no text (i.e. historical source) can be understood the way it was 'originally' meant. An even if they should have been able to 'understand' their sources, which they are not, these textual sources of the past, again, do not refer to any past reality *outside* themselves. Historians are also text *producers*, writing texts which, in turn, cannot refer to any reality outside themselves. According to some theorists, then, there is no connection at all between modern history writing and the past to which historians believe they are referring. The past as an object will be read quite *differently* by each new generation of historians. It has, however, fairly little to do with past reality 'as it really was'. The radical consequence of this must, again, be the 'end of history'.

The so-called 'linguistic turn' has led to drastic developments during the last 20 years or so and represents yet another radical attack on the possibility of history writing in the traditional meaning.

All this, however, *has not* stopped history writing or writing about history. On the contrary, despite much frustration, the enormous amount of books which have appeared in the train of the postmodernist debate represent a striking contrast to the 'end of history' claims of recent theorists.[13] Not only has history not ended, but what we are

12. See, for a short survey, Iggers, *Geschichtswissenschaft im 20. Jahrhundert.*, pp. 87-96. For a more thorough survey, see Berkhofer, *Beyond The Great Story.* One of the most important vehicles for this new and radical development has been the journal *History and Theory* (for the history of the journal during its first 16 years, see R.T. Vann, 'Turning Linguistic: History and Theory and *History and Theory*, 1960–1975', in F. Ankersmit and H. Kellner [eds.], *A New Philosophy of History* [London: Reaktion Books, 1995], pp. 40-69). The label 'linguistic' is, of course, not wholly adequate for a description of what has been going on in the postmodernist discussion. The 'turn' has as much to do with textuality, interpretation and rhetoric as with linguistics. Apparently, the fact that also *historians read texts* has taken a long time to dawn upon some practitioners in the field.

13. Typically, in his survey 'Historiography and Postmodernism', *History and Theory* 28 (1989), pp. 137-53, F.R. Ankersmit takes as his starting point the over-production in historiography.

facing today is rather an ever increasing flow of 'histories' of all sorts. As for theoretical studies there has been a veritable explosion in the production of books and articles. Not bad indeed for a field of studies which is supposed to be dead! One of the stranger phenomena here is that the overwhelming majority of these books and articles deal with the relationship to history of those theorists who have claimed that there is no history.[14]

Yet we should take the philosophers' claim of a dichotomy between language and reality seriously. Even if we do not accept everything, it remains a fact that we have too often overlooked quite a few of the problems raised in 'postmodernist' discussions. What should come out of it is at least an increased methodological awareness of what it is that we are actually doing when we make simplistic statements concerning textual reference and historical reality.

This takes us to the next, and to the historian of ancient Israel perhaps the most important, recent development in history theory: The question of historical 'truth' and the relationship between history and literature. From ancient times philosophers have been stressing the difference between history (fact) and literature (fiction). Since the rise of scientific history in Germany in the late eighteenth and early nineteenth centuries the distinction between fact (= true) and fiction (= not true) has been the chief mainstay of all history writing.[15] Recently, scholars like R. Barthes, H. White and N. Davis,[16] influenced by recent developments in literary theory and genre research have seriously questioned the strict distinction between history writing and fiction.[17] History

14. See typically J. Goldstein (ed.), *Foucault and the Writing of History* (Oxford: Blackwell, 1994).

15. This, of course, does not mean that the truth value of history has not been in stormy weather before. F. Nietzsche's views on history, above all in his *Vom Nutzen und Nachteil der Historie für das Leben* from 1873, are well known. Already in 1921 T. Lessing (*Geschichte als Sinngebung des Sinnlosen* [Munich: C.H. Beck, 1921] claimed that all history writing is mythical and that historians want to create a hope for the future rather than to reconstruct past reality. Since then, discussions about truth and the possibility of a scientific history has been on the agenda with varying intensity. Cf. the surveys in G.G. Iggers, *New Directions in European Historiography* (Hanover, NH: Wesleyan University Press, rev. edn, 1984), pp. 3-42, and in Breisach, *Historiography*, pp. 326-36.

16. Iggers, *Geschichtswissenschaft im 20. Jahrhundert.*, pp. 87-88.

17. It is not without a certain irony that we recollect the Rankean ideal for history writing which put a lot of weight upon the ability to write elegantly and rhetorically

writing represents just another story, but it cannot be more 'true', only 'different'.

The most radical consequence of this 'genre neutralization' would, again, be the 'end of history'. This, however, appears not to be the case, at least not for the majority of scholars.[18] What has happened, though, is that we are now facing a completely new situation concerning the question of historical truth. Future studies must start from the presumption that 'truth' on the one side and 'fiction' on the other is not a valid distinction anymore. In other words, what is at stake here is the belief in a scientific and analytic history, modelled on the sciences, which is precisely what history has mostly been about up until the last 20 years or so.

Can we, as biblical scholars and historians of ancient Israel, allow ourselves to disregard the developments in history theory which I have briefly outlined above? I should think not. As we know, historians have, as a rule, not engaged themselves in philosophical questions.[19] This has now started to change. Whereas theory was formerly the field of philosopers and a few theorist (more often than not within the field of literary theory) today historians, too, point to the necessity of taking also epistemological and ontological presuppositions into some consideration.[20] Even if we cannot really talk of any real consensus, at

when describing the past, and how *imagination* was considered as the historian's most important tool. It is mostly forgotten today that T. Mommsen in 1902, one year before his death, received the Nobel Prize in literature for his *historical* works! The difference between the German historians and recent historians, of course, is that whereas the 'stories' of the former were regarded as providing their readers with direct access to a historical past, the 'stories' of the latter have, according to several theorists, nothing to do with the past.

18. Even H. White, who has been accused of being one of the foremost proponents for the 'end of history movement' has himself made it quite clear that he is not the radical sceptic he has been taken to be: 'I have never denied that knowledge of history, culture, and society was possible; I have only denied that a scientific knowledge, of the sort actually attained in the study of physical nature, was possible. But I have tried to show that, even if we cannot achieve a properly scientific knowledge of human nature, we can achieve another kind of knowledge about it, the kind of knowledge which literature and art in general give us in easily recognizable examples' (*Tropics of Discourse: Essays in Cultural Criticism* (Baltimore: The Johns Hopkins University Press, 5th edn, 1992 [1978]), p. 23.

19. Cf. P. Ricoeur, *The Reality of the Historical Past* (The Aquinas Lecture, 1984; Milwaukee: Marquette University Press, 1984), p. 3.

20. Cf. the statement of R.F. Berkhofer: 'In the end, any textualization, any dis-

least not yet, there can be little doubt that some historians today have realized that the situation has changed completely and that philosophical questions concerning historiography and historical truth cannot any longer be separated from the very task of history writing itself, but are of fundamental significance for what they are actually doing in their daily work.

Such is the situation today that historians simply cannot pretend anymore that nothing has happened. Appleby, Hunt and Jacob sum up the situation to the point:

> In the nineteenth-century sense, there is no scientific history, nor is there even scientific science. But it is possible to know some things more rather than less truly. In their respective realms, both history and science seek to do that. Given the issues about truth and relativism that have been raised late in this century, historians cannot pretend that it is business as usual. It is essential to rethink the understanding of truth and objectivity.[21]

It is precisely the idea 'But it is possible to know some things more rather than less truly' that is important here.[22] Much contemporary theory has been accused of scepticism or nihilism. What we need now is a healthy relativism with a multimethodological approach to history. There is no one method for historical studies any more, but a multitude of different strategies. Pluralism in methodology is final. With the end of scientific history, it follows that there are also several 'truths'.[23]

Summing up so far we can say that the most important thing which has come out of the radicalization of thinking about history during the last 20–30 years is not that 'history has ended' or that history writing has been made impossible. Despite the (quite necessary) postmodernist defiance, history still does not want to tell *any* story about the past, it wants to tell *the most likely story*, to account for the reality of what happened in the past. What is at stake here is that history, on the

course, any scholar must make some commitment about what is real, what is fictional, and what is hypothetical in a represented world' (*Beyond the Great Story*, p. 257).

21. Appleby, Hunt and Jacob, *Telling the Truth about History*, p. 194.

22. One may easily be given the impression that contemporary theoreticians are all 'sceptics'. This, of course, is not the case. For a recent defence of objectivity and authorial intention, see e.g. C.B. McCullagh, 'Can Our Understanding of Old Texts be Objective?', *History and Theory* 30 (1991), pp. 302-23. Cf. also the remarks further below on narrative historiography.

23. Berkhofer, *Beyond the Great Story*, refers to 'the fallacy of a single right or best interpretation' (p. 50).

whole, *has become much more problematic.* This should, however, be regarded as a necessary development, which demands of historians to take, at least a practical, interest also in epistemological and ontological questions.[24] The postmodernist challenge cannot simply be ignored. In the long run this will lead to stale antiquarianism.

III

If there is a crisis in history studies in general, the crisis in ancient Israelite historiography may be judged as even more dramatic. There are various reasons for this. For instance, most biblical scholars are trained as theologians or philologists, not as historians. More important, however, is the possibility that ancient Israelite historiography, similar to much of biblical studies in general, has been, and still is, more firmly embedded in historicist methods and truth values than many other academic disciplines today. This is quite easily perceived when we consider the story of what is 'true' and what is 'not true' in the introductory survey of the development within ancient Israelite historiography presented at the beginning of the present paper.

Apparently, very few biblical historians practising today appreciate that it is their very concept of history that is wrong. To the biblical authors there was no difference between the 'historicity' of, for instance, the Primeval Story and that of other stories in the Hebrew Bible. Subsequently, the process of cutting out bits and pieces of these stories in order to evaluate these as 'true' or 'not true' depending on whether they 'look like' history or not according to truth value standards of the twentieth century, is not only very unfair to the integrity of ancient texts, but also highly anachronistic. One simply cannot take out texts from an ancient culture which, incidentally, 'look like' modern texts and treat these as having a different semantic or cognitive status than other texts from the same culture which are not regarded as sufficiently 'historical' to be bothered with.[25] This, in fact, is one of the

---

24. If only to be able to cope with one's own feeling of being at loss *vis-à-vis* too much relativism or scepticism. Easily accessible introductions to the realism debate, by philosophers who are also 'happy' realists, are: M. Devitt, *Realism and Truth.* (Oxford: Blackwell, 2nd edn, 1991), and F.B. Farrell, *Subjectivity, Realism, and Postmodernism: The Recovery of the World* (Cambridge: Cambridge University Press, 1994).

25. Typically, many scholars working with the Hebrew Bible as a source for the

main reasons why 'historical sources' as the basis for a reconstruction of the history of ancient Israel are now disappearing at such a fast rate that before long there will be no 'historical' texts at all.

However, similar to what has happened in history studies in general, the crisis in biblical historiography clearly has not led to any 'end of history'. Many scholars still write so-called histories of ancient Israel as if nothing has happened,[26] apparently unaware of the fact that there has been a veritable upheaval in the theoretical discussion about the nature of history and the possibilities of history writing in general.[27] In short, the intellectual climate of the last thirty years or so appears not to have caught up on biblical studies at all. To say that historians of ancient Israel are theory weak is, in my view, the understatement of the century. As a genre, most of the so-called 'histories of ancient Israel' represent nothing more than various forms of a retelling of the

reconstruction of the history of ancient Israel regard the Deuteronomistic History as more 'reliable' than the Chronicler. There are several reasons for this. The most dangerous one appears to be that the Deuteronomistic History 'looks' more 'historical' and less 'ideological' in our eyes. Besides, since it is also 'older', it is for some reason regarded as more reliable. It is typical of much traditional historicism, not least in biblical studies since Wellhausen, to regard later texts as inferior to older ones, which, in turn, are regarded as more 'original' and more 'genuine'. This followed as a natural consequence of the strongly genetic approach of classical historicism, but a kind of romanticist Golden Age mentality also plays a certain role here. Already in the forties M. Bloch warned against this 'l'idole des origines' and maintained that the fact that texts are old does not necessarily make them more fit for historical explanation (M. Bloch, *Apologie pour l'histoire* [Paris: A. Colin, 1993], pp. 85-89). It is a good thing that (not many) scholars have now realized that the Deuteronomic History simply cannot be regarded as more 'reliable' than other historiographical texts of the Hebrew Bible (cf. A.G. Auld, *Kings Without Privilege. David and Moses in the Story of the Bible's Kings* (Edinburgh: T. & T. Clark, 1994).

26. M. Weippert, 'Geschichte Israels am Scheideweg', *TRu* 58 (1993), pp. 71-103, p. 72 n. 2, refers to 14 different works which have appeared during the last 20 years or so. He could also have mentioned further works. Cf. also the listing of the most important contributions in this field in J.A. Soggin, *An Introduction to the History of Israel and Judah* (London: SCM Press, 1993), pp. 34-38.

27. There are, of course, a few notable exceptions. See, for instance, K.W. Whitelam, 'Recreating the History of Israel', *JSOT* 35 (1986), pp. 45-70, K.L. Younger, *Ancient Conquest Accounts: A Study in Ancient Near Eastern and Biblical History Writing* (JSOTSup, 98; Sheffield: Sheffield Academic Press, 1990), pp. 25-58, and M.Z. Brettler, *The Creation of History in Ancient Israel* (London: Routledge, 1995), pp. 1-19, and *passim*.

biblical stories, diluted with sparse, desultory analytical remarks, not seldom with disparate references to 'archaeology'. In itself, there may be nothing wrong with this as long as the authors of these books know, or admit, what they are doing. The problem is that they themselves quite often give the impression that what they are doing is not to present us with their versions of the stories of the Hebrew Bible, but to the history of ancient Israel 'as it was'.

Occasionally, historians of ancient Israel do make references to theorists in the history field. One does not, however, always get the feeling that they really have been studying these theorists, or that they themselves have a consistent history theory which can really be said to make an impression on what they write. It is not enough to mention dutifully this or that well-known theoretician in some odd footnote, or in the introduction, something which often seems to be the case with leading scholars in the field. For instance, in the recent *magnum opus* of Ahlström we find a series of references to a bundle of theorists in the introduction to the work.[28] Nevertheless, after having read the book itself, it is very difficult to see that Ahlström himself has a clear view of what he means by 'history'.[29] I suspect that this has to do with Ahlström's hostility towards methodological considerations in general. This hostility is, in Ahlström's *The History of Ancient Palestine*, *inter alia*, revealed in a footnote/anecdote in his work: 'About three and a half decades ago a German student asked me what philosophy I used in studying Old Testament history and religion. My answer was: "None.

---

28. G.W. Ahlström, *The History of Ancient Palestine* (Minneapolis: Fortress Press, 1993), pp. 19-25.

29. Another example is found in J. Van Seters's use of Huizinga (*In Search of History: Historiography in the Ancient World and the Origins of Biblical History* [New Haven: Yale University Press, 1983], p. 1). Here, the problem is not that it is difficult to understand Van Seters's use of history in general, but that Huizinga, who is called upon as Van Seters's prime theoretical alibi, does not really play any role for Van Seters at all throughout his work. Quite another problem is that Van Seters apparently may have read Huizinga out of context (see the pertinent critique of Van Seters in Brettler, *The Creation of History in Ancient Israel*, p. 11). Brettler is probably right when he claims that Huizinga is not so well suited for ancient Israelite historiography because of his sharp distinction between literature on one hand and history on the other. Huizinga should, however, not be too easily dismissed. One remaining value of Huizinga today is in particular to be found in his strongly anti-positivist position (cf. R. Anchor, 'History and Play: John Huizinga and His Critics', *History and Theory* 17 [1978], pp. 63-93, pp. 74-77).

If I have a philosophy, it is that one cannot use any philosophical system." After that our ways parted'.[30]

This attitude, it should be added, is quite common, not only among biblical scholars, but also among practising historians. It is a tendency among many non-historians to refer to 'what is going on in history' as if all historians were now rallying behind the banners of postmodernism. This, of course, is far from being the case, and there is a gap, sometimes even an outspoken ill-will, between what the large majority of historians do and what a quite small number of theoreticians write.[31]

On the whole, this situation is unfortunate, but understandable. Many historians have felt that what is going on in philosophy is more or less irrelevant to what they themselves do. However, as long as these same persons in their very practice also *make* methodological statements based on epistemological and ontological presuppositions, they simply cannot pretend that philosophy is irrelevant. They are all in fact *practising* some sort of philosophy, and it would certainly not hurt their work if they had realized this.

Unfortunately, because of the enormous amount of books and articles being produced these days no one scholar can keep up with what is going on in theoretical studies. This has sometimes led to a most unprosperous development where some scholars 'marry' this or that particular theorist which they have, after much struggle, managed to understand, at least in part. Moreover, adopting uncritically the points of view of other thinkers quite often provides the individual scholar with an abstract straitjacket into which he or she attempts to adjust his or her own thinking and writing. Needless to say, such a procedure is quite unprolific. If one cannot read theoretical studies from the point of view that they should lead to a more acute sense of the theoretical and methodological issues involved, that they should inspire and make one understand more, and that they should make oneself more *inde-*

---

30. Ahlström, *The History of Ancient Palestine*, p. 52 n. 2.

31. For instance, in the presentation (by an aficionado!) of recent trends in history theory, in particular Richard Rorty and Hayden White, K. Jenkins writes of 'the chronic, anti–theoretical nature of mainstream 'history culture' in this country [i.e. England]. . . ' (K. Jenkins, *On 'What is History?' From Carr and Elton to Rorty and White* [London: Routledge, 1995, p. 5]). The same Elton who is being attacked by Jenkins, has, in a recent book (*Return to Essentials: Some Reflection on the Present State of Historical Study* [Cambridge: Cambridge University Press, 1991] characterized recent, theoretical discussions as 'dangerous' and as 'rubbish'.

pendent, one may be better off without any such studies. On the other hand, to reject the insights of those people whose job it is to reflect upon the nature of what it is that historians do, and not to profit from this thinking because one is ignorant or arrogant is a very dangerous business indeed, and will, in the end, only lead to a drastic lowering of the standards of both historical and biblical studies.

Among more methodologically conscious contemporary historians of ancient Israel, like Lemche, Thompson, Weippert and Whitelam, much weight has been given to the so-called *Annales* School with its stress on structures and developments over longer periods ('total history') rather than on events.[32] There are, however, some major problems with this approach, and even if there is a lot to be learnt from 'the *Annales* school', it is, in my view, not particularly suitable for historical studies in relation to the Hebrew Bible. I am here, for practical reasons, referring above all to the use of F. Braudel, who, apparently, has become the hero of quite a few biblical historians during recent years.

Braudel stressed, above all, the necessity to use empirical data, often quantifiable, to be able to identify the structures underlying social and cultural phenomena. Many things could be said about this (lack of theory, statistical primitivism), but this has been done by others and cannot take up my space here. My question would be: where in the Hebrew Bible do we find such (quantifiable!) empirical data? Since biblical historiography is narrative, event oriented and pre-analytical, it simply does not provide us with the kind of empirical data the anti event-oriented and anti-narrative analytical scientist Braudel could use.[33] Even if we also take the archaeological record and extra-biblical sources into consideration, we are still a long way from having enough

32. An easily accessible survey of the *Annales* school is found in Iggers, *New Directions in European Historiography*, pp. 43-79. Together with its many recent ramifications the *Annales* school constitutes what is known today as the 'New History'.

33. Archaeology, can of course, provide us with some information about climate, biology, and geography in Palestine during the Iron Age. Much more difficult is the question of population movements and economic trends—Braudel's second and most important layer in his three-tier model for historical explanation. As for 'traditional' historical categories like politics, culture and intellectual life (Braudel's third layer) we apparently encounter insurmountable methodological difficulties when, for instance, it comes to relating archaeology to biblical texts. It is important to note that Braudel has been criticized also by the younger generation of *Annales* historians (Appleby, Hunt and Jacob, *Telling the Truth about History*, p. 222).

empirical evidence from ancient Israel/Palestine to write anything but a very short and very fragmented history.

And not only fragmentary! Not only are there serious problems with relating the results of archaeology ('archaeological truth') to the Hebrew Bible ('textual truth'), an ever greater problem is perhaps the arbitrariness in ancient Israelite historiography caused by accidental archaeological findings of a few extra-biblical texts. The amount of work done on textual discoveries like those of, for example, Kuntillet Ajrud or Tell Dan may not be at all in proportion to the relative historical value or the representativeness of these texts. However, when such texts have been given so much attention, this is only because of our obsession with 'historical facts'. In sum, the idea of a 'total history' ('structure', 'multiple time', 'the long term') of ancient Palestine, based on the Hebrew Bible, extra biblical texts, or archaeology, is an illusion.[34]

Also, it is important to realize that the differences between the *Annales* school and its less accepted predecessors are not as great as some people assume. Empirical data—*sources*—are as important to Braudel and his followers as they are to researchers pursuing 'traditional' history. The sources may be different, the methods may vary, but in many respects the *Annales* approach, which prospered in the 1950s, 60s, and 70s, represents nothing more than a revised and improved edition of traditional German historiography. 'Total history' has been able to recapture historical reality 'as it was' as little as traditional history. Also the *Annales* approach belongs to 'modernism', to a historical–critical project that has not yet realized that there is a crisis within its walls and that the building is about to collapse. Such an approach can only bring about cosmetic changes in ancient Israelite historiography and *not* the fundamental changes which appear to be needed today.

All this makes it somewhat strange to read today about the so-called paradigm shift in biblical studies, in particular with regard to ancient Israelite/Palestinian historiography. Scholars like Lemche and Thompson have been eager to use the concept 'paradigm shift' of their own contributions to biblical historiography. This, however, is far from being an adequate description of what is really going on. Lemche and

---

34. That a 'total history' in fact is impossible in relation to the classical world has been stressed by R.S. Bagnall, *Reading Papyri, Writing Ancient History* (London: Routledge, 1995), pp. 112-17.

Thompson, apparently unaware of the fact that what we may call a conventional concept of history today is *highly* problematic, still work within the parameters of historical critical research, assuming that history is a science and that one must work with 'hard' facts.

Still profoundly marked by the nineteenth-century absolutist/ historicist/positivist[35] understanding of what it is to be scientific these scholars would, in Kuhnian terminology, qualify as 'normal historians', performing paradigm-based, historical critical research whereas scholars who respond to the postmodernist crisis would represent the beginning of the paradigm shift.[36] At the same time Lemche and Thompson are themselves excellent witnesses to the very paradigm crisis. What these scholars above all show us is, as I have demonstrated in my introductory section above, the full (or near full) consequences of the bankruptcy project historicism and the belief in a scientific history. In this way they have come to represent the first of the last modernists.[37]

In the future we shall, irreversibly, have to adjust to a different view on history from that of the historical–critical methods of the nineteenth century: a history with different 'truths' that are much less (when at all) the result of scientific analyses of empirical data. A history whose epistemic standing should no longer be regarded as part

---

35. This, I am afraid, is where Provan is right when he accuses recent trends in ancient Israelite historiography of being 'positivist' (I.W. Provan, 'Ideologies, Literary and Critical: Reflections on Recent Writing on the History of Israel', *JBL* 114 [1995], pp. 585-606, pp. 601-602). 'Positivism', as we know, is a terribly difficult concept to define. N. Stockman, in a recent study on positivism in the natural and the social sciences (*Antipositivist Theories of the Sciences: Critical Rationalism, Critical Theory, and Scientific Realism* [Sociology of the Sciences; Monograph; Dordrecht: D. Reidel, 1983]), notes that of five recent writers on the phenomenon all use the word positivism of 'unity of science or scientific method', and of 'empiricism in some form'. Three of them also include in the definition that 'science is the only valid knowledge' (p. 7). In the present context, the most useful definition would probably be 'belief in a scientific history'.

36. T.S. Kuhn, *The Structure of Scientific Revolutions* (Foundations of the Unity of Science; Chicago: The University of Chicago Press, 2nd edn, 1970 [1962]). I do not discuss here whether or not Kuhn's work may be useful also for the human sciences. I am simply referring to Kuhn because he has, rightly or wrongly, been brought into the discussion.

37. On how old and new paradigms may exist simultaneously, see Kuhn, *The Structure of Scientific Revolutions*, pp. 84-87.

of science, but as a part of culture.[38] A history characterized by a multiplicity of methods.

IV

Where does all this lead the student of the Hebrew Bible who is also interested in ancient Israelite historiography? Since writing about the history of ancient Israel forms a part of history writing in general, it can hardly be performed in isolation from the rest of academia. As we have seen, recent developments within the philosophy of history have *radically* changed our views on history and history writing. This must have some consequences also for those engaged in the study of ancient Israelite historiography. Are these bleak prospects? On the contrary!

The present status of history, as well as the fact that the historiography of the Hebrew Bible is pre-modern and narrative, make, in fact excellent starting points for a new orientation also in biblical *and* in ancient Israelite/Palestinian historiography. Following their devastating attack on the scientific rationality of much modernist historiography (including structuralist), many postmodernist historians have turned to pre-modern history.[39] One of the lasting consequences of the 'postmodernist' discussions will be the renewed interest in *narrative history*.[40]

The circumstance that the Hebrew Bible is narrative and pre-modern *must* have some consequences for the ways we work with it in relation to historiography. As I have mentioned above, a major problem in relation to that particular scholarly genre called the history of ancient Israel appears to arise from the lack of scholars to realize the truly

---

38. See the useful survey in F.R. Ankersmit, 'Historiography and Post-modernism', *History and Theory* 28 (1989), pp. 137-53.

39. 'Just as postmodernism since Nietzsche and Heidegger has criticized the whole so-called logocentric tradition in philosophy since Socrates and Plato, that is, the rationalistic faith that Reason will enable us to solve the secrets of reality, post-modernist historiography also has a natural nostalgia for a pre-Socratic early history' (Ankersmit, 'Historiography and Postmodernism', p. 153).

40. This interest in narrative history is *not only* a result of postmodernist developments. Historians connected to the *Annales* School have more recently taken a vivid interest in narrative. On this and other recent developments within narrative history ('micro-narrative', 'backward narrative'), see P. Burke, 'History of Events and the Revival of Narrative', in Burke (ed.), *New Perspectives on Historical Writing*, pp. 233-48.

narrative character of the Bible and its world. This is not only strongly anacronistic, but also detrimental to ancient Israelite historiography.

It may be that this unfortunate circumstance is sometimes brought about by religious interests,[41] but for the most part it constitutes an inherent cultural part of Western civilization. We are all 'brainwashed' by German historicism, and we have, according to this mental upbringing, a tendency to classify all written material in categories of true, that is, historical, and not true, that is, fictional. Did this thing happen, or did it not? Did Moses live, or did he not? We are all positivists in a certain sense—some less, some more. Even to use words like 'relativism' and 'scepticism' *is* positivistic, relativistic meaning relativistically 'true', 'historial', 'non-fictional'. In the same manner we use 'minimalist' or 'maximalist'. When we say that something 'is not historical in our sense of the word', or 'not historical in the modern (!) meaning of the word', we may be more right than we realize, but normally we mean that what we are referring to is factually less sound than we should like it to be. Even if it is my firm belief that the future definitely belongs to narrative history,[42] it will take a long time for us fully to learn to respect and to understand that narrative truth is a different truth from that of conventional history, but that it is *not* a lesser truth. It does not help much how many times we say to ourselves that the old categories fact and fiction are not valid distinctions anymore—we are all nursed on historicist milk and weaning is hard.[43] Our culture is *obsessed* with historical facts, and we are, obviously, unable to regain our 'innocence'. We shall continue to be historically conscious in a positivistic sense, to think about history and to write about history. No 'postmodernist' thinker can stop this. Also, much postmodernist thinking has gone too far.

Even if several of the points made by postmodernist theoreticians

41. Cf. J. Barr, 'The Problem of Fundamentalism Today', *The Scope and Authority of the Bible* (Explorations in Theology, 7; London: SCM Press, 1980), pp. 65-90, esp. pp. 87-88.

42. Here, Provan ('Ideologies, Literary and Critical', p. 585) misses the point when he claims that story and history are 'heading at speed in opposite directions'. What we are facing in recent debate is not narrative *instead of* history, but narrative *as* history.

43. 'Every history book available today—including those about the 'end of history'—reflects the enduring power of that nineteenth-century vision of scientific history' (Appleby, Hunt and Jacob, *Telling the Truth about History*, p. 52).

are useful and no doubt represent necessary correctives, many historians still believe in some sort of objective truth, that texts may refer to realities outside themselves, that we can know something about the past (even if far less than what we thought), and that texts have 'meanings'. Even the 'intention of the author', so much despised in recent trends, appears to have a future today.[44] The return to narrative history, then, is *not* completely a return to 'fiction'. Only we must know what it is that we are doing, and that the problems involved are indeed many.

V

My main point above has been that *narrative history* has become important in biblical studies after the decline and fall of 'scientific history'. Even if this goes for all kinds of history writing, it is particularly important for historiographical texts which themselves are pre-modern, pre-critical and narrative.[45]

However, even if narrative historiography has again been put on the agenda in 'postmodernism', it is not always clear what is meant by this concept. Also, the notion of 'narrative' itself is somewhat elusive and difficult to define.[46] In his highly influential article from 1979 Stone defined narrative the following way: 'Narrative is taken to mean the organization of material in a chronologically sequential order and the focusing of the content into a single coherent story, albeit with sub-

44. See, e.g., J.F. Durey, *Realism and Narrative Modality: The Hero and Heroine in Eliot, Tolstoy and Flaubert* (Studies in English and Comparative Literature, 8; Tübingen: G. Narr, 1993). Cf. also for a more comprehensive view the entertaining raillery by V. Cunningham, *In the Reading Gaol: Postmodernity, Texts, and History* (Oxford: Blackwell, 1994).

45. The present state of the history theory discussion also implies that the old discussion whether or not it is appropriate to refer to the biblical texts as 'historiographical', 'historical', or 'history-like' has become obsolete. All cultures have stories about the past, and there is nothing wrong in referring to these stories as 'historiography' as long as we are aware of what is meant by that term.

46. The literature on narrative is, of course, enormous. Since my concern here is with narrative *history*, I do not not intend to go into the more literary aspects of this discussion. Nevertheless, it follows from what I have written above that 'history' and 'literature' cannot anymore be separated as strictly as it has been done. Those interested in narrative in general should consult M.A. Powell, *The Bible and Modern Literary Criticism: A Critical Assessment and Annotated Bibliography* (Bibliographies and Indexes in Religious Studies, 22; New York: Greenwood Press, 1992).

plots'.[47] Even if other definitions could be quoted or given, Stone's definition is more than sufficient for the present purpose, not least because it suits perfectly the kind of literature which we find in the Hebrew Bible.

One particular manner in which narrative history works *is the way in which it uses particular genres*. In order to illustrate how narrative genres operate in the Hebrew Bible, I have taken as an example of a 'single coherent story' narrative the so-called Deuteronomistic Story (in combination with the Priestly Story). As I have mentioned above, it is not problematic to call this history, but it is pre-modern narrative and not modern/logical/analytic. It is descriptive, prescriptive, theological, instructive and didactic, centering around a central theme, with a particular point of view. As an example of a 'sub-plot', I have chosen the story in 1 Kings 3–9 about the Temple building of Solomon.

The so-called Deuteronomic History is probably written late in the sixth century BC. The purpose of this story (the author's intention!) is to explain the situation in which the Judaean nation[48] finds itself, and to show why things went so wrong. The end of the Judaean state, following Nebuchadnezzar's conquest of Jerusalem and the taking of

47. L. Stone, 'The Revival of Narrative: Reflections on a New Old History', *Past and Present* 85 (1979), pp. 3-24 at p. 3.

48. It is, of course, problematic to use such words as 'nation', 'kingdom' and similar 'modern' terms in relation to pre-modern societies. There has been an enormous discussion recently on 'nations' and 'nationalism' with an equally huge bibliography. Leading scholars have maintained that 'nation' is a modern word and should be reserved for this period (in particular for the transition period from agroliteral societies to modern industrial ones). However, since words like 'nation', 'kingdom' and 'state' have been used for such a long time about ancient 'communities' like the 'tribal federations' or 'chiefdoms' of ancient Israel and Judah, I find much of this discussion unprolific or irrelevant, some of it even disappointing (see, for instance, E.J. Hobsbawm's rather old-fashioned 'etymological' approach towards a definition in his book *Nations and Nationalism Since 1780: Programme, Myth, Reality* [repr.; Cambridge: Cambridge University Press, 2nd edn, 1995 (1992)], pp. 14-24). Others, like A.D. Smith, have pointed to the fact that cultural homogeneity (name, descent myths, culture, history, territorial homeland), which persisted for long periods of time in several parts of the world, not least in the ancient Near East, even qualify for the use of the term 'ethnic state'. No one, hopefully, would misunderstand this as having anything to do with the modern nations (A.D. Smith, *The Ethnic Origin of Nations* [repr.; Oxford: Blackwell, 1993 (1986)], pp. 69-91). See also by the same author: 'The Origins of Nations', *Ethnic and Racial Studies* 12 (1989), pp. 340-67.

members of the upper classes to Babylonia, is viewed as the Judaeans' punishment by their national deity Yahweh for their transgressions and their violations of the divine laws during their stay in Canaan, the land given to them by Yahweh. Here the Deuteronomistic Story ends. In the parallel story Chronicles—Ezra—Nehemiah, dealing with the history of God's chosen people from the creation to the restoration of the land during the Persian period, the events are taken even further in time.

Major events of this great biblical story are: Exodus and Wilderness Wanderings, the Conquest of Canaan, the Davidic Empire, the Divided Monarchy, the Babylonian Exile. If the Chronicler is included,[49] we also find a description of the return from Exile and the Resettling of the Land under Ezra and Nehemiah.

What we have here is a kind of history telling which does not pass down the past, but which actually *creates* the past. This, however, is not so unusual.[50] We can say that in the Hebrew Bible we have an early example of 'national' history writing.

The particular genre of this biblical national history does not distingish itself much from similar 'national histories' known from other cultures in many parts of the world. In Scandinavia the Icelandic sagas would probably provide us with the best study material. J. Hutchinson, working with the Gaelic Revival (1890–1921), has pointed to the following 'myths' 'that define the cultural voyage of a nation through time': myth of migration, myth of origins/settlement, myth of a golden age, myth of degeneration, myth of regeneration.[51]

---

49. Even if I use the term 'Chronicler', this does not imply that I assume a common authorship for Chronicles and Ezra/Nehemiah, or even for Ezra and Nehemiah. There is, however, no need to go into this discussion here.

50. Cf. the much referred to collection of essays in E. Hobsbawm and T. Ranger (eds.), *The Invention of Tradition* (repr.; Cambridge: Cambridge University Press, 1983).

51. J. Hutchinson, *The Dynamics of Cultural Nationalism: The Gaelic Revival and the Creation of the Irish Nation State* (London: Allen & Unwin, 1987), pp. 125-26. I am grateful to my friend and colleague Dag Thorkildsen, an expert on Norwegian cultural nationalism, who directed my attention to the work of Hutchinson. Thorkildsen has used Hutchinson's history paradigm to show how the writing of a national history in Norway was meant to provide the country with a national identity, rather than to recreate past reality, and he has also pointed out parallels to the biblical story of ancient Israel (*Nasjonalitet, identitet og moral* [KULTs skriftserie, 33; Oslo: Norges forskningsråd, 1995], pp. 112-13).

When compared to this paradigm, the Story of the Hebrew Bible (the purpose of which is national (re)birth and *not* any return to the past) may look like this:

1. Myth of migration (Exodus and wilderness wanderings).
2. Myth of origins/settlement (the conquest of Canaan).
3. Myth of a golden age (the Davidic empire).
4. Myth of degeneration (inner decay under the divided monarchy, Babylonian exile).
5. Myth of regeneration (future promise through the resettling of the land under Ezra and Nehemiah).

There is, apparently, a common human need which has led to the creation of a particular literary genre for this kind of national history writing. The similarities simply cannot be explained as coincidental.[52]

This theological story does not tell us what Israel's history *really* looked like in ancient times. On the other hand, we must not make the mistake of believing that because the Deuteronomists and their fellow authors expressed themselves through specific genres, everything we find in the Deuteronomic Story is pure fiction. It is the ordering of the different elements that is fictional, and it does not follow from this, as

---

52. I am not going into any discussion here or making any attempt to explain this phenomenon (if it can be explained). A wider discusion of genre would be beyond the scope of the present study. It is with interest we notice that this focusing on genre shines new light on old discussions concerning the nature of history and the question of generalizations. It has been claimed that history must seek generalizations because human action is governed by certain mental and physical laws which it is the task of the historian to discover. This appears to be the point also of A. MacIntyre who apparently sees all human action as the performance of already existing stories, as 'enacted narratives' (*After Virtue: A Study in Moral Theory* [London: Duckworth, 2nd edn, 1985], p. 211). The problem with generalizations in history, however, appears to be that they are insufficiently based on empirical evidence. Apparently, it is not history itself, but history *writing* which is governed by 'unconscious structures' and gives history coherence and meaning. Conceptualized reality is not reality. I do not know if H. White has the correct answer to these questions. His works have, however, been highly influential. White maintains that there exist basic narrative strategies—he calls them fundamental tropes—for *emplotting* events, and that these incompatible forms of emplotment are products of the historian's art in telling about the event. I have a feeling that this view is strongly influenced by structuralism. Cf further H. White's article from 1987: 'The Value of Narrativity in the Representation of Reality', recently reprinted in J. Appleby *et al.* (eds.), *Knowledge and Postmodernism in Historical Perspective* (New York: Routledge, 1996), pp. 395-407.

some scholars have chosen to believe, that there was not an ancient 'kingdom' of Israel at all. Also other 'national histories' are, as we have seen, written according to highly schematized forms. This, however, does not imply that the 'peoples' to which these histories refer did not exist at all prior to the writing of their history.

Even if we do not have at our disposal extra-biblical texts (which we do have for kings like Omri, Ahab, Jehu, Joash, Ahaz, Menahem, Pekah, Hoshea, Hezekiah, Manasseh and Jehoiachin) for David and Solomon, there is no reason to deny the historicity of David[53] or Solomon or the divided monarchy. We do not get access to the 'real' history of David and Solomon through the very late and schematic Deuteronomistic History, but—if one should be interested in such matters—*it is possible to know something.* The Deuteronomistic History simply did not spring from nothing, but must have been based on older traditions. This does not mean, however, that it is likely that we can really reconstruct 'what really happened'. But there is a big difference between knowing something and knowing nothing at all!

I now move to my other example of narrative history, the 'sub-plot' of Solomon's temple building in 1 Kings 3–9.[54] In a similar way as the Hebrew Bible tells its story of God and his people according to a strongly schematized form, the story of Solomon's temple building is apparently written according to a narrative structure common also to other cultures in the ancient Near East. Roughly, the common elements which may be found are: introductory underlining of the necessity to build a temple, visit to the sacred precinct, a dream, the deity reveals

---

53. Because of the several insecurities in relation to the interpretation of the Tell Dan inscription, I do not wish to discuss it here. My personal view today, however, is that I see no reason why this text should not refer to the 'House of David'.

54. Many other examples could have been mentioned in order to show how strongly related is the stereotyped and conventional literature of the Hebrew Bible to that of the ancient Near East. For example, even in a translation into English, no one can fail to notice the many similarites in style and contents between such different texts as, for instance the Egyptian Merneptah stela, dating from around 1200 BC, or the Aramaic/Assyrian bilingual Tell el-Fekheriye inscription, dating from the ninth century BC, and several biblical texts. Among the many valuable contributions to the comparative study of biblical and ancient Near Eastern texts particular mention should be made of the series of summer seminars conducted at Yale University and directed by W.W. Hallo. See, for instance, W.W. Hallo, B.W. Jones and G.L. Mattingly (eds.), *The Bible in the Light of Cuneiform Literature: Scripture in Context III* (Ancient Near Eastern Texts and Studies, 8; Lewiston: Edwin Mellon Press, 1990).

what has to be done, plans for the building, the king's wisdom is emphasized, a builder is hired and materials provided, the temple is finished, sacrifices and consecration ceremonies, gathering of the people, the deity enters his new abode, blessing of the king whose dynasty shall last forever.

The first scholar to see this phenomenon clearly was A.S. Kapelrud in 1963,[55] pointing to the story of the temple building of Gudea, *ensi* of Lagash (twenty-second century BC?) and the temple building of the god Baal in the Ugaritic myths (before the twelfth century BC).

More recently, Hurowitz[56] has analysed more than twenty extra-biblical building accounts, all of which show several basic common topics and events, the major ones being: a reason for the building or restoring, the consent or command of the deity (–ies) in relation to the project, preparation for the project (including workers, materials, laying of the foundation), a description of the building process and the building itself, dedication of the building, celebrations and rituals, a prayer or blessing. Hurowitz has shown how the same pattern is found not only in the story of Solomon's temple building, but also in relation to several other building accounts (the tabernacle, the restoration of the temple by the returned exiles, the repair of the walls of Jerusalem carried out by Nehemiah, and in Josephus's description of the building of the temple of Herod).

The point here is that we are dealing with *literary*, not 'historical' texts. Apparently, there existed a particular building genre in the ancient Near East. When the story of a king's building activities was recorded, this genre was always used. Since we are dealing with literary conventions and not with any historical detailed portrayal of what actually happened, it goes without saying that we face serious problems when we want to use this or similar texts as sources for historical reconstructions of past events.

What happens to history in cases like this? Hurowitz does not reflect upon the historical consequences of his investigation. To him the story of Solomon's temple building represents a literary genre, similar to 'other types of biblical and ancient Near Eastern literary forms, such

---

55. A.S. Kapelrud, 'Temple Building: A Task for Gods and Kings', *Orientalia* 32 (1963), pp. 56-62.

56. V. Hurowitz, *I Have Built You an Exalted House: Temple Building in the Bible in Light of Mesopotamian and Northwest Semitic Writings* (JSOTSup, 115; JSOT/ASOR MonSer, 5; Sheffield: Sheffield Academic Press, 1992).

as treaties and covenants, law corpora, proverb collections and wisdom instructions, letters and the like.'[57] In this, of course, he is quite
right. Nevertheless, if we really *want to* reflect upon the historicity of
1 Kings 3–9, we cannot leave it at that.

Even if specific genres are used, this does not necessarily mean that
we are dealing with 'pure fiction'. Far from it! In my view, there is a
lot of historical 'facts' to be found throughout the Deuteronomistic
History and there is little cause to be equally sceptic as some scholars
tend to be in this matter. For instance, no one appears to deny the existence of Gudea and his temple.[58] Another example (I could mention
several more) would be the seventh century Assyrian king Sennacherib,
a king well documented in the Hebrew Bible. No one, apparently,
would deny that this king built a palace at Ninive because of the highly
stereotyped documentation found in Sennacherib's building inscriptions.[59] There is, consequently, little cause to deny the existence of
Solomon or the fact that he built a temple in ancient Israel even if the
story about this event is narrative and conventional. When we take a
closer look at the story in 1 Kings 3–9 we shall find that there are also
other historical 'facts' to be learnt. For instance, the story reflects the
historical reality that there was an exchange of goods and labour
between ancient Israel and Phoenicia. We do not get a great many
details from the story concerning 'what really happened', but how
important is this? The main point here must be that even if the text
makes use of stereotyped genres, it is not a purely fictional text, but
also a 'historical' one. As a historical text it comes out of the past and
it *reflects* historical reality. This is the kind of 'historical truth' which
we may find in the texts of the Hebrew Bible.

VI

This, finally, brings me to the last point which I am going to take up
here: the relationship between narrative truth and history. What does
it imply for the *historical value* of the Old Testament stories that they

57. Cf. Hurowitz, *I Have Built You an Exalted House*, p. 312.

58. Cf. J.N. Postgate, *Early Mesopotamia: Society and Economy at the Dawn
of History* (London: Routledge, rev. edn, 1994 [1992]), pp. 263-64 and *passim*.

59. For a comprehensive study of Sennacherib's palace see J.M. Russell,
Sennacherib's Palace Without Rival at Nineveh (Chicago: University of Chicago
Press, 1991).

are narrative? What is the relation of these stories to past reality?

The important thing here must be the new view on *historical truth* which I have referred to above, and the fact that we now seem to be heading in the direction of replacing traditional, analytic history with narrative history. Scientific historians' objections to narrative has traditionally been that it belongs to fiction whereas history belongs to science, it is *verifiable*.[60] Being descriptive rather than analytic, they are, simply, 'unhistorical'. As I have shown above, it is exactly this kind of positivistic differentiation between narrative and history that has come under attack in recent years and which cannot any longer be strictly upheld.

We must also face the fact that history is not as important as it used to be. Our obsession with historicity must step down and give way to the recovery of the textual world itself. This does not imply that history has become obsolete, but that we must think about it in a totally different way. Furthermore, since we do not have access to past reality the way we thought we had, we should also reflect upon why and how we approach the past. How interesting is it, after all, to discuss, for example, the historicity of Abraham or whether Solomon built the temple? Are such questions really of any great importance at all? They are most certainly not as important as they used to be.

The decline and fall of scientific history is of the greatest importance to all students of pre-modern texts.[61] Even if we cannot, and should not, let history go completely in our dealings with the Hebrew Bible, we must allow it less space as well as less importance. The narratives of the Hebrew Bible contain *both* fact and fiction at the same time. *Both* of these modes are equally interesting and equally relevant.

Narrative history is not pure fiction, but contains a mixture of history and fiction. Even if we should be less interested in traditional history, we should also realize that there is a lot of it in the biblical stories. Much more than what many scholars tend to believe today.

The fact that the Bible has come much closer to literature, however, does not necessarily make it less 'historical', or less of a representation

---

60. On traditional objections to narrative explanations by historians, see P.A. Roth, 'Narrative Explanations: The Case of History', *History and Theory* 27 (1988), pp. 1-13, esp. pp. 1-2. See also Stone, 'The Revival of Narrative', p. 3.

61. 'Why insist on the Procrustean exercise of rendering histories into a format dictated by the current favorite model of scientific explanation?' (Roth, 'Narrative Explanations', p. 3.).

of past reality. Novels may provide us with some valuable insights here. No one, hopefully, would deny that from reading D.H. Lawrence, *Sons and Lovers* (1913) we can learn a lot about what it was like to grow up in a mining village in Nottinghamshire around the turn of the century, or that Jane Austen's *Emma* (1816) provides us with an excellent 'historical' introduction to the lives of the higher middle classes in its author's lifetime? Most novels are stories which *do* represent past reality, but of which one does not ask the question: did this really happen? How important is it that something really happened as long as it *might have* happened, and in this way convey important pieces of past reality? In many ways the relationship between narrative and reality in the Hebrew Bible is comparable to that of novels. A certain degree of objectivity may be obtained, and since these texts sometimes refer to realities outside themselves, a 'mild' form of realism is possible. It is most certainly true that readers create meaning, but this is not the whole story.

That narratives about the past and narratives from the past may represent past reality[62] is something which has now become more and more clear not only to historical theorists,[63] but also to classical scholars.[64]

---

62. Cf. Iser, who points out that the old distinction between fact and fiction is not very adequate since fiction without any known reality would be incomprehensible (W. Iser, *The Fictive and the Imaginary: Charting Literary Anthropology* [Baltimore: The Johns Hopkins University Press, 1993], p. 1). On the danger of *replacing* history with fiction see D. Lowenthal, *The Past is a Foreign Country* (repr.; Cambridge: Cambridge University Press, 1995 [1985]), pp. 224-31.

63. '. . . history, historical fiction, and fiction all exist along a spectrum ranging from supposedly pure factual representation of literal, historical truth to pure non-literal, invented fictional representation of phantasy. No work of history conveys only literal truth through factuality, and few novels, even science fiction ones, depict only pure fantasy' (Berkhofer, *Beyond the Great Story*, p. 67). A particular challenge, or at least a phenomenon worthwhile to ponder, is the representational status of so-called historical novels when these are based solely on the same sources as those used by historians. When some theorists claim that history is just another story, what is then the relationship between (say) S. Heym, *The King David Report: A Novel* (New York: Putnam, 1973), or J. Heller, *God Knows* (New York: Random House, 1984) to historians' retellings of the history of ancient Israel?

64. 'Narratives—historical and fictional—can be regarded as being spread along a scale with fact (or factual narrative) at one end and fiction at the other. These two poles are not contrary opposites, any more than red and violet are, when we place them at different ends of a spectrum. All stories on the scale produce story worlds' (A. Laird, 'Fiction, Bewitchment and Story Worlds: The Implications of Claims to

It is now time that historians of ancient Israel/Palestine start to think along the same lines.[65]

VII

The main point of this paper is that writing about the history of ancient Israel forms a part of history writing in general and should not be performed in splendid isolation from the rest of academia. The crisis in ancient Israelite/Palestinian historiography can only be solved through an increased epistemological and ontological awareness also among biblical scholars. The apparent shortcomings of traditional historical approaches *vis-à-vis* recent developments within hermeneutics, linguistics and genre theory (historical 'true' versus fictional 'not true') have led to an increased crisis in history. History shall no doubt recover from this crisis, but it will never be the same again. However, the belief in a scientific and analytic history, modelled on the sciences, will never recover.

The much vaunted 'paradigm shift' in contemporary ancient Israelite/ Palestinian historiography is non-existent. Rather, all authors of so-called histories of ancient Israel/Palestine are still profoundly marked by a nineteenth-century absolutist/historicist/positivist understanding of what it is to be scientific. These scholars would, therefore, in Kuhnian terminology qualify as 'normal historians', performing paradigm-based research.

The recent 'reciprocal concern with the historicity of texts and the

---

Truth in Apuleius', in C. Gill and T.P. Wiseman (eds.), *Lies and Fiction in the Ancient World* (Exeter: University of Exeter Press, 1993), pp. 147-74 at p. 174). The whole volume contains valuable contributions to the relationship between fact and fiction in the classical world.

65. This does not imply that there are not many problems with narrative history. For an attempt to deal constructively with the several objections raised against the representational legitimacy of historical narrative see A.P. Norman, 'Telling it Like it Was: Historical Narrative on Their Own Terms', *History and Theory* 30 (1991), pp. 119-35. Quite another matter is the adequacy of narrative in relation to dealing 'with the central issue of how we can systematically and objectively study the history of societies in all their complexity and multifaceted reality' (C. Lloyd, *The Structures of History* [Studies in Social Discontinuity; repr.; Oxford: Blackwell, 1995 (1993)], pp. 67-68). No doubt this objection is valid, but it does not really concern us here since we are dealing with an example of an *ancient* society where we do not have at our disposal sufficient material to write a 'total' history anyway.

textuality of history'[66] has, among other things, led to a renewed interest in narrative history. Narrative history is not pure fiction, but contains a mixture of history and fiction.

The fact that narrative history (always regarded as 'unhistorical' by positivists and 'normal historians') has again been put on the historical agenda, is extremely important to students of the Hebrew Bible, the historiography of which *is* narrative and pre-modern. As examples, I have used the Deuteronomic History and the story about the temple building of King Solomon in the present context. The major problem in relation to that particular scholarly genre called the history of ancient Israel appears to be that the scholarly world has failed to realize the truly narrative character of the Hebrew Bible and the way these narratives make use of certain stereotyped literary genres.

In the same way as there is no one approach to the past—to history— there is also no one truth. Since 'truths' may be of different kinds, it is important to realize that we today can no longer make the claim that traditional historical truth is more 'valuable' or more 'correct' than narrative truth.

Since very few positivistic facts indeed are verifiable, the kind of historical reality which narratives reflect provides us with the most relevant and the most interesting approach to the ancient Israelite/ Palestinian past.

If historical (verifiable) truth should be our only concern, the history of ancient Israel should not only be very short (written on ten pages or so), but it would also be utterly boring.

66. Berkhofer, *Beyond the Great Story*, p. 243, quoting L.A. Montrose.

INSCRIBED SEALS AS EVIDENCE FOR BIBLICAL ISRAEL?
JEREMIAH 40.7–41.15 *PAR EXEMPLE*

Bob Becking

1. *Introduction*

Is it still possible to write a history of Israel and how do I think the Old Testament text can be used in such a history? My answer to this question would be positive but depends on three features: (1) What is meant by 'Israel'?; (2) What is meant by 'history writing'? and (3) How is the Old Testament text used as a historical source?

1.   When Israel is construed as a political or ethnic term, many confusions arise as has been made clear by Philip Davies.[1] Interpreting the population of the central hill country during Iron Age I as Israelites, for instance, is premature. Using Israel as a political term would exclude the kingdom of Judah and confine the historical enterprise to the rather limited period of the existence of the Northern Kingdom. Therefore, when Israel is taken as a geographical term, my answer to the first question would be a firm and definite 'yes': it *is* possible to write a history of events and processes that took place in the area from the beginning up to the turn of the era, although it might politically be correct to speak about the history of ancient Palestine.[2]

2.   The enterprise of this historical reconstruction should be carried out normally as if it were a historical reconstruction of whatever period or people. It is because of the legacy of biblical history writing that

---

1.   P.R. Davies, *In Search of 'Ancient Israel'* (JSOTSup, 148; Sheffield: Sheffield Academic Press, 2nd edn, 1995), pp. 47-56.
2.   See now K.W. Whitelam, *The Invention of Ancient Israel: The Silencing of Palestinian History* (London: Routledge, 1996) and the remarks by N.P. Lemche, 'Clio is Also among the Muses! K.W. Whitelam and the History of Palestine: A Review and a Commentary', *SJOT* 10 (1996), pp. 88-114; esp. pp. 113-14; see also below in this volume, pp. 124-51.

such a statement has to be made. Although history-writing in general can be and has been abused for ideological purposes, this is especially the case when it comes to the question of the historicity of the traditions collected in the Old Testament. Both (traditional Christian) faith (or the lack of it) and various kinds of territorial claims have played the role of a hidden agenda in the process of the reconstruction of the history of Israel. This point can be clarified by referring to Huizinga's definition of history: 'History is the form in which a civilization accounts for its past'. This clause is famous and also ambiguous especially when it comes to the reconstruction of the history of ancient Israel/Palestine. The question is: whose civilization? Ours? The civilization of Iron Age and/or Persian period Israel? In case the last option is meant, the question arises: should the Deuteronomistic History not be considered as a form in which an exilic or post-exilic community accounted for its past? In that view the biblical texts are a clear form of history-writing. In some sense of the word the Deuteronomists were the first historians.[3] In case the first option is meant, several approaches are possible as is clear from the variety of books in the *Gattung* 'A History of Israel'. But one way or the other, when we want to account for the Jewish part of the foundations of the European civilization, a critical stand is needed. Problems arise when the two options are conflated. This happens when the history of ancient Israel is described as if it were in every dimension a part of our past. The concepts 'biblical Israel' and 'historical Israel', to use the terminology coined by Philip Davies, are conflated in the hybrid 'ancient Israel'.[4] The clearest example of this confusion and conflation still is the volume by Bright written in an emic mode.[5] In view of these ambiguities, I think that the definition of Huizinga will no longer provide a methodical basis for the writing of a 'history of ancient Israel/Palestine'.

A more solid base can be found in the philosophy of history of R.G. Collingwood.[6] The main point in Collingwood's approach is the search for a way out of the dilemma between 'realism' and 'scepticism'. This

---

3.   This is, as such, the strong point in the argument of B. Halpern, *The First Historians: The Hebrew Bible and History* (San Francisco: Harper & Row, 1988).

4.   Davies, *In Search of 'Ancient Israel'*.

5.   J. Bright, *A History of Israel* (Philadelphia: Westminster Press, 3rd edn, 1981).

6.   R.G. Collingwood, *The Idea of History* (Oxford: Oxford University Press, 1946).

antagonism differs from the debate between 'maximalists' and 'minimalists'. The antagonism 'realism' versus 'scepticism' has to do with the nature of historical knowledge and not so much with the question whether a source is to be evaluated as reliable in giving information on the past. 'Realism' supposes that the past is an objective reality. Knowledge of the past can be reached analogously as knowledge of the present can be reached. 'Realism' thus denies the categorical difference between past and present. 'Scepticism' is related to a basic mistrust in the knowability of the past. A scepticist only reckons with entities that are present. A final consequence of this sceptical position would be that it is impossible to do history. Collingwood tries to overcome this dilemma by elaborating a view on the character of so-called historical sources. These traces of the past are available and knowable in the present. It is possible to go to the British Museum, for instance, and ask for clay tablets. These traces are not the past as such. All the historian has in hand is the evidence mirroring the past. The evidence makes it possible to know the past but only in a restricted way. The task of the historian is to collect the evidence and then construct a personal image of the past. In this reconstruction models and imagination play a role. The historian cannot do without metaphorical language. Collingwood is very much aware of the subjective character of such a reconstruction. Here, some criticism of two models present in the field is needed. The first model for historical reconstruction is summarized in the often quoted phrase of Gerhard von Rad: 'Die historische Forschung sucht ein kritisch gesichertes Minimum; das kerygmatische Bild tendiert nach einem theologischen Maximum'.[7] The use of the noun 'gesichertes' hints at the fact that von Rad too was to some degree aware of the subjective character of any historical reconstruction. He fails, however, to see that the only thing that is certain is the available evidence. The sketch he is giving of the history of Yahwistic faith in biblical times[8] is much more than a mere exposition of evidence; it is a historical reconstruction in which von Rad's own faith often operates as a model for understanding. On the other hand, a reconstruction of

7. G. von Rad, *Theologie des Alten Testaments. Band I: Die Theologie der geschichtlichen Überlieferungen Israels* (Munich: Kaiser Verlag, 6th edn, 1969). p. 120; ET *Old Testament Theology* (trans. D.M.G. Stalker; New York: Harper and Row, 1962), I, p. 108: 'Historical investigation searches for a critically assured minimum—the kerygmatic picture tends towards a theological maximum.'

8. Von Rad, *Theologie*, pp. 1-115.

the kerygmatic image of the Old Testament should also be based on evidence. The second model to be criticized is to be found in a more recent thought-provoking monograph by Philip Davies. He, correctly, sees 'ancient Israel' as a product of the mind of biblical scholars. He fails to see, however, that what he calls 'historical Israel' is a product of the mind too. In his interesting and informative chapter on 'historical Israel' he is using the language of realism. Here, he is searching for what was 'really there'. In fact, however, he is using archaeological remains, cuneiform inscriptions etc. as evidence on which he builds his own reconstruction of Iron Age Palestine.[9]

This implies that history writing is not an objective science. Two remarks should be made here. (1) The non-repeatability of the events. A scientist can repeat an experiment. We are not in the position to ask the Assyrians to conquer Samaria again and give us the correct date or dates. We have to deal with the existing traces. A detective pursuing a murder inquiry is even better off than a historian, since this police-officer is in a position to check eye-witness reports. (2) There is always the person of the historian who deals with the existing evidence. Apart from social biases and personal interests, the historian is always a subjective interpreter who is relating data. Historian A may relate date 1 with date 2, while historian B relates 1 with 3, etc. This kind of small scale differences or preferences will lead to large scale differences when it comes to reconstruction. This can easily be shown by referring to the discussion on the interpretation of the Tell Dan inscription(s).[10] On a methodical level, it is here that the discussion between 'maximalists' and 'minimalists' finds its place.

Do these observations imply that 'anything goes'? Is any reconstruction of the past a possibility that should be considered? No! History writing should be based on an ongoing discussion or even debate that has as its aim intersubjective knowledge of the past. This implies that I cannot defend my position or reconstruction by merely saying 'Well, that is the way it is, that is how I feel it must have taken place'. Personal insights and subjective reconstructions should be related to the rules of the game, so that other scholars can at least react to it. These rules are, among others: (1) proper classification of the evidence available into primary source, secondary source etc.; (2) appropriate

9.   Davies, *In Search of 'Ancient Israel'*, pp. 57-71.
10.   I would like to refer to the discussion in a volume on the Tell Dan inscription(s) to be edited by F.C. Cryer, autumn 1997.

treatment of archaeological and epigraphic material—this implies a sound stratigraphic analysis and a paleographic discussion of inscriptions before constructing extensive historical conclusions; (3) making explicitly the implicit suppositions on time, space and society in which the event or the process had taken place.

3.   After having discussed the question of what should be meant by the two ideas 'Israel' and 'history writing' a remark on the Old Testament text as a historical source should be made. The metaphor 'source'—though used widely—is as such misleading, since it yields the image of a well from which historical information is constantly flowing. In my view the Old Testament text should be treated as evidence. The Old Testament supplies its readers with a diversity of traces of the past that are one way or another mirroring the past. These traces can be and have been treated differently. The difference in the treatment is mostly related to the ideology of the historian, be it minimalistic or maximalistic or something in between. I do not think that a theoretical discussion is fruitful here. This statement does not imply that I stand opposed to theoretical discussion. How I would like to deal with the evidence from the Old Testament will be shown in an example.

2. *The Gedaliah Incident*

Jeremiah 40.7–41.15 relates the assassination of Gedaliah who was appointed by the Babylonian overlord Nebuchadnezzar as governor over the Judaeans remaining in Judah after the conquest of the city of Jerusalem. The full and detailed story in Jeremiah has a parallel in the short report in 2 Kgs 25.22-26. In 2 Kings only the core of the narration is related while in Jeremiah various details are given. I see four main differences between the two textual units. (1) In Jeremiah a great number of names are given of the persons involved in the incident. In 2 Kings only the main characters are known by name. (2) Jeremiah relates a temporary emigration into various territories among whom Ammon, Edom and Moab are mentioned by name. This detail is absent in 2 Kings. (3) The author of the book of Jeremiah informs us about the political background of the assassination of Gedaliah. Johanan the son of Kareah, with the chiefs of the army, is said to have informed Gedaliah about his coming fate:

Do you know, that Baalis, the king of the Ammonites, has sent Ishmael,
the son of Nethaniah in order to make an end to your life? (Jer. 40.14)

(4) Finally, Jeremiah relates the slaughter by Ishmael of a group of
pilgrims on their way to Jerusalem. Surprisingly, the Gedaliah-incident
is not mentioned in 2 Chronicles. A remark in Josephus (*Ant.* X 9.7)
on the deportation of Ammonites in the 23rd year of Nebuchadnezzar
is seen as the Babylonian answer to the assassination of Gedaliah.[11]
Are these reports reliable and who is relying on whom?

2 Kgs 25.22-26 has generally been considered as part of DtrH. In
view of the religious character of this composition, DtrH cannot be
viewed as a primary historical source. Its framework might contain
reliable historical data, though. Nicholson[12] and Seitz,[13] among others,
noted an interesting contrast in the final compositon of 2 Kings 24–25
between the failure of leaders as Gedaliah and the foretaste of hope
provoked by the amnesty for Jehoiachin. On the date of the final composition of the DtrH there is a lively debate among scholars. Adherents
of the Cross-school reckon with a pre-exilic Dtr1 and an exilic Dtr2.
Within the perimeters of this hypothesis 2 Kgs 25.22-26 is exilic.[14]
Adherents of the Smend-school operate with a model in which an exilic
history writing was edited extensively and variously even after the
exile. Within this concept 2 Kgs 25.22-30 is seen as part of DtrN, a
nomistic editor writing around 560 BCE.[15] Würthwein, however, pleads
for a post-Deuteronomistic and thus post-exilic origin of 2 Kgs 25.22-

---

11. J.M. Berridge, 'Ishmael', *ABD* 3 (1992), p. 512; U. Hübner, *Die Ammoniter:
Untersuchungen zur Geschichte, Kultur und Religion eines transjordanischen
Volkes im 1. Jahrtausend v. Chr.* (Abhandlungen des Deutschen Palästina-Vereins,
16; Wiesbaden: Harrasowitz, 1992), pp. 203-205; G. Barkay, 'A Bulla of Ishmael,
the King's Son', *BASOR* 290-291 (1993), pp. 112-13.

12. E.W. Nicholson, *Preaching to the Exiles: A Study of the Prose Traditions in
the Book of Jeremiah* (Oxford: Basil Blackwell, 1970), p. 132.

13. C.R. Seitz, *Theology in Conflict: Reactions to the Exile in the Book of
Jeremiah* (BZAW 176; Berlin: de Gruyter, 1989), pp. 215-21.

14. See, e.g., R.D. Nelson, *The Double Redaction of the Deuteronomistic
History* (JSOTSup, 18; Sheffield: JSOT Press, 1981), pp. 86-89; S.L. McKenzie,
*The Trouble with Kings: The Composition of the Book of Kings in the
Deuteronomistic History* (VTSup, 42; Leiden: Brill, 1991), pp. 136-37.

15. E.g. W. Dietrich, *Prophetie und Geschichte: Eine redaktionsgeschichtliche
Untersuchung zum deuteronomistischen Geschichtswerk* (FRLANT, 108; Göttingen:
Vandenhoeck & Ruprecht, 1972), pp. 140-43.

26.[16] Special attention should be paid to the view of Begg who argued for the possibility that DtrH ends with the rather negative note in 2 Kgs 25.21b and that 2 Kgs 25.22-30, labelled by him as the 'Babylonian apologetic' reflects the concern of the compiler of the Enneateuch (Genesis–Kings).[17] Unfortunately Begg does not date this final compiler but it stands to reason that the compilation took place after the final redaction of the DtrH and might be a post-exilic addition. The Book of Jeremiah cannot be seen as a primary historical source. The abundance of details in Jer. 40.7–41.15 gives the impression of an eyewitness report. This observation functions as the corner-stone in the more traditional biographic interpretation of the narration under consideration and of the whole of Jeremiah 37–44. Holladay has summarized and defended this position. Although he admits that Jeremiah 37–44 forms a biographical composition, the alleged eye-witness-character of the narratives convinces him of the authorship of Baruch.[18] Scholars like Pohlmann,[19] Thiel[20] and Seitz,[21] though operating with different models for reading texts, agree on the insight that in the *Scribal Chronicle* in Jeremiah 37–43 material from the tradition and elements of the redaction are conflated. It should be remarked, however, that the book of Jeremiah was not composed to relate history but to proclaim a certain belief-system. Its aim is to convince the post-exilic community in Yehud of the conviction that the exile has to be seen as divine punishment for a disobedient people. The post-exilic

16. E. Würthwein, *Die Bücher der Könige: 1. Kön. 17–2 Kön. 25* (ATD, 11.2; Göttingen: Vandenhoeck & Ruprecht, 1984), pp. 479-80.

17. C.T. Begg, 'The Interpretation of the Gedalajah Episode (2 Kgs 25,22-26) in Context', *Antonianum* 62 (1987), pp. 3-11.

18. W.L. Holladay, *Jeremiah 2: A Commentary on the Book of the Prophet Jeremiah Chapters 26-52* (Hermeneia; Minneapolis: Fortress Press, 1989), esp. pp. 286-87.

19. K.-F. Pohlmann, *Studien zum Jeremiabuch: Ein Beitrag zur Frage nach der Entstehung des Jeremiabuches* (FRLANT, 118; Göttingen: Vandenhoeck & Ruprecht, 1978), pp. 108-22; K.-F. Pohlmann, 'Erwägungen zum Schlusskapitel des deuteronomistischen Geschichtswerk', in A.H.J. Gunneweg and O. Kaiser (eds.), *Textgemäss* (Festschrift E. Würthwein; Göttingen: Vandenhoeck & Ruprecht, 1979), pp. 94-109.

20. W. Thiel, *Die deuteronomistische Redaktion von Jeremia 26-45* (WMANT, 52; Neukirchen Vluyn: Neukirchener Verlag, 1981), pp. 52-61.

21. Seitz, *Theology in Conflict*, pp. 273-79.

date of the final redaction of Jeremiah—and of most of the tradition in Jeremiah—has been made probable by the redaction-historical investigations.[22]

The relation between the two textual units has been interpreted differently. According to Gray[23] and many other scholars[24] the account of the Deuteronomistic redactor is quite obviously a summary since Jeremiah is much better informed. M.A. O'Brien[25] extends this line of thought by stating that 2 Kgs 25.22-26 was added to 2 Kgs 25.1-21 on the basis of the Jeremiah account. Theoretically, the opposite position is also a possibility. To my knowledge the thesis that Jer. 40.7–41.15 is a redactional elaboration of 2 Kgs 25.22-26 has not been defended.[26] A common source behind the two texts has been supposed by Mowinckel.[27] This view did not find many adherents.[28] In case the majority view is correct, an exilic date for 2 Kgs 25.22-26 is hardly defendable since the unit must be post-Jeremiah. Moreover, it is hard to understand how a 'historian' living in the Babylonian exile had access to a story about a prophet who at the time was living in Egypt.

This analysis, superficial as it may be, makes clear that a gap in time of at least half a century exists between the alleged moment of the assassination of Gedaliah and the first writing down of the texts

22. See in general R.P. Carroll, *Jeremiah: A Commentary* (OTL; London: SCM Press, 1986).

23. J. Gray, *I & II Kings: A Commentary* (OTL; London: SCM Press, 3rd edn, 1977), p. 770.

24. E.g. Dietrich, *Prophetie*, p. 140 and n.12; Pohlmann, *Studien*, pp. 110-11; Pohlmann, 'Erwägungen zum Schlusskapitel', pp. 94-109; Thiel, *Jeremia 26-45*, pp. 54-55 n. 12; Nelson, *Double Redaction*, p. 86; Würthwein, *Könige*, p. 479; Begg, 'The Interpretation of the Gedalajah Episode', pp. 4-5; Seitz, *Theology in Conflict*, pp. 215-21. This is only a small selection.

25. M.A. O'Brien, *The Deuteronomistic History Hypothesis: A Reassessment* (OBO, 92; Freiburg: Universitätsverlag, Göttingen: Vandenhoeck & Ruprecht, 1989), p. 271.

26. Begg, 'The Interpretation of the Gedalajah Episode', p. 5, only toys with the idea.

27. S. Mowinckel, *Zur Komposition des Buches Jeremia* (Kristiana: Jacob Dybwad, 1914), pp. 29-30.

28. G. Wanke, *Untersuchungen zur sogenannten Baruchschrift* (BZAW, 122; Berlin: de Gruyter, 1971), pp. 115-16; M. Cogan and H. Tadmor, *II Kings: A New Translation with Introduction and Commentary* (AB, 11; Garden City: Doubleday, 1988), p. 326.

concerned. This implies that the information in the Jeremiah narrative as well as in the report in the book of Kings is based on memory. Memory is an important source for the historian. Many details on World War II are only known through oral history. Memories include recollections of the past that would have been overlooked in an approach that accounts only for official documents. Memory, however, is limited and—more importantly—recollections do not have the character of copies of reality. They are products of the mind. Memory is steered by the active involvement of the person who recollects its observations, with the events in which this person was involved. This statement can easily be proved: (1) by referring to the often biased descriptions in the oral history of World War II and (2) by an experiment. You can ask a group of Old Testament scholars for their recollections of the day President Kennedy was assassinated. It might be interesting to compare and contrast these pieces of memory with each other and with other pieces of evidence about the event. The information on the assassination of Gedaliah is based on the memory of persons who were in one way or another involved in the incident. Besides, the interim period between event and description had been a turbulent time for those responsible for this tradition.

For the modern historian these observations have two implications. (1) The historicity of the assassination and its details have to be confirmed by other sources. (2) In the post-exilic period it has been part of the religious tradition of Jerusalemite Yahwism to believe that after the sack of Jerusalem a non-Davidic ruler did not succeed in governing the area for a long period while at the same time there is a thread of hope provoked by the amnesty for the Davidic Jehoiachin.[29] This tradition was thus one of the ways in which the post-exilic community accounted for its past.

3. *Inscribed Seals*

A multitude of seals has been uncovered in Israel/Palestine through archaeological excavations. A great number of seals likewise showed

---

29. See K. Baltzer, 'Das Ende des Staates Juda und die Messias-Frage', in R. Rendtorff and K. Koch (eds.), *Studien zur Theologie der alltestamentlichen Überlieferungen*, (Neukirchen Vluyn: Neukirchener Verlag, 1961), pp. 33-43; Nicholson, *Preaching to the Exiles*, p. 132; Begg, 'The Interpretation of the Gedalajah Episode', pp. 3-11; Seitz, *Theology in Conflict*, pp. 215-21.

up in the hands of antiquities dealers. Their provenance is very uncertain. It is not clear how many of these seals are forgeries. Most of these seals bear an inscription. Generally the inscription gives the name of the owner with the name of the father. A second important group gives the name of the owner with the owner's public office as in the seal on the cover of the *Journal for the Study of the Old Testament*: *lšm' 'bd yrb'm*, 'belonging to Shema the servant of Jeroboam'.[30] The vast majority of the seals bear an iconic representation. These seals are of interest for the historian for three reasons. (1) Sociologically: they are to be seen as evidence for the growing complexity of the society in Israel/Palestine during Iron Age IIB and C. To a certain degree they are symbols of power for the ruling class.[31] (2) The iconic representations give an insight into the symbol system that was in use in the area under consideration. Shifts in the repertoire might indicate changes in the belief system as has, for instance, been argued by Keel and Uehlinger for a process of astralization during the final part of the Iron Age.[32] (3) The inscriptions on the seals have provided us with a great number of names, many of whom are known from the Old Testament. Two warnings are necessary here. First, the over-whelmingly overrepresentation of -*'el* and -*yhw*/-*yw* as theophoric

30. Inscribed seal from Megiddo, first half of the eighth century BCE; E. Kautsch, 'Ein althebräisches Siegel vom Tell el-Mutsellim', Mitteilungen und Nachrichten des deutschen Palästina-Vereins 10 (1904), pp. 1-14; G.I. Davies, *Ancient Hebrew Inscriptions: Corpus and Concordance* (Cambridge: Cambridge University Press, 1991), No. 100.068.

31. See, e.g., N. Avigad, 'The Contribution of Hebrew Seals to an Understanding of Israelite Religion and Society', in P.D. Miller, P.D. Hanson and S.D. McBride (eds.), *Ancient Israelite Religion* (Festschrift F.M. Cross; Philadelphia: Fortress Press, 1987), pp. 195-208; H. Weippert, *Palästina in vorhellenistischer Zeit* (Handbuch der Archäologie II.1; Munich: C.H. Becksche Verlagsbuchhandlung, 1988), pp. 674-78; and the conclusions in D.W. Jamieson-Drake, *Scribes and Schools in Monarchic Judah: A Socio-Archaeological Approach* (JSOTSup, 109; SWBA, 9; Sheffield: Almond Press, 1991), pp. 136-59.

32. O. Keel and C. Uehlinger, *Göttinen, Götter und Gottessymbole: Neue Erkenntnisse zur Religionsgeschichte Kanaans und Israels aufgrund bislang unerschlossener ikonographischer Quellen* (Quaestiones Disputatae, 134; Freiburg: Herder Verlag, 1992), pp. 322-429.

elements in these names lead Tigay[33] and de Moor[34] to the conviction that these inscribed seals plead for an early shift to monotheism (probably already before the Iron Age). This view should be questioned since it is based on the disputable assumption that every *Yh(wh)* and *'l* in the onomasticon would refer to the same deity which was the only deity to be revered. Secondly, any premature identification of an individual name attested in a seal inscription with a person known from the biblical records should be avoided.

4. *Gdlyhw, Yšm'‛l* and *B'lyš'*

In relation with the possible (non-)historicity of the Gedaliah-incident three inscribed seals should be discussed.

a. *Gdlyhw*
In Lachish the imprint of a seal was excavated dating from the second half of the seventh century BCE.[35] The date is anchored by the stratigraphy of the excavation. Paleographically, the script belongs to the Iron Age IIC/III period.[36] The inscription reads:

> *lgdlyhw / [']šr '1 hby[t]*
> Belonging to Gedalyahu, who is over the house

A majority of scholars identify *Gdlyhw* with Gedaliah, the assassinated governor.[37] Some have their doubts.[38] The stratigraphy of the find is

---

33. J.H. Tigay, *You Shall Have No Other Gods: Israelite Religion in the Light of Hebrew Inscriptions* (HSM, 31; Atlanta: Scholars Press, 1986); J.H. Tigay, 'Israelite Religion: The Onomastic and Epigraphic Evidence' in: Miller, Hanson and McBride (eds.), *Ancient Israelite Religion*, pp. 157-94; see also Avigad, 'Contribution', pp. 195-97.

34. J.C. de Moor, *The Rise of Yahwism: The Roots of Israelite Monotheism* (BETL, 91; Leuven: Uitgeverij Peeters, 1990), pp. 10-41.

35. Edited by S.H. Hooke, 'A Scarab and Sealing from Tell Duweir', *PEQ* 67 (1935), pp. 195-96. See also S. Moscati, *L'epigrafia Ebraica Antica: 1935–1950* (BibOr, 15; Rome: Pontifico Istituto Biblico, 1951), pp. 61-62 (No. 30); Davies, *Ancient Hebrew Inscriptions*, p. 139.

36. L.G. Herr, *The Scripts of Ancient Northwest Semitic Seals* (HSM, 18; Missoula: Scholars Press, 1978), p. 91.

37. Already by Hooke (ed.), 'A Scarab', pp. 196-97; see also Moscati, *L'epigrafia*, p. 61 (with lit.); J. Gray, *I & II Kings*, p. 771; B. Oded, 'Judah and the Exile', in J.H. Hayes and J.M. Miller (eds.), *Israelite and Judaean History* (London: SCM Press, 1977), p. 276; D.J. Wiseman, *Nebuchadrezzar and Babylon* (Oxford:

consistent with an early sixth century BCE governor. The problematical thing, however, is the fact that various Gedaliahs are known from this period, some of whom are definitely not identical with the assassinated governor, but others might be. Arad Ostracon 21.1-2 mentions a *gdlyhw [bn] 'ly'r* who is not identical with assassinated governor.[39] A jar handle excavated at Gibeon (seventh/sixth century BCE) contains the inscription *m[gd]lyh[w]*.[40] A bulla of unknown provenance from the early sixth century BCE reads *lḥnnyhw bn gdlyhw*.[41] A bulla probably from the Tell Beit Mirsim area and stemming from the late seventh, early sixth century BCE has the inscription *lgdlyhw 'bd hmlk*.[42] From the same archive a bulla with the inscription *lgd[ly]hw hw[š]'yhw* is known.[43] Finally, a seal of unknown provenance reading *gdlyhw bn šby* is known[44]; this seal cannot be related to the assassinated governor in view of a different name for the father. This survey makes clear that Gedaliah was a relatively popular name around 600 BCE which makes any identification problematic. In case the identification is correct, a remark should be made on the office held by *Gdlyhw*. He has been in the position of 'majordomo', a 'steward' or a

Oxford University Press, 1985), p. 38; Cogan and Tadmor, *II Kings*, p. 325 (with some hesitation); S.C. Layton, 'The Steward in Ancient Israel: A Study of Hebrew *('ašer) 'al-habbayit* in its Near Eastern Setting', *JBL* 109 (1990), p. 637; Davies, *In Search of 'Ancient Israel'*, p. 76 n. 4; R. Althann, 'Gedaliah', *ABD* 2 (1992), p. 923; P.J. King, *Jeremiah: An Archaeological Companion* (Louisville: Westminster/John Knox Press, 1993), pp. 98-99; G.W. Ahlström, *The History of Ancient Palestine from the Paleolithic Period to Alexander's Conquest* (JSOTSup, 146; Sheffield: Sheffield Academic Press, 1993), p. 799.

38. E.g. N. Avigad, 'Baruch the Scribe and Jerahmeel the King's Son', *IEJ* 28 (1978), p. 52 n. 1.

39. Y. Aharoni, *Arad Inscriptions* (Jerusalem: Israel Exploration Society, 1981), pp. 42-43; Davies, *Ancient Hebrew Inscriptions*, 2.021.

40. J.B. Pritchard, 'More Inscribed Jar Handles from El-Jib', *BASOR* 160 (1960), p. 4; Davies, *Ancient Hebrew Inscriptions*, 22.058.

41. N. Avigad, 'The Seal of Jezebel', *IEJ* 14 (1964), pp. 193-94, B, Pl 44.C; Davies, *Ancient Hebrew Inscriptions*, 100.218.

42. N. Avigad, *Hebrew Bullae from the Time of Jeremiah: Remnants of a Burnt Archive* (Jerusalem: Israel Exploration Society, 1986), p. 24 no. 5; Davies, *Ancient Hebrew Inscriptions*, 100.505.

43. Avigad, *Burnt Archive*, p. 48, No. 41; Davies, *Ancient Hebrew Inscriptions*, 100.541.

44. N. Avigad, 'Another Group of West-Semitic Seals from the Hecht Collection', *Michmanim* 4 (July 1989), p. 9; Davies, *Ancient Hebrew Inscriptions*, 100.874.

'prefect of the palace'. This office is mentioned several times in the Old Testament and is known from epigraphic evidence. The function can be interpreted as that of a senior officer in the palace.[45] If that is correct, one wonders why the Babylonian king would have appointed a former high officer in such a delicate position as the governor of a conquered area.

In the Old Testament five different persons go by the name of Gedaliah. In addition to the assassinated governor are known: (1) The son of Amariah and grandfather of Zephaniah (Zeph. 1.1); (2) A descendant of Jeshua who was divorced from his foreign wife in connection with the measures alleged to be taken by Ezra (Ezra 10.18); (3) A levitical singer from the Jeduthun family living after the exile (1 Chron. 25.3 and 9) and (4) Gedaliah, the son of Pashur, who is presented as a senior officer in the reign of Zedekiah and was, with three other officers of high rank, responsible for the incarceration of the prophet Jeremiah (Jer. 38.1-6). It is astonishing that an identification of this Gedaliah with *gdlyhw* / *[']šr 'l hby[t]* has not been proposed until now. In my view he is a better candidate for identification than the assassinated governor. The data in the book of Jeremiah tally with what is known about the function of a 'steward'. By way of an aside, I would like to make a comment on a remark by Davies who connects the Jaazaniah mentioned in 2 Kgs 25.23 and Jer. 40.8 with a seal inscription reading *ly'znyhw 'bd hmlk,* 'belonging to Yaazanyahu, the servant of the king'.[46] This seal was excavated at Mizpe and can be dated to the first half of the sixth century BCE. Although the identification proposed is not without its problems—other persons are known from inscriptional evidence—Davies infers from the indicator 'servant of the king' that Jaazaniah was serving Gedaliah as a king. He then concludes that Gedaliah might have been installed by the Babylonians as a king and not merely as governor. On this tricky basis he argues that '. . . the biblical literature is concealing the fact, maybe because its authors did not regard him as Davidic?'.[47] This is, I think, making clear that 'historical Israel' is not unlike 'ancient Israel' a product of the mind. Moreover, Davies overlooks the possibility that the seal

---

45. See Layton, 'The Steward in Ancient Israel', pp. 633-49.
46. R. Hestrin and M. Dayagi-Mendels, *Seals from the First Temple Period* (Hebrew; Jerusalem: Israel Museum, 1978), No. 5; Davies, *In Search of 'Ancient Israel'*, p. 76 n. 4, incorrectly renders the name as *y'zyhw*.
47. Davies, *In Search of 'Ancient Israel'*, p. 76 n. 4.

might be slightly older than the destruction of Jerusalem and that its owner kept it as a memento of better times.

Therefore, on a scale of one to ten, the probability of the identification of *gdlyhw 'šr 'l hbyt* with the assassinated governor is in my view two, or low probability.

b. *Yšm''l*

Ishmael, the son of Nethaniah, the son of Elishama, one of the royal line, is presented as the person who killed Gedaliah. In 2 Kgs 25.25 the genealogy is much longer than in Jer. 40.14 where the Masoretic Text reads 'Ishmael, the son of Nethaniah'. The Old Greek version did not contain the words the 'son of Nethaniah'. I will not discuss here the complex text-critical issues related to the book of Jeremiah[48] but only refer to the possibility that in some Jeremiah traditions the identity of Gedaliah's killer was no more than 'Ishmael', which as such makes an identification with an individual known from extra biblical material more difficult.

The name Ishmael occurs frequently both in the Old Testament and in inscriptions from the Iron Age II–III. In the Old Testament six individuals go by the name Ishmael: (1) The son of Hagar and Abraham; (2) The murderer of Gedaliah; (3) A Benjaminite from the family of Saul, but ten generations later (1 Chron. 8.38; 9.44); (4) The father of Zebadiah, a senior officer under Jehoshaphat in Judah (2 Chron. 19.11); (5) One of the 'officers over one hundred' operative in the revolt against Athaliah (2 Chron. 23.1); (6) Ezra 10.22 mentions a priest Ishmael who was found guilty of marrying a foreign woman.[49] Several Ishmaels are known from Hebrew inscriptions.[50] Some of them are

---

48. On them, see most recently A. Schenker, 'Der nie aufgehobene Bund: Exegetische Beobachtungen zu Jer 31,31-34', in E. Zenger (ed.), *Der Neue Bund im Alten* (Quaestiones Disputatae, 146; Freiburg: Herder Verlag, 1993), pp. 85-112; B. Becking, 'Jeremiah's Book of Consolation: A Textual Comparison: Notes on the Masoretic Text and the Old Greek Version of Jeremiah xxx-xxxi', *VT* 44 (1994), pp. 145-69; H.-J. Stipp, *Das masoretische und alexandrinische Sondergut des Jeremiabuches* (OBO, 136; Freiburg: Universitätsverlag /Göttingen: Vandenhoeck & Ruprecht, 1994).

49. See J.M. Berridge, 'Ishmael', *ABD* 3 (1992), p. 512; E.A. Knauf, 'Ishmael', *ABD* 3 (1992), pp. 512-13.

50. See Davies, *Ancient Hebrew Inscriptions*, p. 380; Barkay, 'A Bulla of Ishmael', p. 109.

attested in the period surrounding the fall of Jerusalem.[51] None of them is explicitly stated to be the son of Nethaniah. Otherwise, the name Ishmael is attested throughout the West-Semitic languages from Amorite to Safaitic.[52] A few years ago a bulla with an inscription was purchased in Jerusalem. The inscription has been edited by Barkay[53] and reads as follows:

lyšm''l bn hmlk
Belonging to Ishmael, the king's son.

Since the bulla has been purchased nothing is known about the circumstances in which it was found. This implies that a relation with the stratigraphy of a certain tell and thus the allotment to an archaeological period is impossible. Barkay offers a superficial paleographic analysis on the basis of which he considers the script to be typical of seals from the late Judaean Monarchy. He therefore dates the bulla to the end of the seventh or the early sixth century BCE. A survey of the characters in the inscription gave me no reason to doubt this observation. The indicator 'the king's son' is known from the Old Testament[54] as well as from 18 seals and bullae.[55] The interpretation of the indicator is not clear. The interpretation rests on the question whether the word *bn*, 'son', should be taken literally or metaphorically. Two claims are made.[56] (1) The term refers to members of the royal family who fulfilled certain duties at the court. (2) The term does not as such refer

---

51. For instance the ten different Ishmaels known from the archive edited by Avigad, *Burnt Archive*, Nos. 78, 79, 80, 81, 82, 89, 101, 102, 162, 173.

52. See E.A. Knauf, *Ismael: Untersuchungen zur Geschichte Palästinas und Nordarabiens im 1. Jahrtausend v. Chr.* (Abhandlungen des Deutschen Palästina-Vereins; Wiesbaden: Harrasowitz, 2nd edn, 1989), p. 38 n. 170; M. Dijkstra, 'Ishmael', in K. van der Toorn, B. Becking and P.W. van der Horst (eds.), *Dictionary of Deities and Demons in the Bible* (Leiden: Brill, 1995), cols. 844-45.

53. Barkay, 'A Bulla of Ishmael', pp. 109-14.

54. Five individuals are known as a 'king's son': Jotham (2 Kgs 15.5; 2 Chron. 26.21); Joash (2 Kgs 22.26; 2 Chron. 18.25); Jerahmiel (Jer. 36.26; see also Avigad, 'Baruch the Scribe', pp. 54-56; Avigad, *Burnt Archive*, pp. 27-28); Malchiah (Jer. 38.6; see also the same person and title on a seal known from a sale catalogue referred to by Barkay, 'A Bulla of Ishmael', p. 111) and Maaseiah (2 Chron. 28.7).

55. See the outline in Barkay, 'A Bulla of Ishmael', p. 111.

56. See A. Lemaire, 'Note sur le titre BN HMLK dans l'ancien Israël', *Sem* 29 (1979), pp. 197-99; Avigad, *Burnt Archive*, pp. 27-28.

to a member of the royal family. It denotes a ceremonial function probably in relation with the security of the court. Two features plead for the second interpretation, though not decisively. In view of the formal structure of the seals and bullae under consideration the term *bn hmlk* most likely refers to an office and not to relationships within the royal family. Not all the names known from the inscriptions and from the Old Testament are known as the names of a member of the royal family. This is, however, due to the fact that we do not possess a full genealogy chart of the Judahite royal family.

Barkay suggested identifying *yšm''l bn hmlk* with Ishmael the son of Nethaniah.[57] This identification is possible. Is it probable? Against the identification pleads the following: (1) The provenance of the bulla is uncertain with even the possibility of a forgery. (2) The name Ishmael was probably even more popular than the name Gedaliah. From that point of view the difference in the indicator, *bn hmlk* versus 'son of Nethaniah', is difficult to explain.

Therefore, on a scale of one to ten the probability of the identification is in my view five.

c. *B'lyš'*

The name of the Ammonite king Baalis (Jer. 40.14) is unique in the Old Testament. Until recently, a comparable name did not occur in the Ammonite inscriptions. Besides, the Babylonian documents of the period do not refer to an Ammonite king. In Tell el-'Umeiri, Transjordan, a bulla with a seal impression was excavated in 1984.[58] The inscription reads:

> *lmlkm'r 'bd b'lyš'*
> Belonging to Milkomor, the servant of Baalisha.

The seal and its inscription are assumed to be Ammonite.[59] This can be supported by the fact that Tell el-'Umeiri was part of the Ammonite

---

57. Barkay, 'A Bulla of Ishmael', pp. 109-14; supported by King, *Jeremiah*, pp. 98-99.

58. Edited by L.G. Herr, 'The Servant of Baalis', *BA* 48 (1985), pp. 169-72; see also L.T. Geraty, 'A Preliminary Report on the First Season at Tell el-'Umeiri', *AUSS* 23 (1985), pp. 98-100; W.E. Aufrecht, *A Corpus of Ammonite Inscriptions* (Ancient Near Eastern Texts and Studies, 4; Lewiston, NY: Edwin Mellen Press, 1989), pp. 308-09; Hübner, *Ammoniter*, pp. 86-87.

59. Cf. F. Israel, 'Les sceaux ammonites', *Syria* 94 (1987), p. 144; Aufrecht, *Corpus*, pp. 308-09; Hübner, *Ammoniter*, pp. 86-87.

areas in Transjordan.[60] The paleography of the inscription parallels the Ammonite script of circa 600 BCE.[61] Because of the theophoric element *mlkm,* the first name in the inscription *mlkm'r* can be considered as Ammonite.[62]

Soon after the finding of the inscription, identification of *b'lyš'* with the Baalis of Jer. 40.14 was surmised. Even during the campaign at Tell el-'Umeiri, Boling suggested it to Herr, the editor of the text.[63] The identification is accepted by most of the scholars.[64] Some, however, have their doubts.[65] As far as I can see, there are three arguments against it: (1) The absence of the indication 'king' for *b'lyš'* (2) The orthography of the name. In Jer. 40.14 Baalis is spelled with a *sāmek,* the inscription reads a *shin.*[66] (3) The final *'ayin* disappeared in Jeremiah 40. There are also three arguments in support of this identification. (1) It should be noted that in this kind of inscription *'bd* usually means 'servant; minister of the king'.[67] (2) In an analysis of the depictions on the seal Younker showed that 'It is likely, that the seal motifs represent the royal insignia of the kingdom of Ammon'.[68]

60. See the preliminary excavation report of Geraty, pp. 85-109.

61. Cf. Herr, 'The Servant of Baalis', p. 172.

62. L.T. Geraty, 'Baalis', *ABD* 1 (1992), pp. 556-57.

63. See L.G. Herr, 'Is the Spelling of "Baalis" in Jeremiah 40.14 a Mutilation?', *AUSS* 23 (1985), p. 187.

64. E.g. by Geraty, 'A Preliminary Report', p. 98; W.H. Shea, 'Mutilation of Foreign Names by Bible Writers: A Possible Example from Tell el 'Umeiri', *AUSS* 23 (1985), pp. 111-15; Herr, 'The Spelling of "Baalis"', pp. 187-91; A. Lemaire, 'Recherches actuelles sur les sceaux nord-ouest semitiques', *VT* 38 (1988), p. 221; G.A. Rendsburg, 'More on Hebrew *šibbōlet*', *JSS* 33 (1987), pp. 255-58; G.A. Rendsburg, 'The Ammonite Phoneme /Ṯ/', *BASOR* 269 (1988), pp. 73-79; Aufrecht, *Corpus,* p. 309; Holladay, *Jeremiah 2,* p. 296; Hübner, *Ammoniter,* pp. 203-205; King, *Jeremiah,* pp. 98-99.

65. E.g. M. Weippert, 'The Relations of the States East of the Jordan with the Mesopotamian Power During the First Millennium BC', in A. Hadidi (ed.), *Studies in the History and the Archeology of Jordan III* (Amman: Department of Antiquities, 1987), p. 101 n. 51.

66. See Weippert, 'Relations of the States', p. 101 n. 51. He compares Ba'alis with the Ugaritic personal name *b'ls.*

67. Herr, 'The Servant of Baalis', p. 171: 'a very prominent government official'; Geraty, 'A Preliminary Report', p. 98. See also *HALAT* III, p. 732 s.v. *'ebed* I, 3; Aufrecht, *Corpus,* pp. 32.309.

68. R.W. Younker, 'Israel, Judah and Ammon and the Motifs on the Baalis Seal from Tell el-'Umeiri', *BA* 48 (1985), pp. 173-80.

(3) The script of the inscription corresponds with the Ammonite script of circa 600 BCE, which suits the period.[69] The arguments in support of the identification seem to be more convincing than the arguments against it.

With regard to the difference in spelling between *b'lyš'* and Baalis, I would like to make the following remarks. (1) The /š/ in **ba'ᵃlîša'* goes back to a proto-semitic /ṯ/.[70] This consonant is rendered with a ṯ in Ugaritic and Old-South Arabic; with a *shin* in Assyrian; Old Aramaic, Hebrew and in the inscription of Balaam from Deïr 'Allah; with a *tau* in the Official Aramaic of the Achaemenian period, but with a *sāmek* in the Aramaic part of the bilingual inscription from Tell Fekherye.[71,72] These differences make it possible to assume that in Ammonite the *shin* was pronounced in such a way, that Judaeans rendered it with a *sāmek*. Maybe, the Ammonites still pronounced it as the proto-Semitic unvoiced interdental /ṯ/. (2) The Shibbolet-incident in Judges 12 indicates, that there existed a diversity in pronunciation of the interdental /ṯ/ between Ephraimites and Gileadites.[73] (3) The decay of the final *'ayin* is more difficult to explain. Possibly the variant-readings in the Old Greek tradition—βελισσα; βελισαν namely βελισα[74]—preserved a reminiscence to the original form of the name.

Therefore, on a scale of one to ten, the probability of the identification is in my view eight.[75]

---

69. Cf. the remarks by Herr, 'The Sevant of Baalis', p. 172.

70. The name Elisha, for instance, is written in Liuhyanite: *'lyṯ'*.

71. Editio princeps: A. Abu-Assaf, P. Bordreuil and A.R. Millard, *La statue de Tell Fekherye et son inscription bilingue assyro-araméenne* (ERC Cahier, 10; Paris: Editions Recherche sur les Civilisations, 1982), see especially the outline on p. 44.

72. Cf. Rendsburg, 'More on Hebrew *ssibbaolet*', pp. 255-58; Rendsburg, 'The Ammonite Phoneme/Ṯ/', pp. 73-79. But see the critical remarks of A.F.L. Beeston, '*Šibbōlet*; a further comment', *JSS* 33 (1987), pp. 259-61; Geraty, 'Baalis', p. 557.

73. See recently J.A. Emerton, 'Some Comments on the Shibboleth Incident (Judges XII 6)', in A. Caqout, S. Légasse and M. Tardieu (eds.), *Mélanges bibliques et orientaux en l'honneur de M. Mathias Delcor* (AOAT, 215; Neukirchen Vluyn: Neukirchener Verlag, 1985), pp. 149-57; A. Lemaire, 'L'incident de *šibbōlet*: perspective historique', in Caqout, Légasse and Tardieu (eds.), *Mélanges bibliques et orientaux*, pp. 275-81; Rendsburg, 'More on Hebrew *šibbōlet*', pp. 255-58; Beeston, '*Šibbōlet*', pp. 259-61; Rendsburg, 'The Ammonite Phoneme/Ṯ/', pp. 73-79.

74. See J. Ziegler, *Jeremias–Baruch–Threni–Epistula–Jeremias, Septuaginta auctoritate societas litterarum Gottingensis* (Göttingen: Vandenhoeck & Rupprecht, 1957), XV, p. 419.

75. See also B. Becking, 'Baalis, the King of the Ammonites: An Epigraphical

d. *Confirmation?*

In my view it is not 100 per cent certain that the names *Gdlyhw, Yšm''l* and *B'lyš'* can be identified with Gedaliah, Ishmael and Baalis.

5. *Historicity of the Gedaliah Incident*

Even if it could be proved that *Gdlyhw, Yšm''l* and *B'lyš'* are indeed identical with Gedaliah, Ishmael and Baalis, this does not prove the historicity of the Gedaliah incident.[76] The inscriptions can make clear that persons by these names actually lived in the period under consideration. It should be noted that the Babylonians pursued a system of local governorship in occupied territories which make the appointment of an individual like Gedaliah plausible.[77] That, however, does not imply that acts pursued by these individuals as reported or narrated in later narratives are thus historical. By way of an analogy: when you read on a wall in a dead end street in Oxford the words 'Sebastian was here' written in typical twentieth century CE characters, that does not prove the historicity of the narratives in *Brideshead Revisited*, although many scenes from that novel could eventually and possibly have happened in the first part on the century mentioned. This is, however, not a honest analogy, since Waugh's novel is ahistorical and does not claim that the characters had actually lived. The report in 2 Kings and the story in Jeremiah are based on historical characters and thus are limited in the sense that they had to deal with the characteristics of the individuals.

Is it still possible to write a history of Israel and how do I think the Old Testament text can be used in such a history? After this small exercise, my answer to this question is still positive. Now I want to add that the writing of such a reconstruction of a part of the past requires a discussion on a multitude of evidence in minute detail and thus a balanced philosophy of history to supply us with the rules of the game of historical reconstruction.

Remark on Jeremiah 40.14', *JSS* 38 (1993), pp. 15-24.

76. *Pace* Hübner, *Ammoniter*, pp. 203-205; Barkay, 'A Bulla of Ishmael', p. 113; King, *Jeremiah*, pp. 98-99.

77. See, e.g., Oded, 'Judah and the Exile', p. 275; Wiseman, *Nebuchadrezzar and Babylon*, p. 38; *pace* Davies, *In Search of 'Ancient Israel'*, p. 76 n. 4.

MADONNA OF SILENCES: CLIO AND THE BIBLE

Robert P. Carroll

Every new generation must rewrite history in its own way. (R.G. Collingwood[1])

History. . . is a nightmare from which I am trying to awake. (Stephen Dedalus[2])

Once historicity is allowed to intrude difficulties multiply. (Ernest Best[3])

The work is a tissue of fictions: properly speaking it contains nothing that is true. However, in so far as it is not a total deception but a verified falsehood, it asks to be considered as speaking the truth: it is not just any old illusion, it is a determinate illusion. (Pierre Macherey[4])

1. *Historical Preamble*

Regularly I visit the Kelvingrove Art Gallery in Glasgow because it is very close to the University of Glasgow where I work and on each visit I inevitably go into the Scottish Gallery in the east wing of the building where there is a display of art relating to Scotland. Two notices in that gallery warn spectators against naive readings of Scottish culture, especially in relation to tartan and the kilt. The first notice is entitled 'Myths and Realities' and contains the following observation:

. . . the myths and realities of tartan and the kilt. . . whose *bogus but entertaining tales of the past* have developed into universally accepted 'tradition' [emphasis added].

1.   *The Idea of History* (Oxford: Clarendon Press, 1946), p. 248.
2.   J. Joyce, *Ulysses* (London: The Bodley Head, 1960 [1922]), p. 42.
3.   'The Reading and Writing of Commentaries', *ExpTim* 107 (1996), p. 359.
4.   *A Theory of Literary Production* (trans. G. Wall; London: Routledge & Kegan Paul, 1978), p. 69.

The other notice is about 'Tartan' and includes the following statement:

> By the 1820s there were arguments about and research into the origins of tartan and *a colourful history was created*. . . [emphasis added].

On every occasion when I read those notices I wonder whether the same could not be said about the stories in the Bible. Did the biblical writers, whoever they were and whenever they wrote, create 'a colourful history, with bogus but entertaining tales of the past which have developed into a universal tradition'?[5] That for me is one of the central questions in any discussion about historiography and the Bible.[6]

It is a question I ponder regularly but am never certain as to what the answer to it might be. If a gun were put to my head and I had to give a straight, honest answer to the question I would be hard put to provide an adequate or satisfactory answer. I would still have to confess to *not* knowing how best to answer that question. Now I know all the answers other biblical scholars would give and I am familiar with the answers provided by theologians who have a special, but partisan, interest in the Bible. Such answers are often, if not inevitably, constructed out of 'paraphrases of the Bible' and are highly determined by credal, confessional and catechetical readings imposed upon the biblical text, so are (in my opinion) obsolete and irrelevant to serious contemporary academic and cultural historians writing on the Bible. As each generation has to rewrite history for its own time (Collingwood) I do

---

5.   Throughout this paper I use the circumlocution '*biblical* writer' because it is both conventional and convenient to do so, and not because I imagine that whoever the writers of the 'original' texts now constituting the Bible may have been had the slightest idea (or intentionality) that they were writing something to be called, at a later date, 'the Bible'. On this point see P.R. Davies, *Whose Bible Is it Anyway?* (JSOTSup, 204; Sheffield: Sheffield Academic Press, 1995), pp. 15-16.

6.   As my first paper on the subject of historiography in the initial session of a new seminar on 'Biblical Historiography', this paper is necessarily inchoate, exploratory and questing. It would require a further paper from me to entertain the wide range of current theoretical work on historiography or to do it justice in relation to the Bible. Interested parties may care to anticipate that paper by reading A. Grafton, *Forgers and Critics: Creativity and Duplicity in Western Scholarship* (Princeton, NJ: Princeton University Press, 1990); J. Appleby, L. Hunt and M. Jacob, *Telling the Truth about History* (New York: Norton, 1994); K. Jenkins, *On 'What is History?': From Carr and Elton to Rorty and White* (London: Routledge, 1995); L. Gossman, 'The Rationality of History' in *idem* (ed.), *Between History and Literature* (Cambridge, MA: Harvard University Press, 1990), pp. 285-324; and all the writings of Hayden White on historiography.

not find the parroting of ancient answers satisfying in any sense and the repetition of such answers in our time is, in my judgment, a betrayal of the present for an imagined past. I know that there is a problem of historiography here and I recognize the problematic nature of the question, but I remain uncertain as to my own (considered) answer to whatever and however the question of 'the Bible and its relation to history' may be posed. So in this paper I shall attempt to set out *some* of the issues *as I see them* which I think bear directly on the current discussion about the Bible and history. I have entitled it 'Madonna of Silences: Clio and the Bible' in recognition of the fact that the silence of history on so much of what the biblical writers represent as 'the story of Israel' raises a number of questions about the nature of representation in the Bible, and also in acknowledgment of the continued influence on my thinking of the writings of the poets I have used Auden's phrase 'Madonna of silences'.[7]

I live and work in Glasgow, Scotland, although I am not myself Scottish. I am Irish and being from the Republic of Ireland I tend to find that all things Presbyterian are alien to me.[8] However, living in Scotland I am deeply aware of the fact that in the eighteenth century James Macpherson (1736–96) *invented* (that is to say, created) the character Ossian, the famous third-century Celtic poet (trumping the English Cadmus, perhaps?).[9] This figure proved to be enormously

---

7. The phrase 'Madonna of silences' comes from Auden's poem 'Homage to Clio' (*Collected Shorter Poems 1927–1957* [London: Faber & Faber, 1966], pp. 307-10, citing p. 308). Madonna, used because it is appropriate to do so in Ireland, here is *not* a reference to a contemporary American pop singer and self-publicist. Clio is, of course, the muse of history.

8. I am however deeply conscious of the contribution made to Irish republicanism by eighteenth-century dissenting thought (including Presbyterian thinkers) and bemoan the loss of that independence of thought in the centuries since. I also regret that the recent volume of work on ethnicity in biblical studies (M.G. Brett [ed.], *Ethnicity and the Bible* [Biblical Interpretation Series, 19; Leiden: Brill, 1996]) could find no place for a consideration of the Irish dimension in contemporary biblical scholarship. For a nod in the direction of Irish religious thought see the two volumes edited by Enda McDonagh: *Faith and the Hungry Grass: A Mayo Book of Theology* (Blackrock, Co. Dublin: The Columba Press, 1990); and *Survival or Salvation? A Second Mayo Book of Theology* (Blackrock, Co. Dublin: The Columba Press, 1994).

9. See J. Macpherson, *The Poems of Ossian: and Related Works* (ed. H. Gaskell, with an introduction by F. Stafford; Edinburgh: Edinburgh University Press, 1996). For a discussion of Macpherson's creation see H. Gaskell (ed.), *Ossian*

seminal and significant in the subsequent history of Scottish literature and Ossianic societies sprang up all over the place.[10] Like the stories of the invention of the kilt,[11] Ossian was pure invention yet had *real* effects and flourished as a 'living person' in the imagination of writers and poets. Does the figure of Ossian provide an analogy for biblical characters? Did the biblical writers create (invent) Abraham and David, Moses and Ezra and then did those characters resonate as 'real persons' for generations of readers and hearers of the Bible? How could we tell whether they did or did not? What means do we have for exploring the past of a collection of writings, such as constitute the Bible, in terms of the historical (in any sense of actually having happened or existed *outside of the text* as opposed to having been invented by imaginative writers) or in terms of the invented? We know about Ossian. We know about the kilt. But do we know about the Bible? It is this deep agnosticism (in the sense of genuinely *not* knowing) which is at the root of the problem and the fundamental problem *as I see it* is to determine how to overcome our essentially agnostic position in order to make *reliable* judgments about the historical nature of the contents of the Bible. I do not find that the ready dismissal of the problematic nature of the question about history in favour of a quasi-*religious* reading of the Bible as being necessarily historical, so typical of much of contemporary biblical scholarship, is any solution at all to the problem. Of course, this presumption in favour of reading the Bible *as historical* is also a direct inheritance of the post-Enlightenment construction of biblical studies as being of necessity *historical*-critical. As Hans-Georg Gadamer has noted 'the criticism that historical-scriptural studies have exercised on the canon has set the theological task of recognizing biblical history *as history.*'[12] Perhaps then the current reaction

Revisited (Edinburgh: Edinburgh University Press, 1991); and the chapter on 'Ossian as a Poetry of Knowledge' in J. McGann, *The Poetics of Responsibility: A Revolution in Literary Style* (Oxford: Clarendon Press, 1996), pp. 33-40.

10. This paper was first presented at the SBL International Meeting in Trinity College Dublin (on 22 July 1996) and it is a nice coincidence that Oisín House abuts on to the College (at 212-21 Pearse Street), thus illustrating my point about the continued influence of the figure of Ossian (son of Fingal and father of Oscar).

11. On this see H. Trevor-Roper, 'The Invention of Tradition: The Highland Tradition of Scotland' in E. Hobsbawm and T. Ranger (eds.), *The Invention of Tradition* (Cambridge: Cambridge University Press, 1983), pp. 15-42.

12. H.-G. Gadamer, 'Supplement I Hermeneutics and Historicism (1965)' in idem (ed.), *Truth and Method* (London: Sheed & Ward, 2nd edn, 1989; Stagbooks

against treating the Bible as reflecting the genuinely historical is part
of a postmodernist questioning of the project of modernity. It is the
eclipse of history in the context of reading and interpreting the Bible.

2. *History and the Bible*

There is already on the market a serious amount of literature on the
subject of the Bible and historiography.[13] To this literature I would
wish only to add my own observations on the debate in order to clear
a little bit of ground for developing my own thinking about this vexed
issue. Everybody is in agreement that there are fragments and pieces
of historical information (data) embedded in the Bible, but nobody
seems to be able to agree on what such embeddedness signifies. There
are traces, perhaps even a spiral, of a history of the ancient Near East
in the Bible, but do they amount to the whole story of the Bible? Some
of the names of biblical kings have been found in the Assyrian and
Babylonian annals, but have any of the biblical stories and narratives

edn, 1993), pp. 505-41, citing from p. 523 (emphasis in original).
    13. I have no wish to produce here an H.H. Rowley-type footnote, running for
many pages, listing all the relevant works of recent years, but see among so many
others T. L. Thompson, *Early History of the Israelite People: From the Written and
Archaeological Sources* (Studies in the History of the Ancient Near East, 4; Leiden:
Brill, 1992); N.P. Lemche, *Early Israel: Anthropological and Historical Studies on
the Israelite Society Before the Monarchy* (VTSup, 37; Leiden: Brill, 1985); P.R.
Davies, *In Search of 'Ancient Israel'* (JSOTSup, 148; Sheffield: JSOT Press, 1992);
J. Van Seters, *In Search of History: Historiography in the Ancient World and the
Origins of Biblical History* (New Haven: Yale University Press, 1983); G. Ahlström,
*The History of Ancient Palestine from the Palaeolithic Period to Alexander's
Conquest* (Sheffield: JSOT Press, 1993); K.W. Whitelam, *The Invention of Ancient
Israel: The Silencing of Palestinian History* (London: Routledge, 1996). See also the
swingeing critiques of some of these writers' works in W.G. Dever, '"Will the Real
Israel Please Stand Up?" Archaeology and Israelite Historiography: Part I', *BASOR*
297 (1995), pp. 61-80; *idem*, '"Will the Real Israel Please Stand Up?" Part II:
Archaeology and the Religions of Ancient Israel', *BASOR* 298 (1995), pp. 37-58;
and I.W. Provan, 'Ideologies, Literary and Critical: Reflections on Recent Writing
on the History of Israel', *JBL* 114 (1995), pp. 585-606 (with responses from
Thompson and Davies on pp. 683-705). There is an excellent analysis of this kind of
critique in Whitelam, *The Invention of Ancient Israel*, pp. 122-75. For more
conventional 'histories of ancient Israel' see M. Grant, *The History of Ancient Israel*
(London: Weidenfeld & Nicolson, 1996 [1984]) and B. Halpern, *The First
Historians: The Hebrew Bible and History* (San Francisco: Harper & Row, 1988).

been found elsewhere outside of the Bible? My problem, however, is not with specific names or allusions to them, but with the range and specifics of the biblical narratives. I think of such narratives as 'the invention of colourful but bogus tales', but not as 'real history'— rather somewhat like Collingwood's notion of 'theocratic history'.[14] The names may be real, only the stories have been invented in order to protect history! I want to focus on the three sample issues (names) in order to focus my own thoughts on the subject as an introductory statement about the problem, but I also wish to set these three examples into a context of treating the Bible as *ideological* literature.[15]

Everybody agrees that the Bible is embedded in history *in some sense*, but there is little agreement about what that sense might be. To use the word 'ahistorical' for the Bible clearly upsets everybody, so it is probably not a good word to use in this debate. While the word 'fiction' strikes me as being a good term for describing the biblical narratives, it tends to upset many scholars who wish to read the Bible as 'straight history' (in Collingwood fiction and history are recognized as being similar).[16] Hans Frei's notion of 'history-like story' is a good one, especially if separated from his own and the Yale School's theological retrieval programme for the Bible.[17] Some of the players in the Bible are historical in a *Shakespearian* sense: Assyria, Babylon, Persia, Greece and Rome were historical entities, so we may assume

14. *The Idea of History*, pp. 14-17.

15. In spite of the strong dislike of some biblical scholars for using the term 'ideology' in conjunction with the word 'Bible' (a word no clearer than history in such a context) I cannot see how it can be avoided. For my thinking about the Bible as ideological literature see R.P.Carroll, 'The Hebrew Bible as Literature—A Misprision?', *ST* 47 (1993), pp. 77-90 and those versions of my South African lectures on 'The Bible and Ideology' which have been published in *JNSL* 19–22 (1993–96). Perhaps it is time to call for a moratorium on the use of such loaded terms as 'history', 'theology' and 'ideology' in Biblical Studies because they are not doing an adequate job of work, but who will start practising such a moratorium consistently and who will sustain it?

16. See his discussion of such matters in the section on 'Historical Imagination' in *The Idea of History*, pp. 231-49.

17. See H.W. Frei, *The Eclipse of Biblical Narrative: A Study in Eighteenth and Nineteenth Century Hermeneutics* (New Haven: Yale University Press, 1974), p. 59. I hope the use of the eighteenth-century German word *Geschichtsähnlichkeit* here does not implicate me in the Frei–Lindbeck retrieval of the Bible for theology project, even though I admire Frei's work very much. Neither a footnote nor an article on historiography is the place to discuss such weighty theological matters.

that the term 'Israel' refers to something historical (in some sense or other)—but defining its historical dimension is currently defeating the members of the Guild interested in historiography.[18] What *is* historical in the biblical narratives? Speaking snakes, talking donkeys, prophet-containing great fish, millions of people leaving a country overnight, forty years of trekking in the wilderness without sandals wearing out? These are surely the stuff of legend.[19] What then? An Israel which in turn destroyed Egyptian and Assyrian forces by no human means other than divine intervention? An Israel which was instrumental in the humiliation of all the empires, including the slaughter of more than 75,000 Persians (Est. 9.5-14), and whose choral activities could be used to generate an 'ambush of YHWH' (2 Chron. 20; music as the continuation of war by other means)? Surely not! What is historical and what is ideological fiction in such stories? It is the sorting out of these factors which constitutes, for me, one of the central elements of 'the problem of the Bible and history' (or even the problematic itself). The mixture of the ideological, the fictional and the historical in the Bible makes it very difficult for modern historians to sort out the one from the others, but sort them out we must or yield the floor to those who are more serious about reading the Bible as non-historical literature or as text.[20]

It is not so much the historical nature of much in the biblical literature which is of the essence here but the ideological aspects of the text which should be the foundation of any and all analyses of the text. A

---

18. I do not share the current obsession for thinking that archaeology can make good the defects of the Bible in the historical reconstruction of whatever gave rise to the writings we now call 'the Bible'. If some epigraphists have found large-scale scrolls (predating the Qumran finds) containing remarkably bible-like narratives I would like to hear about it, but the fragments and brief inscriptions so far unearthed are a long way from the developed narratives characteristic of the scrolls which went into the making of the Bible.

19. As I understand the essential argument of Provan's article, 'Ideologies, Literary and Critical', he would claim that such events were historical rather than legendary because the 'miraculous' must be factored into any competent historical reading of the Bible by historians today.

20. Sorting out this mixture in the Bible might be likened, in one sense, to a similar activity in current Russian historiography now that the collapse of the Russian empire has given historians access to the Russian archives. Unfortunately there are no such 'biblical' archives available from which to correct the ideological distortions of the writers whose works now constitute the Bible.

character such as Nebuchadrezzar may well have been a historical figure, but are the biblical tales in which he appears historical? Is the Nebuchadrezzar who is a friend (or acquaintance) of Jeremiah (well, his protector at least: Jer. 39.11-12) and the patron of Daniel historical? Like Shakespeare's great historical plays, the characters reflect (in the sense of bearing the names of) historical figures, but the dramas in which they appear are constructed by the dramatist—there can be no confusing of Shakespeare's *Macbeth* with the noble Scottish king of that name. Ought there to be such confusion between the Nebuchadrezzar of history and the much more famous biblical Nebuchadnezzar? Ought we not to be able to distinguish between the two in such a way that the 'realities' of both figures are preserved without the boundary between the two being taken away? Or is the matter more complicated than such a simple solution suggests, so that we really cannot distinguish between history and fiction in this manner? That is one way of avoiding having to decide the issue. But if there are differences between history and fiction, how and with what terminology are we to recognize these differences and similarities? How may we not move ancient boundary posts while remaining true to contemporary historiographical values and judgments?

That is the background for the analysis which follows. While big questions tend to make for awkward and imprecise answers, even small issues can be confusing when associated with the Bible. However, in order to illustrate the current state of my thinking on the vexed question of the Bible and historiography I have chosen to focus on three biblical characters as one way of explaining what I see to be some of the main aspects of the central problem. The three characters are Balaam, Omri and Baruch. Perhaps any three other figures from the Bible would make similar points because it is the problematic of the topos which interests me. While it would be tempting to focus on the Tell Dan inscription because, apart from being an up-to-the-minute, contemporaneous issue, it nicely illustrates that 'whoring after certainty' aspect of our discipline which so complicates the Guild's historiographical approaches to the Bible, my three chosen characters will more than adequately permit me to make the few points I wish to contribute *at this point* to the current debate.

Balaam Ben Beor

Reading the Bible from Genesis to Chronicles (from right to left, as it were) we first encounter Balaam (Bileam) ben Beor in Numbers 22–

24. This figure also appears in the Deir 'Alla texts which most scholars date to the seventh century, though a few are inclined to date them much earlier, but the biblical grand narrative (or primary narrative) sets Balaam's story in a period centuries before his actual 'historical' existence.[21] Here is a nice example of the complexities of the problem of a split-level reading of the Bible: if we follow historical-critical datings and readings of the text we run into fewer problems than if we accept the biblical narrative at face value. But if we move away from the biblical narrative to our own reconstruction of the story, then we have changed that narrative to something more in keeping with our own way of doing history. Change the story and then we may arrive at any conclusion we choose to make. If we agree on the strength of the Deir 'Alla texts that there was an actual historical Balaam, then what are we to make of his appearance in the biblical text at a juncture centuries before his time? The *recontextualization* of Balaam renders him unhistorical in some sense, does it not? If modern historians were to place Horatio Nelson's naval battles during the Armada period or in the time of World War I or if they were to make Henry VIII follow William IV would we still call such errors historical writing? Would it not be a case, at best, of historical fiction in which historical figures are set into stories of an ideological, fictional or entertaining nature? Would that not be to write *bogus history*? So while there may well be 'historical characters' written about in the Bible, the *recontextualization* of such characters may not reflect any degree of historical accuracy at all. As with the recognition that the historical events and characters represented in the writings of William Shakespeare or Charles Dickens have been transformed in many different and creative ways, so we have to recognize the fact that while the biblical writers knew about such historical characters or events (that is, these figures or events are

---

21. There is little agreement on when this inscription should be dated (archaeological finds tend to generate just as much disagreement among experts as does the interpretation of documents). The literature on Balaam is quite extensive and much also has been written about the relationship of the biblical Balaam to the Deir 'Alla texts, see E.W. Davies, 'Excursus on the Deir 'Alla Texts' in *Numbers* (New Century Bible Commentary; London: Marshall Pickering, 1995), pp. 281-84; J.A. Hackett, *The Balaam Text from Deir 'Alla* (HSM, 31; Chico, CA: Scholars Press, 1980); J. Hoftijzer and G. Van der Kooij, *The Balaam Text from Deir 'Alla Re-evaluated* (Leiden: Brill, 1991); M.S. Moore, *The Balaam Traditions: Their Character and Development* (SBLDS, 113; Atlanta, GA: Scholars Press, 1990); R. Nuilleumier, 'Bileam zwischen Bibel und Deir 'Alla', *TZ* 52 (1996), pp. 150-63.

not just simply inventions) they exist now in and as *invented* stories.[22] The historical may have been rendered unhistorical by contextualization in the Bible. So to the big question about whether a history of Israel can be written I am tempted to give the answer: 'Yes, if by history you include bogus history!'. But I think such bogus history is inevitably *unreliable* history and it should be indicated as being such in the books written about history in the Bible.

Perhaps I should define here what I mean by the phrase *bogus history*. Bogus qualifies the term history, thereby rendering it not-history or false history, where historical characters are taken out of their historical context and assigned to narrative contexts where they are out of context in historical terms. Bogus also qualifies all those scholarly antics whereby fragmented texts are restored to read whatever will make the artefacts conform to *an imagined narrative* constructed from the biblical text—where blanks are filled in from artefacts discovered from outside the Bible, but where in the absence of such artefacts the biblical text is deemed to be reliable. The practice of the continual correction of the text by means of extra-textual sources combined with the presumption in favour of the historical reliability of the biblical text unless proved otherwise, plus the selective use of evidence in order to rush to judgment about the necessary connection between a name or word found on an inscription and a similar name or word in the biblical text all seem to me to represent the mechanisms whereby bogus biblical history is constructed by modern 'biblical' historians. I think the whole operation is a sham and can only produce bogus history. I do recognize, however, the relativity of all such judgments and that one person's bogus history is another person's 'truth from god'. Perhaps 'real' history is never more than a mixture of true and false opinions constructed out of historical facts, conventional judgments and a skilful manipulation of legendary material. As Erich Auerbach writes: 'To write history is so difficult that most historians are forced to make concessions to the technique of legend.'[23] So why not settle

22. This is the point I tried to make in my commentary on Jeremiah: see R.P. Carroll, *Jeremiah: A Commentary* (OTL; London and Philadelphia: SCM Press and Westminster Press, 1986), pp. 55-64.

23. In 'Odysseus' Scar' in *Mimesis: The Representation of Reality in Western Literature* (trans. W.R. Trask; Princeton, NJ: Princeton University Press, 1968 [1953]), p. 20. The context of Auerbach's remarks on the difficulty of writing history (the rise of National Socialism in Germany in the 1930s) should be noted. Of

for treating the Bible as 'legendary history', that is 'bogus but entertaining tales of ancient Israel's past as imagined by her writers'?

The story of Balaam ben Beor raises many other interpretative
issues for biblical scholarship. The discovery of the Deir 'Alla text
makes the figure of Balaam an intertextual one, not only in the Bible
(that fact is known already) but between the Bible and non-biblical
texts. In the matter of intertextuality the historical aspect of textual
figures becomes far less important than the literary reception of such
characters. As a character in biblical narratives Balaam is a very complex figure, reflecting different and contrary evaluations of such
foreign seers. As an intertextual figure outside the Bible Balaam also
represents a character inserted into the story of Israel's past and
assigned an important role in the pre-conquest narratives associated
with the legendary figure of Moses. He takes on an almost legendary
aspect himself, as one of the figures who in ancient times appeared to
have opposed Israel but failed to arrest its onward march of triumph
through the desert into the land. Nearly all the subsequent treatments
of him represent him as having been an anti-Israel figure; hence he fits
into the triumphalist ideology represented by the narratives of the past
as a counter-balance to the point of view of him as a magician working
his bad magic against Israel. His oracles are too valuable to be ditched
just to square the tradition and represent him as a 'bad man' speaking
against Israel. On the contrary, controlled by Yahweh he can only utter
blessings for Israel. Placed in the desert trek period, he becomes part
of the foundational legends of Israel's past. But is it history as such?

At this point I am reminded of nothing so much as that discussion
between Catherine Morland, Miss Tilney, Henry Allen and the others
in Jane Austen's *Northanger Abbey* where the women fall to arguing
about history and fiction.[24] Reading the Bible *as history* is somewhat
like sharing Miss Tilney's opinion:

> 'Historians, you think,' said Miss Tilney, 'are not happy in their flights of
> fancy. They display imagination without raising interest. I am fond of
> history—and am very well contented to take the false with the true. In the
> principal facts they have sources of intelligence in former histories and

relevance to this debate but beyond the scope of this paper is L.G. Perdue, *The
Collapse of History: Reconstructing Old Testament Theology* (OBT; Minneapolis:
Fortress Press, 1994).

24. J. Austen, *Northanger Abbey* (The World's Classics; London: Oxford
University Press, 1930), chapter 14, pp. 110-21.

records, which may be depended on, I conclude, as anything that does not actually pass under one's own observation; and as for the little embellishments you speak of, they are embellishments, and I like them as such. If a speech be well drawn up, I read it with pleasure, by whomsoever it may be made—and probably with much greater, if the production of Mr. Hume or Mr. Robertson, than if the genuine words of Caractacus, Agricola, or Alfred the Great.'[25]

It is very much a case of being 'well contented to take the false with the true' and of recognizing that 'as for the little embellishments. . . they are embellishments and I like them as such'. Of course it would greatly help if historians of the Bible were to admit more openly than they do to the existence of the 'false' and 'the embellishments' in the Bible in order not to mislead naive readers into thinking that there are no such things in the book. Balaam ben Beor is a very good example of one of the problems posed by treating the Bible as history *simpliciter*. He may have been a real person, even a practising seer, in ancient times, but he is out of place in the story in which he appears in the Bible. The biblical Balaam is genuinely false!

Omri

The second figure is Omri, the king whose name is used in the Assyrian annals to characterize the land—'the land/house of Omri'[26]—yet of whose deeds little or nothing is known in the Bible. How can a figure be known to foreigners so well as to give the land its identity and yet be of such little worth to the 'biblical historians' as to be dismissed in a few verses? The nature of that dismissal is clearly indicative of ideological bias against Omri. The stereotypical 'Deuteronomistic' language of the biblical text, 'Omri did what was evil in the sight of YHWH, and did more evil than all who were before him' (1 Kgs 16.25; the whole story of Omri is encompassed in vv. 16-28), reveals the ideological nature of his treatment. The one event of note attributed to him in the Bible is that of the building of the city of Samaria. But that point in itself is enough to condemn him to obloquy (guilt by smear or association tactic) because in biblical symbolic terms Samaria is a

25. Austen, *Northanger Abbey*, p. 113.

26. See A.L.Oppenheim, 'Babylonian and Assyrian Historical Texts' in J.B. Pritchard (ed.) *Ancient Near Eastern Texts relating to the Old Testament* (Princeton, NJ: Princeton University Press, 3rd edn, 1969), pp. 280-85 (the phrase *Bît Hu-um-ri-ia* appears in an inscription translated on p. 285).

metonym of viciousness and representative of anti-YHWHist culture. The failure to treat Omri adequately is a good indicator of the ideological nature of the biblical text and a serious mark against the historical reliability of the biblical writings. As ideological literature, its claims to historical reliability are shot to ribbons and the question arises as to whether it is worthless as history. In modern historiography how much faith is put by modern historians in Soviet historical literature? Should any more faith be put in the biblical documents? Is history then the most useful or accurate term for describing such ideological literature? Of course there are historical data embedded in such literature, but is history *the best category* for describing the Bible? A genuinely historical text (in *our* sense of history, but then it is we who are engaged in this historiographical enquiry) would have devoted many chapters to Omri, whereas a text which can dismiss him so briefly is itself fatally flawed as an ideological document untrustworthy on the subject of history. This is only history in the sense of *unreliable* history (another way of saying *bogus* history). While this may be a modern point of view reading an ancient text, the contemporary historiography issue is one of whether we should be paraphrasing the Bible as if it were history proper in our sense or producing our own values-based histories in relation to the Bible.

It may be argued that the biblical writers were indeed historians (Halpern's point of view shared by many biblical scholars) and that because they were such they chose to include certain factors about the kings and to exclude the bulk of the material constitutes their way of doing history. That would be fine and dandy if we had access to all the other material on Omri, so that we could correct their biases, omissions and slanted history. But we do not have access to the 'Book of the Chronicles of the Kings of Israel' where 'the rest of the acts of Omri which he did' are recorded (1 Kgs 16.27), so we are left with only the heavily ideologically biased biblical text. We cannot do reliable history from such a source. The source is too contaminated with ancient ideology to afford a reliable guide to Omri and his works. This may be all right for 'biblical history', but it is grossly inadequate for modern historians writing modern history, for rewriting history in our own way.

Berekhyahu Ben Neriyahu
The third name which attracts my attention is that of Berekhyahu ben Neriyahu. His name appears on a bulla found among the bullae which

Nahum Avigad locates in sixth-century Jerusalem and which he identifies with Baruch ben Neriah, Jeremiah's scribe and companion.[27] Now this name raises for me all sorts of questions about the use of the category of history for the Bible. The 'old credulists' who oppose the 'new nihilists' (Dever's term)[28] or, in other words, the maximalists versus the minimalists, would use a *totalizing transfer mode* here to read into the name on the bulla the whole story of Jeremiah and Baruch as found in the biblical book of Jeremiah.[29] Apart from the illegitimacy of such a totalizing transfer, I also have many problems with such archaeological *finds*, especially in relation to the regularity with which they turn up in modern Israel. Some of the problems are the standard ones about the importance of *contextualization* for interpreting archaeological finds. All interpretation depends on context, but Avigad is less than forthcoming in his book on the bullae: many of the bullae were purchased by collectors of antiquities from antique shops in modern Jerusalem (Avigad, *Hebrew Bullae*, pp. 11-13), so there is no actual archaeological context for these bullae! As such they are unreliable objects and might as well be fakes.[30] They cannot be counted as serious evidence for anything because who knows which are faked and which are reliable? Such contaminated evidence renders them useless for any argument about the historical nature of the biblical text.

A different point is well made by Avigad himself in the Preface to his book:

> Stratigraphical excavations are often able to provide a sound chronological basis for undated epigraphical discoveries. Mere chance finds do not

27. See N. Avigad, *Hebrew Bullae from the Time of Jeremiah: Remnants of a Burnt Archive* (Jerusalem: Israel Exploration Society, 1986).

28. I really do not approve of the name-calling habit practised by Dever ('"Will the Real Israel Please Stand up?", Parts I and II') and Provan ('Ideologies, Literary and Critical') in the debate about the Bible and historiography. It is so much a case of 'give a dog a bad name, then hang it', a game which is too easily played by everybody for it to provide anybody with an edge in the debate. I assume that the emotional appeal of name-calling opponents is a clear indication of the ideological nature of the debate in current biblical scholarship.

29. This is not the place to go into the current debate about the interpretation of the book of Jeremiah, for that see R.P. Carroll, 'Surplus Meaning and the Conflict of interpretations: A Dodecade of Jeremiah Studies (1984–95)', *Currents in Research: Biblical Studies* 4 (1996), pp. 115-59.

30. On this point see G. Garbini, *History and Ideology in Ancient Israel* (London: SCM Press, 1988), pp. 38-47.

ordinarily enjoy such an advantage, but among this new group of Hebrew
bullae there are two items which serve to provide for the entire assemblage
with a dating more precise than that which would derive from a normal
stratiagraphical context, *for these bullae bear the names of personages
known to us from the Bible* (Avigad, *Hebrew Bullae*, p. 9; emphasis
added).

Now here Avigad is dating the archaeological finds from the biblical
text and then using the finds to confirm and illuminate the text. This
is, of course, an all too typical example of the kind of circular argumentation which passes for logic in Biblical Studies. The dating of the
production of the book of Jeremiah is not a fixed historical fact. On
the contrary, it is an open question. So when bullae are 'found' which
include, among many other names, the names of figures to be found in
the book of Jeremiah, that 'finding' may not have any significance at
all for such dating purposes. That factor has to be decided by other
means, such as logic and argument or the use of coordinating data.
But Avigad already *knows* that the book of Jeremiah is straight history and therefore that it provides him with a cross-reference for
dating *with certainty*—'is certain' says Avigad.[31] I find that to be an
illegitimate use of texts and archaeological 'finds' as well as being an
unacknowledged theory-laden approach to both. While the rightness
of Avigad's position may still be argued for, it is the assumptions and
the lack of arguments which bother me the most.

Dating finds from the Bible without any obvious connections between
the Bible or the 'finds' strikes me as being an ideological activity
much more than it is a historical activity. What are the warrants and
assumptions involved in such activities? Of course it is a very common
assumption: I find it in Israel Finkelstein's book *The Archaeology of
the Israelite Settlement* where the very term 'settlement' reflects a
reading of the Bible and can hardly reflect the archaeological remains
available for interpretation.[32] Finkelstein himself says, on p. 22, 'We

31. Cf. Avigad's penchant for using the word 'certain' in such statements as 'One
fact, however, is quite certain. . . ' and 'In any event. . . is certain' in *Hebrew Bullae*,
pp. 128, 130. Too many circular arguments and assumptions of 'it is reasonable' are
used by Avigad to impress the cautious reader of his book.

32. I. Finkelstein, *The Archaeology of the Israelite Settlement* (Jerusalem: Israel
Exploration Society, 1988). It is the presumption that everything found when dug up
by archaeologists is Israelite (as the title asserts) unless there are good reasons for
arguing that it is not is the focus of my complaint here. On this point see Whitelam,
The Invention of Ancient Israel, pp. 179-203.

will hardly touch upon biblical evidence at all' (and why should we in a book on archaeology?), but whence the notion of 'an Israelite settlement'? Now I do not belong to that happy group of optimistic biblical historians who believe that we can avoid the problems of biblical historiography by switching from the biblical text to archaeology and the study of material remains.[33] I tend to regard archaeological data as being even more difficult to interpret than texts, even though both activities require fundamentally sophisticated hermeneutic tools to have any sense made of them at all. If I may express the matter thus: a shard is a shard is a shard, but a Rosetta Stone is a Rosetta Stone is a Rosetta Stone (with due thanks to Gertrude Stein for a remark not dissimilar to the one I have used here). Shards lacking writing are harder to interpret and less interesting than shards with writing on them, but both types of artefacts require considerable hermeneutical skills in order to be interpreted accurately. In all such interpretative activity there is much room for disagreement and for the production of competing points of view.

Avigad and Finkelstein strike me as following bad procedural methods at certain points in their writings, bad practice quite typical of 'biblical' archaeologists. So I have many problems every time some archaeologist or other comes up with yet another discovery which somehow 'proves' the Bible to be right or historical.[34] The newspapers are always full of this kind of reportage: for example, the recent piece in *The Times* on 'biblical lions found'—what, pray, is a biblical lion?— or *The Times's* report some years ago about the finding of the golden calf written about in the Bible. The bad practice which then under

---

33. I do not appreciate the claims of Dever (in his voluminous writings on the subject, especially in '"Will the Real Israel Please Stand up?", Parts I and II') that in order to write 'a history of ancient Israel' one must be an archaeologist. This privileging of archaeology as the only legitimate source for writing such a history is not only a question-begging activity, it is also a good example of the fallacy defined by the phrase 'he who drives fat oxen must himself be fat'. It will not do either as argument or good practice, but it is a very effective political method of excluding by diktat the awkward dissenters in the Guild from participating in the debate.

34. This craze for proving the historicity of the Bible is a cultural thing: see J. Pemble, *The Mediterranean Passion: Victorians and Edwardians in the South* (Oxford: Oxford University Press, 1987), esp. pp.182-96; also B. Kuklick, *Puritans in Babylon: The Ancient Near East and American Intellectual Life, 1880–1930* (Princeton, NJ: Princeton University Press, 1996).

writes much 'history writing' on the Bible is that bits of archaeological 'data' are linked *directly* to any bit of a biblical narrative which is deemed suitable for the find because of some superficial or imagined similarity (the *bytdwd* inscription from Tell Dan is a good example of the social practice described here). So there may have been a scribe called Berekhyahu ben Neriyahu who lived and worked in the some (unspecified) period (earlier or later than the Persian?) and whose name is used in the Jeremiah literature, but what are the actual historical connections between this figure behind the (constructed) bulla and the book of Jeremiah? Many answers may be given to that question, not simply the one assumed by Avigad. Some of the shifts in interpretation which Avigad makes in his assumptions would require warrants and justifications which he fails to produce for his reading of the Bible and the bullae.[35] It is at best one possible interpretation of the 'finds', but there are many other interpretations which may equally fit the bullae (including the treatment of them as faked). In my judgment, the names on the bullae seem to reflect biblical names from all over the Bible so do not constitute anything remotely close to the specific information Avigad seems to imagine for them. My principal objection to his hermeneutics is this: from such bits of baked clay he reconstructs the world. The mouse has given birth to a mountain! Such baked clay is by definition undatable (does thereby hang a tale?). But it is the Bible which drives his interpretation.[36] I think a collection of bullae (whether faked or found), without precise datable contextualization, cannot yield so much reliable information. I suspect that ideology is behind such reconstructions and so I would read Avigad (and to some extent Finkelstein) as tending towards an indulgence in the production of ideological literature (propaganda in other words) in relation to the Bible.

---

35. See Avigad, *Hebrew Bullae*, pp. 120-30.

36. This is often the case. An example which comes to mind will be found in the 'Conclusion' to K.A. Kitchen, *Ancient Orient and Old Testament* (London: Tyndale Press, 1966), pp. 171-73, where, in the closing sentences, it is suddenly made explicit that the book is a work of (Christian) apologetics for 'the historic Christian faith'. What drives the interpretation of the data throughout the book is now revealed and readers can begin to understand the passion with which the historical-critical point of view is denounced and dismissed.

3. *Conclusion*

So where do my three examples take me? The various notions of unreliable or bogus history, ideological literature, propaganda, recontextualization and the totalizing transfer of discrete categories constitute for me only the beginnings of an exposition of the problematics of reading the Bible as history. They also help to point away from the category of history in the direction of what I would call 'ideological literature' or, if you wish, 'propaganda'. It is as propaganda that we should be reading the Bible and the categories of propaganda analysis should be our guidelines in this discussion (start reading the writings of George Orwell). I take propaganda to be *bad* or *bogus* or *contaminated* history at best, where there is a strong wish to retain the term 'history' for the Bible. But what is the Bible propaganda for? This is a question which invariably will have many different answers, especially if the proper distinction between writers and canonizers/gatherers/collectors is maintained. I would tend to say that the Hebrew Bible is propaganda for the temple cult/guild based on Palestinian territory, even if focused on diasporic values and communities, hence the empty land focus.[37] While propaganda makes for very bad history writing (historiography), I do not know if bad historiography is better treated as history or as fiction (Collingwood says that bad art is not art at all, but does the same judgment follow for bad history?). If I knew a better term than history I would use it for the Bible. I would prefer some such categorizing terms along the lines of 'sacred scripture', 'ideological literature', 'propaganda', 'myth', 'theocratic history' if a blanket term must be used for the Bible. Or following Pierre Macherey how about 'sacred fiction' as a term to describe what the collectors-canonizers of the biblical books have put together? To the question 'can a history of ancient Israel be written?' I am inclined to answer 'No', unless it is allowed that a bogus or unreliable history is still an adequate account of history. The many silences still remain and militate strongly against treating the Bible as reliable history.

---

37. On this topos see R.P. Carroll, 'The Myth of the Empty Land' in D. Jobling and T. Pippin (eds.), *Ideological Criticism of Biblical Texts* (Semeia, 59; Atlanta, GA: Scholars Press, 1992), pp. 79-93; H.M. Barstad, *The Myth of the Empty Land: A Study in the History and Archaeology of Judah during the "Exilic" Period* (Symbolae Osloenses Fasc. Suppl. XXVIII; Stockholm: Scandinavian University Press, 1996).

The propaganda aspect may be taken further: it appears in Samuel–Kings to reflect an ideology of prophetism.[38] Even the annals of the kings are contaminated by being constructed from narratives about prophets. That is, we do not have a genuine history of the kings of Israel–Judah but stories about prophets shape the stories of the kings to the detriment of the representation of the monarchy. This has to be propaganda reflecting the writers' (the Deuteronomists?) obsession with prophets and prophecy, but it is no way to produce a history of the so-called kingdoms. It is in fact an alternative to whatever that history may have been and as such is essentially propaganda for a specific ideology of prophecy. We need to write our own histories of the past and it does not seem to me to be a feasible project that we should reiterate the biblical propaganda as our own version of that ancient history. At best what I think we have with the Bible is 'a Mexican standoff' in the matter of historiography.

I think the collection of books constituting the Bible (in the various canons which we have) contains 'a tissue of fictions', or a sacred fiction as a collective work gathered together centuries after its inscription, but for millennia readers have been prepared to read it *as if* it contained nothing but true historiography. This conglomerate of 'verified falsehood' now confronts the academic historian with the demand to decide whether 'true' or 'false' is the correct term to use in its evaluation. If historiography is the category wherein the judgment must be made, then it is time for historians to make up their minds, to clamber off the fence and to declare their opinion as to what kind of historiographical literature the Bible might be. Even if the Bible is declared to be a fiction, a great concatenation of novelistic fictional fabrications, 'a tissue of fictions', it still stands as major literature in some sense or other. As the narrator of *Northanger Abbey* musing on the way the friendship between Catherine (Morland) and Isabella (Tilney) developed, including the reading of novels, praises the novel as affording such extensive and unaffected pleasure, responding to the young lady's riposte 'Oh! It is only a novel!', with the fine observation,

> in short, only some work in which the greatest powers of the mind are displayed, in which the most thorough knowledge of human nature, the

38. This is not the place to explore this point, but see B. Peckham, *History and Prophecy: The Development of Late Judean Literary Traditions* (The Anchor Bible Reference Library; New York: Doubleday, 1993)—a book too long and too complex to be discussed here either.

happiest delineation of its varieties, the liveliest effusions of wit and humour are conveyed to the world in the best chosen language.[39]

Would such a judgment do for the Bible? Could the Madonna of silences yield the floor to the literary judgment of the Bible as literature? Or is this debate about the Bible and historiography about bigger things than history or the Bible?

39. Austen, *Northanger Abbey*, chapter 5, p. 30.

WHOSE HISTORY? WHOSE ISRAEL? WHOSE BIBLE?
BIBLICAL HISTORIES, ANCIENT AND MODERN

Philip R. Davies

1. *Addressing the Questions*

The thematic questions of this volume are (1) whether a history of ancient Israel can be written and (2) how the Old Testament/Hebrew Bible can be used in such a history. My immediate answers are as follows.

1. Histories of ancient Israel certainly *can* be written, and the multitude of such enterprises testifies to that, but 'a history' (of anything) means both *someone's* history, and indeed a history *of something*. 'Ancient Israel' is not an agreed historical datum. For some it is more or less the society described within the biblical books. For others it is an as yet little known and relatively short-lived highland kingdom of the Iron Age. Most historians operate, sometimes even critically, between these two poles. But precisely what 'ancient Israel' is, or was, is currently at the core of discussion about modern historiography.

Histories of *an* ancient Israel, then, are possible; *the* history of *the* ancient Israel is not.

2. Regardless of who one is or what one's Israel is, for a modern *critical* history, the Old Testament/Hebrew Bible can be used in reconstructing history in two ways, primary and secondary. In the primary respect, the writings in this collection are part of the intellectual history of an ancient society that identified itself (among other things) as, or as part of, 'Israel', and the first task of the historian is to discover (or provide) the historical context of these writings, on the principle that the historical testimony of any work will be relevant in the first instance to the time in which it was written. Unfortunately, the literature in the Hebrew Bible/Old Testament very largely does

not identify its authors, nor the time, place or occasion of their production. For that reason, determination of the historical setting of any biblical text is difficult. The task is, moreover, made even more difficult because the historical framework into which they need to be fitted cannot be derived from the texts themselves, because that would already imply their use in a secondary respect (see next paragraph). Put simply: texts cannot verify their own historical value.

In the secondary respect, what these writings may say about historical events might be used to build a picture of the periods *which they claim to be describing*. A basic assessment of the validity of any text will be provided by the results of the primary exercise, when the date, setting, genre and authorship have been decided (in most cases, of course, provisionally). But even then, a reasonable amount of independent data is needed to gauge how far these stories provide a reliable account. The nature and extent of such data is in many cases so restricted that this exercise will be fairly piecemeal—although it has tended to be remarkably more successful in *disposing* of the historical reliability of some texts than in enhancing it. Some items narrated in the biblical literature accord with episodes narrated in other ancient literature, or implied by non-literary data. But such cases are actually rather rare, too rare to justify an appropriation of biblical narrative as a basis for critical historical reconstruction. Moreover, even cases where independent testimony is available, discrepancies in detail or evaluation remind us of the tendency of all literary sources to tell us what the author wanted to have happened rather than what we want to know.

I would therefore have to conclude that the use of biblical historiographical narrative for critical reconstruction of periods that it describes (rather than periods in which it was written) is precarious and only possible where there is adequate independent data. If we have no positive grounds for thinking that a biblical account is historically useful, we cannot really adopt it as history. True, the result will be that we have less history than we might. But what little we have we can at least claim we know (in whatever sense we 'know' the distant past); this, in my opinion, is better than having more history than we might, much of which we do not know at all, since it consists merely of unverifiable stories. Herodotus knew the difference.

2. *History and Bible*

Contrary to the principle just set out, many modern 'histories of ancient Israel' deal largely with the secondary use of biblical narrative, basing their accounts on what the narratives say happened rather than on the evidence of such narratives for the ideas of their own time. They take *as the basis of their history* a set of writings whose own historical context and authorship are unclear and unexamined. Moreover, the 'Israel' that explicitly or implicitly promotes the agenda of the scholarly 'history of Israel' is actually a creation of authors of texts in the Hebrew Bible, and not something generated from research into contemporary historical archives or artefacts, whose date and provenance is usually known.

Without external data it is technically impossible to write a critical history of ancient Israel. The picture of Israelite history famously developed by Julius Wellhausen was based on a source-critical analysis superimposed on a history derived from the biblical material. It was a brilliant exercise in using the contradictions of the narratives to reverse their own account and to put the development of law later than prophecy. The principle that sources tell us about the time they were written was explicitly embraced. But how could documents be dated in the first place? To do this, Wellhausen needed to accept the reliability of some narratives. Why were 1 Samuel and Ezra historically reliable but not Genesis? Why were the prophetic books taken as evidence of the monarchic period? Because Wellhausen's source-critical analysis was not applied in the same way to other 'historical' books, the results of his reconstruction of Israelite religion were methodologically insecure. Put simply, Wellhausen separated out the Pentateuchal documents and assigned them to various points in a history narrated by other books. The success of demonstrating the historical unreliability of one part of the literature depended on assuming the historical reliability of the rest! The one exception was the books of Chronicles.[1]

To be entirely fair to Wellhausen, he worked before the advent of Near Eastern archaeology. He deserves such criticism a good deal less

---

1.   It would be interesting to speculate how Chronicles would fare without our knowledge of Kings. The differences allow us to devalue Chronicles; but if it were the only account it would probably be accorded much greater historical value. On the other hand, the existence, and generally low estimate of Chronicles' historical reliability should not automatically enhance the historical value of Samuel and Kings.

than his successors who, having at their disposal a range (however limited) of non-biblical data relating to the periods and areas which the biblical narratives claim to describe, still choose to slot these data in the biblical schema instead of using them to construct an independent one. Such data *do* point to the existence of a kingdom called 'Israel',[2] and we can be reasonably confident in our limited knowledge of this kingdom from these sources, because the dating and locus of the sources is known (or largely agreed on), and the sources emanate from various directions; in the case of non-literary sources, additionally, there is no possibility of *deliberate* deception (forgery excluded!). Only texts, as a rule, can *consciously* lie. But do these various sources refer to what the biblical narratives call 'Israel'? Not exactly. The sources offer the beginnings of an opportunity to interrogate these biblical narratives for their basic schematization and categorization, but the challenge has until recently been declined by modern 'biblical historians' who prefer the much easier (and more popular) recourse of taking the biblical parameters as the grid on which all the data, biblical and non-biblical, are laid out. For the biblical literature, it is of course a home game, from which an honourable draw is the worst that these narratives usually manage.

To challenge the primacy of biblical narratives in setting the agenda for 'ancient Israel's history' is not anti-biblical, despite some of the rhetoric currently in flow, but a methodological procedure. Any modern critical history of ancient Israel has to start, then, by evaluating the biblical profile by testing it with non-biblical sources. We cannot take the biblical story as a 'first draft'. To assign to non-biblical data the role of 'elucidating', 'confirming' (or equally, of 'denying') the biblical narrative (or 'biblical record'[3]) will mean that the many remaining gaps in our knowledge are occupied by biblical data. More importantly,

---

2.   There exists a widespread perception that in my *In Search of 'Ancient Israel'* (Sheffield: JSOT Press, 1992) I denied the existence of an ancient Israel. That perception represents a very serious misreading of the book, and so we seem to be dealing with that unfortunate phenomenon whereby books are labelled and discussed without reference to the contents and by those who have not read them.

3.   The word 'record' is quite often used with reference to biblical sources. I allude to it here merely to be able to make the point that whether it is a record is precisely the issue! While 'narrative' or 'story' are neutral with regard to historical reference, 'record' implies an event, as does 'testimony' (beloved of more conservative-evangelical writing) or 'witness'. The word 'account' lies ambiguously between the two.

because less often debated, major biblical *categories* like 'pre-exilic', 'United Monarchy', 'Canaanites' and 'Israelite' remain in place, though historically unclear, inaccurate or inappropriate.[4] If the fate of the non-biblical data is to be made to fit into the remnants of a framework *which they themselves have not sponsored*, then they are not being properly utilized. Their capacity to generate different frameworks, categories and interpretations is hamstrung. It may be impossible to construct an Israel in detail equal to biblical dimensions on the basis of the few data—though archaeologists such as Dever are keen to do so[5]—but that is what the method demands.[6]

What has emerged from the current unscientific[7] process of modifying the biblical story through sporadic, eclectic use of non-biblical data is a range of conclusions, from a maximal evaluation of the historicity of the biblical sources to a minimal one. The range is possible because the synthesis of a fairly comprehensive *literary* pattern in the

---

4.   Unfortunately even competent archaeologists can fall unwarily into the trap, speaking, for instance, of the 'united monarchy' period, although the archaeological record gives no warrant for such a description. For example, I. Finkelstein, 'The Archaeology of the United Monarchy: an Alternative View', *Levant* 28 (1996), pp. 175-97. I single out Finkelstein not so much as the most recent, but as a scholar whom I would certainly *not* accuse of misuse of the biblical sources. Indeed, his article implicitly undermines the notion of a 'united monarchy'.

5.   See W.G. Dever, 'The Identity of Early Israel: A Rejoinder to K.W. Whitelam', *JSOT* 72 (1996), pp. 3-24.

6.   It has been pointed out that since the biblical story is the only one we have, there is no choice. That is an argument one could make from the Aeneid about the origins of Rome or of Maori oral traditions about the arrival of Polynesians in New Zealand. Since modern Westerners do not accept either of these sources as historical, we actually prefer to maintain our relative scientific ignorance of these important historical events to a fuller 'knowledge' that we deem unscientific. Whether because the biblical narratives are written in prose or, more probably, because their story is part of our cultural prehistory, or because belief in their historicity is a religious commitment, these narratives escape the brutal interrogation they require as to whether the story they are telling should be setting the agenda for part of the history of the ancient world.

7.   To use the word 'scientific' these days in connection with biblical studies (*pace Bibelwissenschaft* and *sciences religieuses*) is to incur the almost automatic accusation of being positivistic. But science derives from *scientia*, 'knowledge' and, I submit, retains essentially that sense (my argument is not etymological). I think there is such as thing as historical knowledge, and, like the natural sciences, it is a function of method. What you 'know' depends on how you come to 'know' it.

Bible and a set of suggestive but partial non-biblical data permits a wide range of choices. The individual historian is permitted by this procedure to pick and choose the evidence, interpret it, and exegete the relevant biblical texts, all in such a way that a greater or lesser measure of congruence or dissonance between Bible and non-Bible is arrived at. In all this, the real point of dispute becomes not method (there *is* no method in this process) but the question of how one treats the Bible. As Whitelam has pointed out, biblical history has largely been a subdiscipline of theology and not of history. The accusations of 'minimizing' that greet this programme are at first sight puzzling, until it strikes one that what is being minimized is not *history* (despite the naive [or disingenuous?] claims of Halpern[8]) but *the Bible*! What is ostensibly an argument about history turns out to be an argument about sacred scriptures.[9]

Only this conclusion explains why the label 'minimalist' has emerged in what should be a complex discussion of what is in reality a spectrum of views. Such ridiculous terminology only betrays the extent to which the writing of histories of ancient Israel is still driven by an agenda concerned with the reliability of the biblical sources—an issue in which a historian has to be impartial. The related label 'sceptic' reveals even more clearly a religious dimension to this debate. It is only in religious language that to believe is good and to doubt bad; for a historian, to doubt is good and to believe is bad! The label 'sceptic' honours a historian—unless a biblical one, where faith in biblical narratives is expected!

In fact, to abandon a biblical profile and create one instead from other sources is not only possible, but has been done on quite a large scale already. Some decades ago, the 'patriarchal age' and the 'conquest' were regular ingredients of 'histories of Israel', and that either might be totally unhistorical was inconceivable. The arrival of Thompson's *Historicity of the Patriarchal Narratives*[10] was met with some

8.   B. Halpern, 'Erasing History', *Bible Review* December (1995), pp. 26-47 (the title says it all).

9.   Perhaps this is not so strange, on reflection. Since the Reformation, an incredible weight has been placed on the literal, historical reading of the Bible (and the Bible itself has borne an additional weight as the defining document of Christian belief). For average Israelis, too, biblical studies is simply their own history.

10.   T.L. Thompson, *The Historicity of the Patriarchal Narratives: The Quest for the Historical Abraham* (Berlin: de Gruyter, 1974); see also J. Van Seters,

resistance, even though the ground had been prepared by Gunkel, Alt and Noth. The same was true of Gottwald's *Tribes of Yahweh*.[11] The thesis that the Israelites did not come from outside Palestine was initially curious, and indeed, unacceptable[12] because it so totally contravened a basic tenet of the biblical definition of Israel. Attempts to salvage 'two legs, or a piece of an ear' remain on the margins of the debate. 'Biblical historicity' is not a *principle*. It should not even be a bone of contention among historians. It is simply a *possibility* that needs to be tested. And to a considerable degree that testing has been done, with widely agreed results. Historians cannot write a critical history in which a 'patriarchal age' and an Israelite 'conquest of Canaan' figure. They have had, in such cases, to create a new framework from non-biblical evidence. It is not unreasonable to extend the analysis to biblical texts about the monarchic period. It is not unreasonable to argue that these narratives are pretty unreliable. But it is *unreasonable* to protest at such a procedure or to call names at those whose method is entirely justified.

It is unfortunate that while biblical studies has recently embraced and applied literary, anthropological and sociological theory, there are too few biblical historians who care about the principles, methods and techniques of history. The whole discipline of 'biblical history' is concerned with the *outcomes* of history writing rather than with the questions of what historical knowledge is and how we arrive at it. For while history is not a natural science, it does constitute a form of social knowledge, always provisional and never final, which is attained by the application of explicit methods and arguments that guarantee and authorize that knowledge. More discussion about historical method and less about the historicity of individual persons and events is badly needed.

3. *Ownership of History*

Ancient Ownership
The question of 'whose history' or 'history of what' can be asked of both ancient and modern historians of Israel. The former were clearly

Abraham in History and Tradition (New Haven: Yale University Press, 1975).

11. N.K. Gottwald, *The Tribes of Yahweh: A Sociology of the Religion of Liberated Israel* (Maryknoll: Orbis, 1979).

12. The theory was first developed, of course, by G. Mendenhall, 'The Hebrew Conquest of Palestine', *BA* 25 (1962), pp. 66-87.

for the most part members of one or more intellectual elites. Their individual and class interests, psychological, political economic, are for the modern historian to discover. Their narrative(s) in Samuel–Kings contain(s) a thread consisting of names of kings and their deeds, partial, sometimes confused, but partly verified and perhaps further verifiable—although it needs to be acknowledged that the chronologies of the kings (biblical versions differ) are the result not of careful contemporary recording but subsequent scribal editing in the interests of a wider historical schema.[13]

This thread, then, is possibly the relic of contemporary annals. But it has been hugely embellished with accounts of fabulous empires, a fabulously wise and wealthy monarch who had a magnificent temple built in Jerusalem; of prophetic miracles and confrontations, and of cult reforms. The plot of the books of Kings (the same is true of Chronicles) is dictated by clear ideological considerations to which the name 'Deuteronom(ist)ic' is given. Such 'Deuteronomic' ideas are that 'Israel' is a single twelve-tribe nation latterly divided into two kingdoms, that it settled throughout the whole of Palestine and that 'Israelite' and 'Canaanite' are distinct ethnic and cultural entities, that a Davidic line is the only legitimate one (and that all the Judaean kings belonged to it). The exploits of Joshua, the institution of the 'judgeship', the 'empire' of David and Solomon and the conflict between prophet (a Deuteronomistic category) and king are by-products of this ideology.

This is *a* history of *an* Israel; surely not a history that Judaean peasants might have told, or a merchant from Jaffa, or a priest of a local sanctuary, or a foreign mercenary, or a pragmatic royal political adviser, or any number of religious intermediaries. This history is one of innumerable possibilities, but the one that came down to us. The idea that we can filter its point of view, its ideology, throw away the 'story' and keep the 'facts' is risible. There is no *objective* history of Israel any more than there is an objective 'ancient Israel'. Modern historians need to write their own story (or stories), and define their own ancient Israel. The story written by an ancient elite (or elites) cannot pre-empt our own attempts to reconstruct, our own stories of the past, neither because it just happened to be the best preserved, nor because it is Scripture.

13. See J. Hughes, *Secrets of the Times: Myth and History in Biblical Chronology* (Sheffield: JSOT Press, 1990).

Modern Ownership

Nor, of course, will moderns all agree on what story they wish to tell. Whose history, or what history, are *we* moderns telling? This question has two meanings: who are the people, or what is the territory, about which we are writing a history?; and who are 'we'? The problems inherent in the use of the name 'Israel' are widely understood. Is 'Israel' essentially an ethnic designation, a cultural one or a geographical one? Each of these alternatives (which are not entirely exclusive of each other) implies a different kind of history: a national history, a regional history, or an intellectual/cultural history.[14] In each case, fundamental difficulties have to be overcome: what *is* the territory we can call 'Israel' in antiquity (and is the term appropriate for more than a few centuries of human history?); what sort of identity, if any, was implied by the self-designation 'Israelite' in ancient times? Where and when does 'Israelite culture' begin and end, and how does one characterize and identify it? This last question is surely *the* fundamental question for a modern historian of ancient Israel: what exactly do we now mean by 'Israel'?

For many historians, a history of ancient Israel is simultaneously of a people and of a land between the Mediterranean (mostly confined, however, to the upland areas) and the Jordan (and perhaps a little beyond) between the hills of the Carmel range and the Upper Galilee and the Sinai peninsula. But neither the area west of the Jordan nor its population constituted any more of real entity in the past than they do now. An 'Israel' covering the whole of Palestine is a myth, if by 'Israel' we mean a single people, society or state. Within the area defined just now flourished briefly a mountain kingdom known (among other things) as Israel. In the surrounding territory lived Philistines, Phoenicians, Arameans, Hittites—people differentiated by ethnic and cultural identities as well as political allegiances. Under what name can any history link their fortunes?

Most modern 'histories of Israel' *do* cover a geographical area consisting of Palestine, treating both it and its inhabitants as 'Israel'. This is actually a kind of colonialism, and the term is apposite, because our European historiographical tradition belongs with colonialism, and because the issue of the ownership of history is most acute in areas

---

14. A similar dilemma underlies the apparent contradiction of such categories as 'non-religious Jew' or 'Arab Israeli' (remember that 'Israeli' and 'Israelite' are identical in Hebrew).

once colonized and now trying to reassert an independent history.[15] The history of the Bible's use is also a colonial one (intruders always win over the indigenous people) and it has subsequently served colonialism, both Christian and Jewish, internal and external, very well. The modern historian of 'ancient Israel' lives, however, in a postcolonial world, and should realize perfectly well the contemporary implications of retrospectively colonizing the whole area west of the Jordan with 'Israelites'.

For 'history', as every historian should know, is not about the past but about the present.[16] Histories have frequently had identity-forming functions and as such aim to promote ideological and political conflict. The island lying to the west of Britain may be called 'Ireland', 'the island of Ireland'; its northern region may be known as 'Northern Ireland' or 'Ulster' or the 'Six Counties'. Each term implies a different history, and the choice of use will often betray one's political allegiance to a 'loyalist' or 'republican' (or 'Protestant' or 'Catholic') cause. Whether or not 'Ireland' is a unity is an issue for which a large number of people have been murdered and, as I write, are still being murdered. Whether 'Israel' is 'Palestine' is only one of a number of such cases. Thus, there is an Israeli history of Israel/Palestine. But there *can* be a Palestinian one, too. How can they accept the Zionist history without condoning their own lack of political rights? No-one has a right to deny them a story. The recovery of marginal histories, for example by feminists and by third world historians, and the recognition of those marginal histories by academic institutions and by governments further illustrates the politics of history and confronts every would-be 'biblical historian' or 'historian of ancient Israel' with a challenge to be aware of whose history he or she will be writing. We need *multiple* histories, because there can be no neutral history. Whoever says there can will probably claim to be able to tell it, and ought to be ignored.

15. The expression 'land of the Bible' represents merely a different kind of colonialism, the religious imperialism of Judaeo–Christianity. Its use even in Amihai Mazar's *Archaeology of the Land of the Bible* (Garden City: Doubleday, 1990)— though whether author's or publisher's choice is unknown—reveals just how easily this territory is assimilated to the literary world of the Bible.

16. The reader is referred to the excellent demonstration by K.W. Whitelam, *The Invention of Ancient Israel: The Silencing of Palestinian History* (London: Routledge, 1996).

Writing a 'history of Israel', then, may be interpreted as a theological statement, and will inevitably constitute a political one. The resulting story will also be only one of many possible ones. And yet, cannot one history be better than another? Should we merely accommodate an ever-growing plurality in a celebration of postmodern entropy? Or can any historian of this particular piece of the earth's surface we are concerned with lay claim to a 'better' history than another? Can academic historians do anything except add to the pile of histories?

That is the question driving the remainder of this essay. I do not believe that the role of the historian is merely to tell stories over again, however much these stories accommodate ever more data and ever more sophisticated levels of theoretical explanation. To explain what *I* think modern historians of ancient Israel should do I need to propose a revision and clarification of terminology.

4. *History, Historiography and Metahistory*

Many problems in scholarship begin at the level of terminology (as I have shown above). Abandoning, then, whatever use I may have adopted previously in this essay (for the benefit of simplicity or convenience), I now propose some basic distinctions and definitions. First, I think it is necessary to distinguish 'history' and 'historiography': the former to refer to 'the past' and the latter to refer to a narrative which claims to relate that past.

The following quotation illustrates the distinction rather well: 'To suggest that many things in the Bible are not historical is not too serious. But to lose biblical history altogether is to lose our tradition'[17]. With these words, Frank Cross employs two different senses: 'not historical' means 'not belonging to history' in the sense I am defining 'history', that is, not part of the past. 'Biblical history', on the other hand, means the biblical story.[18] Cross implies that the biblical story

17. In 'Are the Bible's Stories True?', *Time* 15 December, 1995, pp. 46-53, quoted on p. 53.
18. The suggestion that while parts of the biblical story can be rejected as unhistorical, we should not reject the total story as incoherent. Should a historian decide at some point that although such-and-such a biblical datum ought to be dismissed as unhistorical, to do so would destroy the framework and so it must be regarded as historical?

loses its value if too much of it turns out to be unhistorical. Here he illuminates, in fact, an important aspect of modern biblical history writing. Biblical scholarship wants to hold onto its received story (because that is the theological value it has acquired) but also wants its received story to be validated as a critically reconstructed history. What Cross (and others) dream of is *a history that has critically-secured data but the old biblical framework.* In other words, a 'history' (story) that is history (real past). This wish explains, I think, why 'history' remains particularly ambiguous in some areas of biblical scholarship.

There is, however, yet a third meaning of 'history': the name of a *discipline* taught in schools and universities. It is this usage that makes possible a confusion in the meaning of the term 'historian'. For we can, and do, refer both to Thucydides and Livy or to Braudel and Collingwood—and many of our fellow academics—as 'historians'. But while modern historians may write stories about the past, they very often do other things that do not result in stories and do not pretend to be narratives. Historians also deal with the philosophy of writing about the past, about method, about very circumscribed pieces of data or moments of time. They argue about interpretation and the evaluation of data. In doing so they would claim, I think, neither to be writing a story of the past, however brief, nor discovering the past as something objective, beyond the limits of the methods of the human sciences. In such activities, Thucydides might be their subject at times, but he would not be their colleague.

There are, therefore, three senses in which the word 'history' is used and at least two possible areas of confusion, as 'history' and 'historian' enjoy different meanings. A preliminary task in fulfilling the agenda set for the contributions in this volume is to point to the potential muddle and mischief and suggest some precise terminology. I turn now to the three terms under discussion.

History

Of the three possible meanings of 'history' just outlined (the past, a story about the past, a discipline), I propose that we think of retaining the first and using different terms for the other two. The only reason for this is that there are alternative names for the others which still retain the verbal element 'history' in them. I am not suggesting that my preferred usage is the 'right' one, or the only one; I merely propose to use the word in one sense only, and that this sense might be the most appropriate, at least for the purposes of the kind of discussion in which I am engaged.

A particular advantage of using 'history' to mean 'the past' is that this sense is both the most basic (logically) and the most problematic. Any definition of 'history' invokes 'the past' in some way, and yet the term 'the past' is one of the most elusive of all signifiers. The singular noun plus definite article imply some kind of unity, and not just a temporal unity but a metaphysical one. This 'past' insinuates itself as a massive whole to which we have different degrees of privileged access, and yet which we somehow acknowledge as beyond our total control or even comprehension. As 'past' it seems invulnerable to the manipulations of human consciousness: we experience the present, we create the future: the past we cannot change. Rather like the idea of an infallible and all-knowing god, 'the past' is an indispensable resource for ideologues: the terms signifies some kind of objective truth to which a hierophant has access and can impart to others. (It is here that the use of the term 'competence' comes into play; those who espouse such a view of the past can best attack opponents on such grounds because such an attack also reinforces the idea of the past as a set of objective data which the historian controls.)

I invoke deities and use the word 'hierophant' with deliberation, because the notion of an objective past, an objective 'history' makes sense only if it is indivisible and universal. Such a past could not belong to anyone, and is beyond the power of any human or group of humans to conceive. It could only mean the totality, to the very minutest detail, of everything that has happened. But in order for 'history' in this sense to be invoked as a reality this totality must be comprehensible as a whole. As Berkeley clearly understood, such a notion implies a transcendental observer, for only from a transcendental position could such an objective 'history' be grasped. No human can understand 'all history'.

This is not an idle argument. The belief in a single transcendental being who can comprehend, indeed controls, all history is precisely a biblical belief: it is one of the major tenets of biblical historiography. Modern 'biblical historians' do not merely parrot the biblical framework in their own historiography: they often subscribe to the same belief in the same god, and thus they also inherit the possibility of a notion of objective history. When I claim, then, that there is no 'objective' history I am implying a world-view incompatible with that of the biblical writings (except perhaps Qoheleth) for whom history was defined by divine deeds (or so they claimed in their writings; they may have thought differently). So a certain kind of religious belief *might* well dictate a certain definition of 'history'.[19]

But whether or not there is a being that can do so, no human can see the past *sub specie aeternitatis*. As Cross observed, we are born into narratives about the past; history is already 'storied' for us; we learn about it as story. We may believe we can ask with Ranke 'how it actually happened'. But what is the 'it'? 'It' must remain an Idea, accessible to human knowledge only through representation, through signifiers such as relics, texts and memories. The advent of film and videotape has made little difference: the camera cannot present more than an eye can see, and cannot escape the partiality of an observer. The form in which this ideal 'history' must be clothed to be humanly apprehended is historiography.

Historiography

By this term I designate a particular kind of writing about the past. The various ways in which this can be done have been brilliantly illuminated by Hayden White in his study of nineteenth-century historiography.[20] Its genres are narrative ones, telling the story of something, be it an institution, a nation, an epoch or a person. The beginning and ending of the story will be selected with some degree of arbitrariness, selection of the data known will be determined by considerations of relevance to the plot; gaps will be filled by deduction or surmise; and, in general, the finished product will employ all the characteristics of a narrative: plot, sequence, character, point of view, and so on. Most important of these is, of course, plot. But historiography is a *meta-genre*: it comprises a number of genres, as it has done over different periods. It also partially embraces overlapping genres concerned with the past, such as myth, legend, historical fiction and autobiography.

---

19. This is not an issue specifically between religious believers and non-believers, but about the discourses that surround a discipline that combines religious and secular elements to a peculiar degree. Both Dever and Halpern have indicated (in personal communication) that they are either agnostic or atheist; this does not prevent them from arguing for what I would regard as a view of history that is theistic (as, I would argue, was Karl Marx's also).

20. H. White, *Metahistory: The Historical Imagination in Nineteenth-Century Europe* (Baltimore: Johns Hopkins University Press, 1973).

Sometimes these genres have indeed fallen within the orbit of historiography: while modern biblical historians conventionally distinguish
myths, legends/sagas and historiography in, for example, Genesis 1–
11, Genesis 12–50 and 2 Kings respectively, these generic distinctions
are not clearly marked by the literature itself: we cannot see signs that
these authors made such distinctions. In the Hellenistic age, it is true,
historiographers claimed to tell the truth while others merely offered
tales. Although abundant evidence of what we would now call plagi-
arism, distortion and invention in these authors shows that these charges
were largely rhetorical, there is at least a conceptual distinction between
true and untrue writing about the past. Thucydides wrote only about
the very recent past, to which he was a witness or had access to
witnesses; other historians in ancient or mediaeval times were dependent largely on older sources which they had little means of evaluating
other than by common sense.

Thus the conventions of historiographical genres vary over time and
culture. Ancient historiography cannot be transformed into modern
historiography any more easily than a Euripides drama can into
Shakespeare or Shakespeare into Beckett. The conventions of modern
historiography are different, both because of our sense of the past as
something objective, our attachment to objectivity itself, our access to
many different forms of information from the past, and our rational
disposition that requires us to 'show what we know'; for although
rhetoric in historiography still plays well, we pride ourselves that we
argue and deduce what happened in the past from evidence and by
method. At least, that is how the genre of *critical* historiography works.
There are other genres, found especially in the media and the more
popular forms of sensational literature.

Critical historiography is now typically practised as an interdiscipli-
nary academic exercise and patronized by the state or the consumer,
rather than a divine, royal or ecclesiastical patron. Critical historiography is no longer the rehearsing of older stories, transcribing of
memories, inculcating of moral values or the inventing of appropriate
episodes. Modern readers and writers of history now claim to judge a
historiographical work on the basis of its accuracy and its intention to
report the past 'as it was'.

Yet critical historiography remains narrative, and its methods do not
guarantee reliability (analogy and probability are two of its necessary
but fallible rules). Few readers of historiography are competent to

debate every issue in such a work; and so we react to this type of story as we do to narratives generally: namely, we respond to its ideology and its rhetoric. The same facts can portray Oliver Cromwell or Christopher Columbus or Josef Stalin as villain or a hero (or both); Napoleon's place in European history depends on whether or not the twentieth century is brought into view. Most people's idea of Claudius is from Graves; and of Caesar from Shakespeare. Because it is narrative, historiography attracts us and in attracting us it unties our disbelief or our ignorance and confronts us with what we like to think of as a real past, just as our own memories of childhood do.

For this reason, it is better not to confuse historiography and history. Neither should it be concluded that one historiography is no better than another. Comparison and evaluation is possible, as with most narratives, on the basis of conformity to criteria that the genre invokes. We cannot compare fairly a critical historiography with a piece of historical fiction or with an ancient Hellenistic historiography, but we can compare any modern historiographies that claim to be critical ones. That is because there exist conventions to the genre of 'critical historiography' (the word 'critical' is hardly ever used, but the claim exists in the form of generic markers), and even if we cannot challenge a historiography on the basis of our command of all the surviving data, we can judge it on whether or not it adheres to the dominant requirements of the genre. These are: to contain nothing that the data contradict, never to promote the improbable over the probable (without specific argumentation), to evaluate all sources of information critically, and to exclude obvious bias from description. Generic features include footnotes, bibliographies, discussion of alternative interpretations, and priority of primary over secondary sources. These features invoke a particular relationship between 'history' and 'historiography, that can form the basis for comparison and evaluation.

It is also possible to compare the modern genres of historiography with ancient ones—favourably, if we use the criteria of the modern genres. An ancient historiographer might well have disliked our modern ones for lack of edifying prose, or moral example, or splendour of theme. Critical historiography makes claims to knowledge (of a certain kind) and invites discussion about how such knowledge is obtained. But historiographical genres did not (and do not) always claim superiority on the basis of their claim to knowledge. Fashion, political correctness, chauvinism and other kinds of prejudice have usually produced a more favourable reception.

So what is the point of continuing to write critically-informed stories about the past? One obvious reason would seem to be that previous stories are not good enough, and this may be the case in two ways. More data (hard or soft, artefactual or theoretical) are becoming available which contradict or challenge or render inadequate earlier historiographies, or previous critical historiographies are methodologically defective. But new historiographies also arise because previous accounts fail to satisfy aesthetically or ideologically, and a better narrative for the same data needs to be attempted. Such a motive is not as frivolous at may seem, for as long as there is the implicit (or explicit) claim that a historiography *is* history, historiographers have the power to manipulate people's ideas in a way that is dangerous. To say simply 'but these are the *facts*; this *happened*' in the context of a narrative which interprets these 'facts' is to impose not just data but a worldview. If there can be no historiographies which are objective and reliable, then at least let there be enough historiographies so that the reader can see how loosely interpretation may sit on data and may realize that history-as-story is never the same as history-as-fact. Let there be fascist and Marxist, Zionist and Palestinian, Western and Oriental historiographies, minimal and maximal, so that, indeed, no reader may ever pardonably be deluded into believing in objective historical truth.[21]

---

21. I cannot praise variety more eloquently than Diana Edelman ('Saul ben Kish in History and Tradition', in V. Fritz and P.R. Davies [eds], *The Origins of the Ancient Israelite States* [JSOTSup, 228; Sheffield: Sheffield Academic Press, 1996], pp. 142-59: 'There can never be a definitive reconstruction of the past; there can only be a range of creative associations by individuals who have been influenced by their own life experiences as well as by the data they believe to be reliable and choose to link together in chains of meaning.

'It is possible, but not necessarily preferable, to create a "history by consensus", in which a majority of individuals agree that one creation of events best suits the evidence. Such a consensus cannot guarantee, however, that the creation accurately captures the actual events. Most histories are created by linking together individual data into chains of cause and effect based on logical processing; real life does not necessarily operate by the same neat, rational principles. What is plausible then, is not necessarily what actually happened. Ultimately, it is the meaning assigned to actual events rather than the events themselves that holds importance for humans and influences their lives. The attempt to establish a 'history by consensus' whose accuracy can never be verified, is a potentially dangerous goal. Such a consensus obscures the

Metahistory

I use this term not in the sense adopted by Hayden White, but to denote the academic discipline that studies historiography and its relation to history. What goes on in university history departments (and in sociology and archaeology too) is not always the production of new narratives. It may be the application of a theory or a model to a set of data, or a comparison of one historiographical account with another, and both with the data they employ. It may be concerned with factors that historiographic narratives commonly exclude, such as climate, diet or comparative data. As an academic discipline, 'history' is not necessarily historiography, but may be (and here I think it best fulfils its social responsibility) to investigate and police both history and historiography, to insist again and again on the dangers of mistaking historiographies for history and exposing the ideological factors at work in *every* story about the past. Narrative is not the only possible genre in which historians can work, any more than literary critics. The essays in the present volume make that clear.

Application

If metahistory is to establish itself as the main activity of historians, then we shall see a tension between them and historiographers. The latter will seek, or at least they will achieve, representation of their history as real, as fact, as 'the past', and their stories will create an attitude towards it. Historiographers may well seek to obscure the distinction between their 'historiography' and 'history', to deposit their narrative in that Holy of Holies marked 'The Past'. Many of these perpetrators will be people of integrity and scholarship, who seek to create a story whose elements are derived transparently from knowledge gained and documented meticulously, with methods and prejudices that are not concealed. But for every such historiographer there are a hundred ambitious, demagogic charlatans, seeking to exploit our fascination with this absent cause, 'The Past' and hijack it for political,

---

individualistic and creative nature of the historiographic enterprise, defining an unnecessary orthodoxy that discourages fresh investigations and creative imaginings and which results in a form of thought policing'.

Also relevant to this viewpoint is the following statement of H. Marrou: 'the fruitfulness of historical knowledge is to be found primarily in the dialogue which it generates within us between the Self and the Other' (*A History of Education in Antiquity* [London: Sheed and Ward, 1956], p. xii).

personal or mercenary ends. (For an example, replace 'history' with 'heritage'.) We may cut our teeth on each other within the academy but outside the academy 'history' is still invoked to kill people, to indoctrinate them, to subjugate them, to capture them, to captivate and delude them.

There are three things a historian can (and perhaps should) do these days. One is not to discourage the production of good historiographies, and encourage people to read many of them, so that they may learn in how many different ways 'history' may be represented, and perhaps even ask themselves why these stories differ. The second is to expose deceits practised in the name of history, dispel stories parading as truth, and enforced and fictive identities parading in the form of gene-alogies. And the third is to remain sceptical, minimalist and negative. We need not fear that we will ever be anything but a minority. The invention of history will never cease.

CLIO IS ALSO AMONG THE MUSES!
KEITH W. WHITELAM AND THE HISTORY OF PALESTINE:
A REVIEW AND A COMMENTARY*

Niels Peter Lemche

1. *Introduction*

Many years ago, at the International Organization for the Study of the Old Testament Conference in Edinburgh (1974), a group of young scholars held a separate meeting, the subject of which was a revitalization of the study of Israelite history—in those days considered a moribund affair. An important Assyriologist and historian of the ancient world was invited to become a member of our group, but he declined the offer because it would, in his view, be without perspective to co-operate with theologians, magicians or their likes.

This scholar was, of course, right. In those days the project of changing the direction of historical studies among biblical scholars really seemed to be a hopeless one, and very few had any ideas as to the rather dramatic developments this field was to experience over the next 25 years, although, ironically, 1974 was also the year of the first major attack in modern times on a specific period in Israel's history, the patriarchal age.[1]

Now, two decades later, it is obvious that most of the traditional ideas about the history of Israel have become the victim of progress

    *   A review of K.W. Whitelam, *The Invention of Ancient Israel: The Silencing of Palestinian History* (London: Routledge, 1996). I thank the publishers very much for the ready cooperation in providing me with a pre-publication copy of this book, making it possible within only a few months after its appearance to publish a first edition of this extended review (*SJOT* 10 [1996], pp. 88-119).
    1.   In 1974 T.L. Thompson published his *The Historicity of the Patriarchal Narratives: The Quest for the Historical Abraham* (BZAW, 133; Berlin: de Gruyter, 1974), closely followed by J. Van Seters, *Abraham in History and Tradition* (New Haven: Yale University Press, 1975).

made in historical studies: there is no premonarchic history of Israel left worth speaking about; the Davidic and Solomonic empire is in jeopardy; the history of the divided kingdom—particularly the Judaean part—is being drastically rewritten, the exile is suspected of being mostly an ideological construct, and the Persian and Hellenistic periods, about which the Old Testament itself has very little to tell, are moving into the focus of scholarly attention.

In this situation the present work by Keith W. Whitelam, professor at the University of Stirling, Scotland, should be seen. Whitelam planned to write a major history of Israel, a project which, however, collapsed under the growing impression of the questionable character of the enterprise when viewed in the light of almost two hundred years of studying ancient Israelite history. He has simply drawn the consequence of the absent history of ancient Israel, and has turned to Palestinian history, only to discover that this history does not exist either. At this point the pertinent questions must be: what happened to this history and why has nobody written such a thing?

In order to answer these questions the position of the historical study of ancient Israel in theology and religious studies as part of the study of the Hebrew Bible/Old Testament should be considered, or so Whitelam maintains. Moreover, in modern Israel, founded on the soil of Palestine, the history of ancient Israel has become the discourse of the modern state and society, and part of its identity. The Palestinian inhabitants of this country share this idea, as they see their own history as modern, either as a history of 'depossession and exile' (p. 7),[2] or as part of the history of the Moslem world.

Whitelam does not compose a history of Palestine; rather he paves the way for such a history by exposing the ideological background of the modern study of the history of Ancient Israel. In a way, this history has to be liberated from biblical studies in very much the same way as the archaeology of Palestine had to be removed from the tyranny of biblically-dominated idiosyncrasies.[3]

---

2.   Strange the way exiles can define nations! The paradox could be that biblical Israel arose as part of the exilic experience, very much in the same manner as the Palestinian nation and Palestinian identity of the present age as opposed to, on the one hand Israel and, on the other, the Arab world may owe its existence to the fact that the Palestinians lost their land.

3.   Whitelam refers to the demand made by the well-known archaeologist W.G. Dever for an independent discipline of Palestinian archaeology, not controlled by

Among the students of ancient Israel who are particularly criticized by Whitelam in his introduction, we find the following pedigree of scholars: G.W. Ahlström, E.A. Knauf, N.P. Lemche, T.L. Thompson, and H. Weippert. Whitelam also includes himself among the members of this list especially to be blamed for not having realized the importance of an independent Palestinian history: to be blamed because they—probably more than their colleagues—are supposed to be in possession of insights which should in time have led them to the recognition of the independence of Palestinian history. The titles of two recent history books by T.L. Thompson and G.W. Ahlström must be regarded as paradoxical examples of this, as they promise exactly the opposite of what is intended by their authors.[4]

2. *Partial Texts and Fractured Histories*

In his first chapter (pp. 11-36), Whitelam tunes in on what might in one sentence be called 'the social production of texts': all historical texts are partial, the products of writers who are themselves participants in a specific mental network and writing for the benefit of other members of this network.[5] This goes for modern as well as ancient historical texts. So, instead of starting another unnecessary discussion of the historical importance of narratives about the past in the Hebrew Bible, Whitelam seeks out the basic notions behind the construction of the modern histories of ancient Israel, understood to be a part of what

biblical beliefs and ideas. This demand for the freedom of archaeology is valid although Dever's interpretations at times show a remarkable influence from biblical studies. The same applies to modern historians dealing with ancient Palestine and the history of Israel, as demonstrated many times by Whitelam in this book.

4.   G.W. Ahlström's textbook of Israelite history became *The History of Ancient Palestine from the Palaeolithic Period to Alexander's Conquest* (ed. D. Edelman; JSOTSup, 148: Sheffield: Sheffield Academic Press, 1993). This is only a correct title as long as the pre-monarchic period is intended; thereafter it becomes a rather traditional (from its point of orientation) history of ancient Israel. On the other side, T.L. Thompson recently published a major monograph, *Early History of the Israelite People from the Written and Archaeological Sources* (Studies in the History and Culture of the Ancient Near East, 4; Leiden: Brill, 1992), although the last thing he planned to do was to write a history of the Israelite people. As a matter of fact, Thompson's book is much closer to Whitelam's demand for an independent Palestinian history.

5.   This is of course a truism, relevant to all kinds of literature.

could best be called the discourse of the Western world. This history of ancient Israel was construed over the last two hundred years as an inseparable part of the Western heritage which in those years centred around the nation and the national state and was to be perpetuated in Zionism and the creation of the modern state of Israel, the ideological basis of which (the 'return' to the 'Homeland') is without qualification solidly embedded in this nationalistic ideology of the modern world, an ideology which arose during the eighteenth century to become a dominant ideological factor in the nineteenth and twentieth centuries.

There is no reason to question this view on the emergence of nationalism and historical thinking as presented by Whitelam. Any person with only the slightest knowledge of Western intellectual development over the last two hundred years will have to subscribe to his description. History as a discipline is a fairly recent newcomer to the academic scene, although an antiquarian interest in the past has always been known, generally in the form of chronicles of the past, like Holinshed's famous chronicle of the history of England, which was soon to be adapted in the plays of William Shakespeare. Shakespeare—like the compiler of his source book—can hardly be accused of paying overdue attention to historical facts; he was far more interested in entertaining an audience that was always an eager participant in the vicissitudes of the dramatic plot.[6] Furthermore, the manner in which the genres are blended together is also seen easily in some of the major historiographic works of the eighteenth century, a fine example of which is Edward Gibbon's *Decline and Fall of the Roman Empire*, which has traditionally been admired for its rich style and lively presentation, but today hardly anyone considers it a faithful historical rendering of the past.

The origin of history writing as a part of fictional literature and its

6.   On Shakespeare and Holinshed see, e.g., the review in A. and J. Nicoll, *Holinshed's Chronicle as Used in Shakespeare's Plays* (London: J.M. Dent & Sons, 1927). This example could of course be expanded ad nauseam. The use of history in plays and operas, however, is an excellent testimony to the importance of writing with an audience in mind. An interesting plot will find its audience irrespective of the historical truth, as long as the historical narrative is accepted by the public as something it can identify with and sympathize with. Otherwise, it will be a total disaster. Some 'historical' plays or movies failed at this point, simply because they did not fulfil the last mentioned requirement. Famous among these in recent years is Steven Spielberg's fiasco '1941', which was simply not accepted by the American public.

subsequent liberation as an independent genre can also be traced in the development of the genre during the nineteenth century and the early twentieth century. So it should not be forgotten that as late as the beginning of the present century, the German *Altgeschichtler*, Theodor Mommsen, was awarded the Nobel Prize in Literature, not only because of the historical excellence of his work, but also because of its splendid and rich style. It was recognized to be a major achievement by an independent mind.[7] Happily this tradition of history understood as literature has never totally died out, in spite of present academic preferences. First of all, in the present age of meticulous historical investigations, historical novels or literate biographies of historical persons are still very popular, but also during the twentieth century a number of general-historical books or collections have appeared, such as— among the more successful—the multi-volume history by the Swede Carl Grimberg, who is certainly best known for his vivid style, and not for the precision of his historical judgment.

It goes without saying that the emergence of history as an independent academic discipline and at the same time the public idea of history as the description of the past, however chronologically arranged, could also be traced in art history as well.[8] I shall, for the present, skip this topic. No doubt Whitelam has focused on an important aspect of history writing and understanding of history, although he does not discuss art but politics. His examples are mainly drawn from present-day political disturbances and disquiet which arose because of nationalistic biases nourished by the concept of history among present-day people, for example the discussion in Greece about the Elgin marbles, or the problems created by the emergence of Macedonia in recent years. Whitelam, however, draws special attention to the role of history and archaeology in the modern state of Israel, and in this connection he

7. The Laudatio prepared by C.D. Wisén in 1902 on occasion of this award, includes the following passage: 'Selten fühlt man so lebhaft wie beim Studium von Mommsens "Römischer Geschichte", daß Klio eine der Musen war. Dieses Werk begeisterte uns, als wir es in unserer Jugend kennenlernten; es behält, da wir es in älteren Tagen wieder lesen, seine Gewalt über uns. So groß ist die Kraft der historischen Wissenschaft, wenn sie zugleich große historische Kunst ist.' (quoted on the first page of T. Mommsen, *Römische Geschichte*, I (dtv-bibliothek, 6053; Munich: Deutscher Taschenbuch Verlag, 1976).

8. One has only to study the staging of 'historical' events, on the one hand, in paintings from the Renaissance to the beginning of this century, and on the other in movies of the modern age.

particularly stresses the fairly recent rise to importance of the minor incident of the siege of Masada during the Jewish–Roman war, an event largely ignored by later Jewish tradition, although narrated by Josephus.

He knows that his presentation will stir up a tidal wave of protests, which is only to be expected because of the position in modern societies of biblically-oriented historians who have reconstructed ancient Israel as if it was just another European national state—which it certainly was not.

It is one of the tragedies of this century that nationalism in its most outrageous form was destined to act as the basis of the Nazi 'Blut und Boden' ideology, which included a strange and dangerous combination of the concept of ethnicity with the idea of the national state. The tragedy not only consisted in the way this ideology was abused by Nazi politicians, who were acting according to 'Der Mythus des zwanzigsten Jahrhunderts', but also in the manner in which it has been perpetuated since the collapse of Nazi Germany to form the ideology behind the creation of a large number of new national states. And it is certainly tragic that this Western myth can also be seen to form a part of the ideological back-up for the modern state of Israel, which seems to be founded on the concept of a Jewish people, not to say race, although it should never be forgotten that the term 'Jew' was traditionally not an ethnic but a religious designation. Evidence of this can easily be found in the pages of the Hebrew Bible, which in spite of the rhetorical use of a terminology like the 'sons of Israel', is not really talking about a real society ('nation'). The Hebrew Bible is clearly referring to a religious community, not to a living society of the ancient world.[9] It is also an ironic part of the modern Western *Weltanschauung* that this dimension of the Hebrew text has for a long time been forgotten.

Whitelam, however, also understands that his own accommodation with this tradition of writing histories of the Israelite people is partial, not to be separated from the decline of European colonialism, the European discovery of other people's tradition, and the insecurity presently felt about our situation in the post-war world. While at the

---

9. In my 'The Understanding of Community in the Old Testament and in the DSS', to be published in T.L. Thompson (ed.), *Proceedings of the Copenhagen Congress of DSS Studies* (Copenhagen International Seminar; Sheffield: Sheffield Academic Press, 1996), I have tried to show that the concept of community in the Hebrew Bible is more or less the same as found in the writings of the Dead Sea community, normally considered to be late sectarian Jewish literature.

same time being successfully exported to the rest of the world, basic concepts belonging to European (which in this sense certainly also includes North American) tradition are now in discredit in our part of the world, not least the idea of the nation state. This is obvious in Europe, where we at the same time find a tendency towards a fragmentation of the traditional national states (understood now to be parts of the European Union), and a marked revival of tribalism (at the present called 'regionalism') which demands more political space for the local community. In North America an analogous movement is clearly seen in the attitude of the indigenous population, the Indians, and the rediscovery of their tradition.[10]

Another related issue concerns the question why Palestinian history was ignored except for the episode of ancient Israel. The answer is obvious: the Europeans found no partner in the ancient Palestinian world with whom they could communicate, apart from ancient Israel, the creation of their own mind.

3. *Denying Space and Time to Palestinian History*

This line of thought continues but is at the same time sharpened in the following chapter (pp. 37-70), which is devoted to the two famous logical categories of Immanuel Kant, time and space, which, however, are here understood not to be logical terms but political concepts that have been twisted and bent to suit political purposes.

The first part of the chapter is devoted to 'the denial of Palestinian space'. Here a number of devices have traditionally been employed to escape the fact that the territory of present-day Israel was in fact in antiquity named Palestine. Instead of simply admitting this, European tradition created a tradition of Palestine as—in Whitelam's terms—a construct of the Other, a society peculiarly different from and foreign to Europe. 'Israel' was, at the same time, considered the cradle of European civilization, although this 'honour' was shared by the classical Greek world, considered to be the second cradle of the Western world.

---

10. It is, on the other hand, an ironic fact that this tradition may first and foremost have been rediscovered not by the Indians themselves but by members of the ruling white society, the intruders and masters (it has at least been made publicly known by members of the white majority). It may be considered only another confirmation of the old adage that revolutions start at the top, never among common man who only delivers the soldiers for the revolutions.

By emphasizing this 'otherness' of ancient Palestine, we excluded the Palestinians from the European discourse, and so they became part of the oriental discourse, which has traditionally been seen as foreign and even hostile to European civilization.

Whitelam's argument is a most convincing one, but it begins to crack at exactly this point. His project is a pioneering one and polemical in its planning and execution. He accordingly shows little understanding of why it all happened. Sometimes we get the impression that a treason was more or less intentionally committed. This was hardly the case—or else it only recently became a conscious political device for stating a claim to ownership of the land called Palestine. Most of the background of this mental matrix among Europeans, according to which there is no room for Palestine and Palestinians, could be, on the one side, the communality between the Bible and Western civilization which over a period of almost 2000 years became adjusted to the literary biblical world and, on the other, the fascination of the Europeans with the Oriental world which was at one and the same time understood to be both very foreign and very close to the European civilization. Any student of the Near East will soon have to realize that the people of this region often behave and act in ways which are not much different from our own standards of behaviour, except that they may seem a bit *altmodisch*. On the other hand, they may also react in a manner which we cannot predict and therefore understand. In this way a difference is created exactly at the point where the Europeans believed a communality to exist. The resulting bewilderment probably led to the Europeans totally denying this communality, and thus in the minds of the Europeans the people of the Near East became the principal enemies of Europe, a concept which of course was fed by the tradition of the crusades.

Thus it is hardly because of ill will that the Palestinians were denied their identity, and it is certainly also a question whether they ever had one before the creation of their *Other*, the present state of Israel. European visitors to the region before the middle of the present century hardly found anything which could be compared to a Palestinian national identity; rather they would have thought of the Palestinian population as part of the Syrian one, if not simply as a member of the Arab world, although the concept of Palestine as the Holy Land was of course well known to them. Because of the confusion created by this situation the European *Beobachter* could therefore be led to assume that Palestine was not the home of a nation: a land called Palestine without a proper population of Palestinians would, to a member of the embryonic European national states of the nineteenth century,[11] be a contradiction in terms. For this reason they never understood Palestine to be anything except its biblical and Christian meaning.

However this may be, the effects of European marginalization of the inhabitants of the Near East paved the way for the Zionist slogan of 'land without a people for a people without a land', and for the modern debate not least in Israel about terminology. At this point Israeli historians and archaeologists have only sharpened and actualized what was already prepared by earlier generations of European scholars, including names such as Kathleen (not Katherine!, cf. Whitelam, p. 47) Kenyon, and William F. Albright. These scholars among others paved the way for a more conscious political use of the term 'Land of Israel' such as the one advocated strongly, for example by Anson F. Rainey who in a most absurd way argues that Eretz-Israel must be considered the only non-political term. This line probably met its high point in Moshe Dothan's postulate that after the eleventh century CE the name of Palestine was no longer used as a political term, only to reappear again in the course of the nineteenth century. So there is no room for either a modern or an ancient Palestinian history, in spite of the fact that the term 'Palestine' has been known since Neo-Assyrian times, and is well attested in classical sources, first and foremost in the History of Herodotus.

Herodotus's use of the term Palestine and Palestinians is particularly revealing, as he seems always to use the term in connection with Syria: I 105: καὶ ἐπείτε ἐγένοντο ἐν τῇ Παλαιστίνῃ Συρίη (about Psammeticus meeting the Scythians in the Palestinian Syria); II 106: ἐν δὲ τῇ Παλαιστίνῃ Συρίη (about stelas erected by Pharaoh Sesostris in the Palestinian Syria); cf. immediately before this II 104: Φοίνικες δὲ καὶ Σύριοι οἱ ἐν τῇ Παλαιστίνῃ (about Phoenicians and Syrians living in Palestine who are tracing the habit of circumcision back to Egypt); III 91: Φοινίκη τε πᾶσα καὶ Συρίη ἡ Παλαιστίνη καλεομένη... ('Phoenicia and that part of Syria which is called Palestine'); IV 39: Συρίην τὴν Παλαιστίνην (part of a geographical description of the Levant); VII 89: τῆς δὲ Συρίης τοῦτο τὸ χωρίον

---

11. And it should not be forgotten that these visitors generally belonged among the elite of their respective European countries, i.e. they were themselves infatuated by a nationalistic ideology without much foundation in the real world.

καὶ τό μέχρι Αἰγύπτου πᾶν Παλαιστίνη καλέεται (in A. de Sélincourt's translation [Penguin]: 'This part of Syria, together with the country which extends southward to Egypt, is all known as Palestine'), and in the same passage the expression Φοίνικες μὲν σὺν Συρίοισι τοῖσι ἐν τῇ Παλαιστίνῃ τριηκοσίας (saying that the Syrians living in Palestine contributed 300 triremes to Xerxes' fleet). Cf., finally, also III 5: ἀπὸ γὰρ Φοινίκης μέχρι οὔρων τῶν Καδύτιος πόλιός ἥ ἐστι Συρίων τῶν Παλαιστίνων καλεομένων ('From Phoenicia to the boundaries of Gaza the country belongs to the Syrians known as "Palestinians"').

This evidence drawn from Herodotus shows, however, that Whitelam is right and wrong at the same time, and probably makes it clear—as I already indicated above—that there never was a Palestinian people, except as part of a greater world: for Herodotus as for the European travellers of the nineteenth century they were identified as the Syrians living in that part of Syria which was called Palestine and which is considered to be identical with the territory between the Phoenician cities, that is, Lebanon, and the city of Gaza. Instead of speaking of an independent history of Palestine in Antiquity, we should talk about the history of Syria. Since the Arab conquest this could then be easily extended to expand the history of Palestine to become an inseparable part of the history of the Arab world. Although in danger of repeating myself, this also indicates that there was no Palestinian history before 1948 CE, simply because the nationalism of Europe had not yet reached this part of the world. Palestine as a nation was unintentionally created by the Zionist movement on the basis of a population which counted themselves as Arabs (or Syrians) living in the landscape of Palestine. The failure of the Europeans was simply that in the Zionist declaration, already quoted, 'people' is understood to be synonymous with 'nation', but if you asked an Arab living in, say Nablus around 1900 CE, whether he was a Palestinian, he would probably have understood this to be no more than an indication of his geographical background.

In this chapter Whitelam quite correctly draws attention to the changes brought about in historical studies by the appearance of the French school of *les annales*, and he particularly emphasizes the use of the concept *la longue durée* by the members of this school. This concept which concerns the understanding of time in history has been explained elsewhere but should perhaps be supplemented by an analogous concept called 'the wide space', meaning that a history of, say

Palestine, cannot be confined to this territory alone. To isolate Palestine from its surroundings would leave it alone and barren in the middle of nowhere. A proper history of Palestine would accordingly be to describe its history as a regional variation of the history of Syria, of which it was an integral part. Whitelam's demonstration of the need for an independent Palestinian history points at the necessity of creating an independent Syrian history, not at the usefulness of an isolated history of the landscape of Palestine.

Here, however, we are taught another lesson: such a history has probably been written several times, and with some success, as long as we speak about the Bronze Age.[12] However, for the Iron Age, the scholarly understanding of the history of Palestine and Syria has been permeated by biblical beliefs and considerations which makes such a venture almost impossible.

It goes without saying that a change in attitude as far as space is concerned will at the same time bring about changes in the understanding of time. Also here, the concept of time in the Hebrew Bible prevails to the detriment of a better understanding of the historical processes as such. Most biblical scholars have been using biblical periodizations in their reconstruction of Israel's ancient history: the period of the Patriarchs, the period of the Exodus and Conquest, the period of the Judges, the time of the empire of David and Solomon, and of the divided monarchy, the exilic and post-exilic periods. Whitelam also mentions the ironic fact that even the period of Jewish history which is left uncovered by the Hebrew Bible has got a name which is dependent on the Bible: the intertestamental period!

This situation has only been partly changed by those modern scholars who have destroyed the biblical historical periods one by one. Whitelam obviously thinks that this change has accomplished almost nothing in

---

12. I, having recently contributed to this collection by publishing two descriptions of the history of Syria and Palestine (*Die Vorgeschichte Israels. Biblische Enzyklopädie*, I [Stuttgart: Kohlhammer, 1996]; 'Syrian-Palestinian History: An Overview', in J.M. Sasson [ed.], *Civilizations of the Ancient Near East* [New York: Scribner, 1995], II, pp. 1195-218) have only partially solved the problem of an independent history, as the Palestinian territory in contrast to the rest of Syria always gets a special treatment (a special regional history). As a matter of fact, this should not have happened, or the regional view on history should also have been extended to other parts of ancient Syria.

the direction of a Palestinian history (although some may say: 'Well, it did bring about Whitelam's volume!').

At the end of this chapter Whitelam distances himself in a sarcastic way from the concept of pre-history, as if history did not include also the pre-historic period, which is so called because of the lack of written sources, although this runs contrary to the generally accepted meaning of the term 'history' as it is used by many historians of the present (pre-history concerns periods without written sources while history of course covers the period of written documents).

4. *Inventing Ancient Israel*

In the next two chapters Whitelam brings substance to his argument. He concentrates on two case examples of the eurocentric mode of studying the history of Israel without at the same time allowing for a history of the Palestinians except as part of this history.

The first example includes (in the chapter called *Inventing Ancient Israel*, pp. 71-121) the Late Bronze–Early Iron Age transition and shows how at the same time a fictitious entity was invented called 'ancient Israel' and how the Palestinian people were denied their own history. In this chapter he discusses the three classical constructions of the so-called history of early Israel: Albrecht Alt's immigration model, William F. Albright's conquest model, and G.E. Mendenhall's revolution model. Whitelam's discussion of the three models is, however, not a traditional one. He first and foremost concentrates on the ideological aspect of each of these models. Alt's model goes back to the 1920s, when the Jewish immigration into the British mandate of Palestine after the First World War gained momentum and Alt was evidently impressed by the demographic development in Palestine in his own life-time.[13] Alt was on the other hand also a witness to the Arab

---

13. Whitelam only refers to Alt's seminal article from 1925, 'Die Landnahme der Israeliten in Palästina' (1925), re-published in his *Kleine Schriften zur Geschichte des Volkes Israel* (3 vols.; Munich: Beck, 1953), I, pp. 89-125 but, in its English translation 'The Settlement of the Israelites in Palestine' in the collection *Essays on Old Testament History and Religion* (trans. R.A. Wilson; Oxford: Blackwell's, 1966), pp. 133-70. It is, however, a pity that this English collection does not include Alt's second article on the immigration of the Israelites, 'Erwägungen über die Landnahme der Israeliten' (*Kleine Schriften*, I, pp. 126-75) from 1939, as this article certainly supplements and expands the first article. Sometimes it seems that the English speaking world because of this omission has totally overlooked the second article.

(Palestinian) confusion about how to react to this immigration. He accordingly in his own mind equated the Jews of the twentieth century with the ancient Israelites and the Arabs of the British mandate to the pre-Israelite population, that is, the Canaanites, and he therefore denied the Canaanites, as he did the Palestinians, the ability to form political organizations of more than a very limited extent, such as the city-state.

Among the more sophisticated Old Testament scholars at the time of publication, Alt's model was from the beginning met with an almost universal acceptance, and it was perpetuated and cemented in the works of his student Martin Noth,[14] and yet again in the respected summary of the various immigration theories by Manfred Weippert.[15] Now it has even been adopted by the heirs of Albright. It is, however, a striking fact that this model, although outwardly very different from Albright's conquest model, is ideologically closely related to it, as Albright's model shows the same negative evaluation of the ancient civilizations of Palestine.

We could also say that the attitude to the Palestinians shared by both Alt and Albright is only sharpened in the latter scholar's work, albeit in an incredible—not to say disgusting—fashion. This is illustrated by an extensive quotation from Albright's influential *From the Stone Age to Christianity*[16] where Albright accepts genocide if only the victims belong to an inferior nation, as the ancient Canaanite nation always was to Albright. Although it could with some justice be maintained (although Whitelam does not say this) that Albright did in fact only say what was common in those days, the content of this quotation could be taken—in a different geographical setting and with different actors—as a defence of the ideology behind the Holocaust, in particular because Albright never retracted this utterance.

It is obvious from Albright's writings that he never understood Palestinian culture but always looked upon it from the perspective of

---

14. Especially in his commentary on Joshua, *Das Buch Joshua* (HAT 1.7; Tübingen: Mohr, rev. edn, 1953 [1938]) and *Geschichte Israels* (Göttingen: Vandenhoeck & Ruprecht, 1950; ET; London: Black, 1960).

15. *Die Landnahme der israelitischen Stämme in der neueren wissenschaftlichen Diskussion* (FRLANT, 92; Göttingen: Vandenhoeck & Ruprecht, 1967; *The Settlement of the Israelite Tribes in Palestine* (ET; London: SCM Press, 1971).

16. W.F. Albright, *From the Stone Age to Christianity: Monotheism and the Historical Process* (New York: Doubleday, 2nd edn, 1957), pp. 280-81, cf. Whitelam, pp. 83-84.

the biblical writers. In spite of his very broad orientation in the cultures of the ancient Near East, he never wished to deal with these people, except in their role as primitive forerunners of a lofty and ethical Israel, who were, in Albright's view, the *Übermenschen* of ancient times. Still worse, because of Albright's immense influence and reputation, such views survived to be commonly accepted by his students—such as George Ernest Wright and John Bright—who in the next generation came into possession of some of the most respected academic positions in the United States. In this circle the connection with the ancient Near East was effectively cut off. Only Israel could be understood to be our forefather and provider of the religious and ethical standards of modern man.

This view has been questioned on several occasions by scholars with a different perspective, for example, by Bertil Albrektson and Hans Heinrich Schmid, to mention only a few participants in this discussion,[17] not to speak of several of Mario Liverani's contributions to the study of the religion and ideologies of the ancient Near East.[18] Moreover, it is fatally flawed. At its base stands the conviction that the religious beliefs of the Canaanites were limited to fertility rites, unlike the religion of the Israelites which focused on ethics and morality. It is easy to show that this concept is nonsense, and that also the so-called Israelite religion of the Hebrew Bible contains quite a few elements attributable to fertility worship, whereas religions of the ancient Near East have from their very beginning been preoccupied with questions of an ethical nature.[19]

The conviction that there is no reason to pay any attention to the people of ancient Palestine—that they only got from the superior Israelites what they deserved—continued to rule the scholarly world even after the breakdown of Albright's conquest model. This becomes conspicuous in George Mendenhall's opposition to the idea of an origin of ancient Israel outside of Palestine. To Mendenhall—and after him

17. Cf. B. Albrektson, *History and The Gods: An Essay on the Idea of Historical Events as Divine Manifestations* (Lund: Gleerup, 1967), and H.H. Schmid, *Gerechtigkeit als Weltordnung: Hintergrund und Geschichte des alttestamentlichen Gerechtigkeitsbegriffes* (BHT, 49; Tübingen: Mohr, 1968).

18. To mention here only: 'La concezione dell'universo', in S. Moscati *et al.* (eds.), *L'Alba della* (3 vols.; Torino: UTET, 1976), III, pp. 439-516.

19. I have presented my view on this in my *Die Vorgeschichte Israels*, Part III, 'Elemente des Geisteslebens', pp. 151-207.

to Norman K. Gottwald—the Israelites were mainly of Canaanite origin, and ancient Israel arose in Palestine, not as a special ethnos foreign to Palestine. Although these scholars are without doubt right, they nevertheless contributed to the fallacy of 'biblical' scholarship by attributing the demographical changes of the Late Bronze–Early Iron transition to a religious prime mover, the monotheistic belief in Yahweh, the God of Israel, and to the superiority of this religion's ethical claims to the previous Canaanite religion. There is no need to continue this part of the discussion. Whitelam is obviously right. To students of ancient Palestine it should be obvious that Mendenhall's version is nothing but another paraphrase of Albright's model, which he really never opposed. Instead his principal opponents are—as I have stressed several times—Alt, and after him Gottwald, probably because both scholars were considered to have based their investigations on secular, worldly interpretations of history.[20] It will therefore be difficult for me to disagree with the conclusion to this chapter: there was little love and understanding for the people who inhabited ancient Palestine before and after the so-called Israelite settlement among the scholars who 'created' ancient Israel.

According to Whitelam, the scholars who occasioned the break with the classical tradition also failed at this point, although it could be maintained that he is not totally fair to some among us. It is true that neither Ahlström, Finkelstein nor I realized the ethnical consequences of our own research, but it could also by and large be argued that we paved the way for such an understanding. As such, there is a red thread which runs from my *Early Israel*, from 1985, to Whitelam's *Inventing Ancient Israel* from 1996, which embraces works by Gösta W. Ahlström (1986; 1993), Robert Coote and Keith Whitelam (1987), Israel Finkelstein (1988), Niels Peter Lemche (1991), Philip R. Davies (1992), and Thomas L. Thompson (1992).[21] Ahlström's original question from 1986, 'who were the Israelites?', was only partly answered in the studies which followed, until 1991 when I proposed to see the

---

20. Mendenhall's attack on Gottwald is famous (or infamous): 'Ancient Israel's Hyphenated History', in D.N. Freedman and D.F. Graf (eds.), *Palestine in Transition: The Emergence of Ancient Israel* (SWBA 2; Sheffield, Almond Press, 1983), pp. 95-103.

21. To save space: a fairly comprehensive survey of this development can be found in my 'Early Israel Revisited', *Current Research: Biblical Studies* 4 (1996), pp. 9-34.

adversaries of Israel, the ancient Canaanites, as a construct of the biblical writers, and in 1992, when Philip Davies and Thomas Thompson showed that the ancient Israelites themselves were also fictitious creations of the imagination of the biblical historians. The distance from this position to the one entertained by Whitelam is at one and the same time both short and long. This has not been said in order to diminish Whitelam's accomplishment; it is only mentioned in order to place Whitelam's study in the correct perspective.

5. *The Creation of an Israelite State*

This chapter, in which Whitelam presents his second case study (pp. 122-75), continues the argument from the preceding example and provides the material for his assertion that the idea of ancient Israel is a creation of, on the one hand, European nationalistic thinking, and on the other, Zionist ideologies behind the establishment of the modern state of Israel. Again Whitelam concentrates on the work of Albrecht Alt, this time on his study of the establishment of the Israelite state.[22] Also in this case the same mental matrix seems to be operative according to which the Palestinians are considered to be an inferior race unable to create anything like a nation state. The Philistines (being of European origin—this is not mentioned by Whitelam, but seems to be implied by Alt) had the opportunity but failed by being contaminated by the culture and tradition of the low-ranking Canaanites.

According to this view the Israelites, because of their national unity and in spite of being primitive intruders from the desert, managed to create a comprehensive state—even an empire—where no such thing had previously existed and which was never to reappear (with the implied meaning: not before modern times). Whitelam is here stressing correctly the contradictory nature of the argument which also includes the belief that monarchy was an institution foreign to the mind of this nation called Israel: its God Yahweh was considered to be its only king and ruler.[23] In spite of the fact that the institutions of

22. 'Die Staatenbildung der Israeliten in Palästina' (1930), *Kleine Schriften* II (1953), pp. 1-65 (ET; 'The Formation of the Israelite State in Palestine', in *Essays on Old Testament History and Religion*, pp. 171-237).

23. The *Prüftext* of this was considered to be Judg. 8.22-23, where Gideon refuses to rule the Israelites because in his words nobody can rule Israel except Yahweh.

kingship and a secular state were foreign to the Israelites, they are nevertheless supposed to have grasped the idea to such an extent that they soon became founders of empires and states.

It goes without saying that Alt's original and, for its time, penetrating study has almost universally been accepted since its appearance as providing the best description of the events which led up to the formation of the Davidic state. This is still the case in Old Testament studies although the presentation will undoubtedly be called antiquated among ordinary historians, not least because of its personalized mode of interpreting history as a series of acts done by 'great men'. Alt's approach to history is so far removed from modern historical research that it is in fact ridiculous to find such veneration for his study of the rise of the Israelite state today. Whitelam might have added that it is strange that Alt adopted this mode of interpreting the historical process since he knew very well how to use more advanced historical methodology, as he displayed by his use of *Territorialgeschichte* in his studies on the settlement of the Israelites.

Although all of this is without doubt true, it is nevertheless a fact that to this day all of Alt's basic ideas have survived, among them also the opinion that the Palestinians or Canaanites were no more than a wretched bunch of primitive idol worshippers who were really not worth paying attention to. The argument in this section would probably have been more solid, however, if Whitelam had also referred to the view on the so-called 'syncretism' between Israelite and Canaanite culture which is shared by many Old Testament scholars. According to these scholars, the influence of Canaan distracted the minds of the ancient Israelites and induced them to forsake the Lord and break their oath of allegiance, in consequence of which they lost their ability to defend their empire. Therefore they were soon reduced, after the glorious days of David and Solomon, to becoming citizens of two insignificant states of ancient Palestine, the separate kingdoms of Israel and Judah.[24] In this book Whitelam is not very interested in the evi-

---

24. In a comment in *The Times Higher Education Supplement* from 20 January 1996, I. Finkelstein accused the 'Bible Bashers' (not his expression) of forgetting that there existed in the Iron Age an ancient Israel. Finkelstein, who at the time of his comment (published the day after the appearance of Whitelam's volume) may not yet have read the book, makes the usual mistake of assuming something which we never said. He is simply forgetting that this terminology of 'ancient Israel' is now reserved for the scholarly construction of Israel. We do not deny the historicity of either

dence of the biblical literature, and he accordingly does not include a discussion of ancient Israel's history as it is found in the Old Testament. It is, however, exactly the acknowledgment that the history of Israel in the Old Testament is by all means a religious story which ensures that simple-minded paraphrases of it will, from a historian's point of view, never lead to anything but a false understanding of ancient Palestinian society, including also the two historical states of Israel and Judah.[25]

Instead of this easy and probably more persuasive way of settling with previous scholarship, Whitelam refers to a number of critical issues connected with the biblical picture of the period of David and Solomon. He discusses theories of the origin of states and their application to the history of Palestine, and he shows why this country could never be the home of a great empire, irrespective of whatever claims to the contrary happen to appear in the Old Testament. Most important, Palestine does not possess any resources worth mentioning, and the population is simply too small (in antiquity probably less than half a million) to provide any Palestinian ruler with the manpower needed for creating and maintaining an empire.

Whitelam also refers to previous criticism of the idea of a Davidic empire by, for example, Giovanni Garbini and David Jamieson-Drake,

Mernephtah's Israel (whatever it was) or of the state otherwise known to history as respectively *Bit Humriya* ('the House of Omri') or *Samarina* (Samaria). This in our terminology is historical Israel. For this distinction see P.R. Davies, *In Search of 'Ancient Israel'* (JSOTSup, 148; Sheffield: Sheffield Academic Press, 1992).

25. In his recent article, 'Ideologies, Literary and Critical: Reflections on Recent Writing on the History of Israel', *JBL* 114 (1995), pp. 585-606. Ian W. Provan accuses this writer of playing history off against ideology (p. 585). Nothing can be more wrong as the above remark shows: the ideological framework of the Old Testament historical narrative certainly does not exclude the possibility that historical information is concealed in this narrative. On the other hand, if we do not respect the intentions of the author(s) of the so-called historical literature in the Old Testament (i.e., to compose a narrative of Israel's fate in defence of Yahweh who forsook his country, people and temple) and limit our critical investigations to only a rationalistic paraphrase of this story after having removed selected parts of the narrative (the references to the acts of God), then we have not only destroyed a marvelous narrative, but we have also lost our ability critically to distinguish between history and narrative and thus to reach any historical conclusions worth speaking about. I have so far abstained from a 'dialogue' with the upcoming neo-conservatism of which Provan is an obvious example. I hope to be able to deal with such matters in a comprehensive way in the near future.

without paying too much attention to the obvious problems of either study.[26] It can easily be maintained that Garbini's study is like the curate's egg: good in parts, that is, it is very uneven, some times splendid and ingenious, other times almost ridiculous. Garbini's book was written by an outsider to the field of biblical studies, and he does not always command the specialized tools of the trade. Otherwise, his criticism of the notion of a united Israelite kingdom is precise and cannot easily be dismissed. Jamieson-Drake, on the other hand, bases his criticism of previous scholarship on statistical material drawn from excavations in the territory of ancient Judah in the Iron Age, and he reaches the conclusion that no state existed here before, at the earliest, the first half of the eighth century. If this is true, then there was, of course, no Davidic empire in the tenth century with Jerusalem (in those days an insignificant hamlet, if it existed at all) as its magnificent capital.[27] The problematical character of Jamieson-Drake's statistics, however, has often been aired (orally, as few reviews have so far been published) by professional archaeologists, who argue that the statistical material is limited in extent and hardly allows for a sweeping conclusion like the one proposed by Jamieson-Drake.

At this point we are, indeed, approaching what may today be reckoned the most controversial part of Israel's imagined ancient history. The period of David including the foundation of his great empire has, more than any other part of Israel's ancient history, been decisive for the modern state of Israel's claim to ownership of Palestine. It has, so to speak, provided the historical legitimization of the modern Jewish annexation of this piece of land,[28] and it may therefore be assumed

26. Cf. G. Garbini, 'David's Empire', in his *History and Ideology in Ancient Israel* (London: SCM Press, 1988), pp. 21-32, and D. Jamieson-Drake, *Scribes and Schools in Monarchic Judah: A Socio-Archaeological Approach* (JSOTSup, 109; SWBA, 9; Sheffield: Sheffield Academic Press, 1991). Whitelam, however, ignores H.M. Niemann, *Herrschaft, Königtum und Staat: Skizzen zur soziokulturellen Entwicklung im monarchischen Israel* (Forschungen zum Alten Testament, 6; Tübingen: Mohr, 1993), who reaches results close to Jamieson-Drake's, however based on a study of the Old Testament text.

27. More studies on this period are published in the Proceedings of the Conference on the Formation of the Israelite State held at the German Archaeological Institute in Jerusalem in June 1995: V. Fritz and P.R. Davies (eds.), *The Origins of the Ancient Israelite States* (JSOTSup, 228; Sheffield: Sheffield Academic Press, 1996).

28. Recently epitomized in the celebration of Jerusalem's 3000th anniversary! As if we did not have sources for the existence of this city which are almost a thousand

that in the event the Davidic empire should vanish from the history books, many ordinary people will simply deny Israel the right to its country. The ideology of David as the founder of the Israelite state could in this way turn out to be counterproductive, should this happen. It is also at this point we find the fiercest opposition to the modern so-called 'minimalist' understanding of Israelite history, which is some-times described as the work of dilettantes soon to be forgotten and by no means to be read.[29]

Here we finally arrive at the front-line of the present debate among biblical scholars about the history of Israel; it is probably not a safe place to stay for long. It seems, however, inevitable that the biblical picture of an Israelite empire will not survive for long: indeed, that picture seems beyond salvation, as most historians will soon have to admit. Rhetorical performances do not help, here, only arguments and evidence and so far there is only one source which speaks in favour of the historical David, that is the Old Testament.

The chapter on David and the Israelite state should, however, not be read without criticism, in particular because Whitelam may have missed his target. I am not personally convinced that Whitelam's interpre-tation of the intentions and especially the ideological background of Alt's study of the formation of the Israelite state is correct; and it may only be correct in parts. To me, Alt's reference to the ability of the nomads coming out of the desert to form states and high-ranking societies sounds more like a paraphrase, not of the Old Testament but of Ibn Khaldun's philosophy of the historical development which he

years older (not to speak of archaeological evidence from the MB Period).

29. The malicious attack on P.R. Davies in A.F. Rainey, 'The "House of David" and the House of the Deconstructionists', *BARev* 20 November/December (1994), p. 47, an answer to P.R. Davies, '"House of David" Built on Sand: The Sin of the Biblical Maximizers', *BARev* 20 September/October (1994), pp. 44-54 may serve as a case example. The worth of modern internet communication was proven at the time of publication of this piece as I, in cooperation with my colleague T.L. Thompson, succeeded in publishing an appropriate answer to this infamous attack on the integrity of a leading scholar within less than 48 hours by distributing our opinion of Rainey's attack to a series of electronic networks, including IOUDAIOS and ANE. Over the period lasting from 30 October 1994 to 7 November 1994, more than 200 letters and comments followed, some in favour of Rainey's position, but still more in vehement opposition to his bad manners. The serious discussion among scholars of the so-called Beth-David inscription from Tell Dan is being brought together to be published in book form by F.H. Cryer.

understands to be caused by changing dynasties originating in the desert: when a ruling dynasty is corrupted by the easy life of the settled world it will sooner or later be substituted by another dynasty not yet spoiled by the luxuries of urban life.[30] It is my opinion that Whitelam may himself have created an imagined picture of a rather simple-minded and traditional scholar who has little to do with the Albrecht Alt of history, a leading German scholar of the old school, who undoubtedly commanded classical studies, Islamic history and tradition as well as the study of ancient Near Eastern civilizations.

This is not to say that Alt is not dated and that his programme was not an apologetic and rather conservative and biblicist one, which it indeed was. It is also true that the common ground between Albright and Alt is in many respects far greater than the differences, which all belong within the same generally accepted scholarly interpretation of ancient Israel. My criticism is directed against the way in which Whitelam too easily brushes Alt and his students aside, simply because he does not allow for the complexity of Alt's scholarship.

A related issue which ought to have been part of the discussion concerns the extension of Alt's dependency on previous German scholarship, especially the understanding of the history of Israel in German history books from at least Heinrich Ewald to Rudolf Kittel (who was Alt's teacher). When seen in this light, it becomes obvious that Alt's idea of ancient Israelite state formation was embedded in his own time and tradition and probably not coloured by the events which were to follow. It can only be guessed whether Alt already in 1930 believed in the creation of a future Israeli state in Palestine, thereby denying the Palestinians the right to their own land and history; he would probably himself have maintained that he was certainly not a prophet!

This, however, indicates that if it can be shown that the view on Israelite history and society—'ancient Israel' so to speak—which was formed by Alt and his successors also played a leading part in the imagination of German scholars before Alt, then Alt's understanding

---

30. Cf. his *Muqaddimah*, translated by F. Rosenthal, *The Muqaddimah: An Introduction to History* (3 vols.; London: Routledge & Kegan Paul, 1958). Cf. on Ibn Khaldun's reconstruction of history my *Early Israel: Anthropological and Historical Studies on the Israelite Society Before the Monarchy* (VTSup, 37; Leiden: Brill, 1985), pp. 91-93. The observant reader would probably also recognize the roots of this 'philosophy' in Livy's famous description of the destructive effects of Capua on Hannibal's victorious veterans after Cannae.

of ancient Israel certainly arose as the result of the speculations of previous Christian scholars, and it was not an answer to the expectations about the possible appearance of a future state of Israel to be established on Palestinian soil. Thus I very much doubt whether there can be found traces of Zionist propaganda in Julius Wellhausen's history books,[31] or in the histories of, say Hermann Guthe[32] or Bernhard Stade,[33] to mention only two of Wellhausen's followers.

It is, on the other hand, certain that the ideology of the modern Jewish state was supported by the views prevailing among German scholars above all. Neither should it be forgotten that some of Israel's leading biblical scholars (such as Benjamin Mazar) studied in Germany before the Second World War. It is also certain that a great many German as well as non-German scholars subsequently adopted the ideology of the modern state of Israel and made it into a fixed part of their own picture of 'Ancient Israel'. This is among other examples evident in history books like the one by Siegfried Herrmann.[34] Whitelam's monograph, however, has modern scholarship as its target; he will therefore probably find such a historical digression into the past rather uninteresting. It is, however, possible that he would there have found more persuasive material for his argumentation and, at the same time, made a greater impression on his audience. This is not written in order to diminish the accomplishment of this book, nor to indicate that Whitelam is wrong. The issue is simply that the subject is so controversial that Whitelam's opponents will use whatever mistakes

31. *Prolegomena zur Geschichte Israels* (Berlin: Georg Reimer, 1878), *Israelitische und jüdische Geschichte* (Berlin: de Gruyter, 1958 [9th edn, 1894]). To the contrary, modern Jewish scholars have probably too willingly accused Wellhausen of anti-Semitism, most likely because of his view on the invention of the Torah, as a retrograde religious step. compared to the more original and primitive prophetic religion. Rather than accusing Wellhausen of anti-Semitism, he may be accused of anti-Judaism, since Judaism is seen in contrast to ancient Israel. This part of Wellhausen's thinking goes back to the romantic emphasis on the importance of the primitive compared to the more sophisticated stages in the human evolution. Wellhausen shared this idea of Judaism with an amazing number of other scholars of both the nineteenth and twentieth centuries.

32. *Geschichte des Volkes Israel* (Tübingen: Mohr [Paul Siebeck], 2nd edn, 1904).

33. *Geschichte des Volkes Israel* I-II (Berlin: Baumgärtel,1887–88).

34. *Geschichte Israels in alttestamentlicher Zeit* (Munich: Kaiser, 1973; ET, *A History of Israel in Old Testament Times*, London: SCM Press, 1975).

he makes in order to discredit his project as a whole. It is inevitable that such mistakes will be used to cover up the real achievement of this study, which is the claim that the history of Palestine should be given back to all of its inhabitants and not only to the Jewish part.

6. *The Continuing Search*

The logical continuation of the two examples from the imagined history of ancient Israel already reviewed would be to survey recent trends in historical studies, and although the redundancy is markedly felt in this chapter (pp. 176-222), it presents an intriguing picture of a scholarly enterprise which from the onset did not quite understand what it was aiming at. Two main topics are reviewed in this chapter. First we should mention the development in archaeology marked by the introduction of a number of principles borrowed from the 'New Archaeology' which are linked to a new understanding of historical research as not so much interested in a sequence of isolated events as in understanding societal processes and the factors lying behind these. I have already referred to the school of *les annales*.

Here Whitelam draws heavily on the results and methodologies of this school, as does also the main target of his archaeological section, the Israeli archaeologist Israel Finkelstein,[35] whose publication and interpretation of the archaeological surveys from the so-called West Bank marked a revolution in *biblical* archaeology, and it should—in spite of Finkelstein's intentions—still be called biblical, or this seems at least to be what Whitelam intends to say. It is evident that Finkelstein is showing the way for a more adequate use of archaeology, although he is, as it seems, still part of the biblical discourse. This has been a central point in the criticism of Finkelstein since the publication of his study because it binds him to conclusions about ethnicity which are really no longer part of his archaeological discourse.[36] The development in the Central Highlands of Palestine at the end of the second millennium BCE which are described in detail in Finkelstein's book

---

35. Who is certainly not the only one mentioned. As well as other names referred to by Whitelam may be mentioned A. Mazar and Z. Gal. Finkelstein is, however, obviously the most important figure in this connection.

36. For a more detailed critique of Finkelstein's concept of ethnicity cf. M. Skjeggestad, 'Ethnic Groups in Early Iron Age Palestine', *SJOT* 6 (1992), pp. 159-86.

does not give any indications about the ethnic composition of the people who were the settlers in the new villages of the Late Bronze– Early Iron Age transition. Finkelstein, as well as his more traditionally minded colleagues have, however, not managed to rid themselves of the controlling factor which the Old Testament narrative about the settlement and identity of early Israel constitutes.

There can be no doubt that so far very little has appeared from the so-called 'new archaeologists' which really liberates them from entanglement in the biblical discourse. Finkelstein himself has, on other occasions, tried to adjust his ethnical interpretation to the realities of his archaeological findings but so far not yet succeeded in this venture.[37] It is, however, interesting that in a recent publication from Tel Aviv University which presents a summary and interpretation of the various regional surveys, at least one Israeli scholar, Shlomo Bunimovitz, has managed to write a fine piece of work about socio-demographical developments in the highlands of Palestine without mentioning the Israelite settlement more than once, and then only in quotation marks.[38] Maybe there is hope also in Israel for an independent, that is, non-biblical, study of the history of Palestine.

The second issue discussed in this chapter concerns the development in biblical studies which was probably inaugurated (at least according to Whitelam's chronology) by the appearance of my *Early Israel* in 1985 and G.W. Ahlström's *Who Were the Israelites* in 1986, and which reached its provisional conclusion in Thomas L. Thompson's *Early*

---

37. Cf. Finkelstein's 'New Orleans (not Chicago!, cf. Whitelam p. 259 n. 19) statements', where he advocates a much more cautious approach to the question of the identity of the settlers, Cf. I. Finkelstein, 'The Emergence of Israel in Canaan: Concensus, Mainstream and Dispute', *SJOT* 5/2 (1991), pp. 47-59. However, also in publications following this date, the ethnic label appears in Finkelstein's writing, so in his 'The Emergence of Israel: A Phase in the Cyclic History of Canaan in the Third and Second Millennia BCE', in I. Finkelstein and N. Na'aman (eds.), *From Nomadism to Monarchy: Archaeological and Historical Aspects of Early Israel* (Jerusalem/Washington: Israel Exploration Society/Biblical Archaeology Society, 1994), pp. 150-78. Also here, the Davidic state stands as the ultimate result of the societal developments.

38. S. Bunimovitz, 'Socio-Political Transformations in the Central Hill Country in the Late Bronze-Iron I Transition', in Finkelstein and Na'aman (eds.), *From Nomadism to Monarchy*, pp. 179-202. This volume, as the title indicates, is otherwise almost totally confined to the biblical discourse of ancient Israelite history.

History of the Israelite People, which was published in 1992.[39] Common to these scholars, and including also Whitelam himself and Robert Coote as well as Israel Finkelstein, was an outspoken awareness of the impossibility of maintaining the biblical narrative as a primary historical source. Increasingly, these scholars and their colleagues have been forced to lower the time of composition of the biblical narrative successively to the late monarchic period (thus Finkelstein[40]), the Period of the Exile (thus John Van Seters[41]) and especially the Persian (so Philip. R. Davies and Thomas L. Thompson[42]) and Hellenistic periods (so Lemche[43]).

None of them, however, drew the obvious conclusion of their interpretation of the biblical material, or so Whitelam maintains. He is partly correct, although it must also be said that if we were to apply the principles of *la longue durée* also to the study of early Israel, it was in any case only a matter of time before we had arrived at the same point as Whitelam. When I and my colleagues published our respective studies on the Late Bronze–Early Iron Age transition in Palestine, none of us were prepared for what was to come. This was inevitable, as none of us intended to 'deconstruct, not to say 'destroy', the early history of early Israel. On the contrary, we were looking for traces of this very Israel, but—as it turned out—in vain. There is nothing wrong about this when seen in the perspective of *la longue*

39. Lemche, *Early Israel*, cf. n. 30 above; G.W. Ahlström, *Who Were the Israelites* (Winona Lake: Eisenbrauns, 1986); T.L. Thompson, *Early History of the Israelite People*.

40. For example in his *Settlement*, p. 22.

41. *Abraham in History and Tradition* (New Haven: Yale University Press, 1975); repeated in *In Search of History: Historiography in the Ancient World and the Origins of Biblical History* (New Haven: Yale University Press, 1983); *Prologue to History: The Yahwist as Historian in Genesis* (Louisville: Westminster, 1992), and *The Life of Moses: The Yahwist as Historian in Exodus-Numbers* (Kampen: Kock Pharos, 1994).

42. Davies, *In Search of 'Ancient Israel'*; Thompson, *Early History*. It will only be fair to say that Thompson since 1992 has moved not only in the same direction as me (cf. the following note) but even bypassed his Hellenistic dating.

43. Cf. N.P. Lemche, 'The Old Testament-A Hellenistic Book?' *SJOT* 7 (1993), pp. 163-93. R. Coote, however, proves to be an exception to this view since he favours a very early date of the history writing in the Old Testament, in fact the time of the united monarchy; cf. R. Coote and D.R. Ord, *The Bible's First History* (Philadelphia: Fortress Press, 1989).

durée. Rather, it should serve as a warning to the scholars who try to defame the contributions of the so-called 'minimalists' (considering themselves to be 'maximalists') as the result of an entirely negative attitude to the Hebrew text of the Old Testament. This was never the case—on the contrary, fifteen years ago all of us believed that we could use the biblical narrative for historical purposes—but since we like Per Gynt with his onion carried on with our rather traditional historical-critical investigations, we ended up in a situation where not a single bit of our subject, that is, the biblical version of Israel's early history, remained intact.

Whitelam will probably not object to any part of this description of recent research which also includes his own pioneering work. It was probably the only possible way to go. Already in the 1960s and 1970s some scholars presented syntheses which were at least approaching what was to become mainstream among critical students of the Hebrew Bible of the 1980s and 1990s. Among these we may count Heike Friis of Copenhagen and Bernd Jörg Diebner of Heidelberg.[44] The fate of both scholars, including their marginalization (in the case of Diebner probably self-inflicted), tells us what may happen to scholars who are not on-line, who stand up like prophets at the wrong moment and in the wrong manner.[45] It is of course preposterous that Anson Rainey,

44. Cf. H. Friis, *Die Bedingungen für die Errichtung des Davidischen Reichs in Israel und seiner Umwelt* (Dielheimer Blätter zum Alten Testament, 6; Heidelberg, 1986), originally written in Danish in 1968, but never published. As far as B.J. Diebner is concerned, since the mid-1970s he has published his ideas almost exclusively in his own journal, *Dielheimer Blätter zum Alten Testament*, thereby effectively preventing them from being known to the English speaking world.

45. In this light probably Diebner's repeated attacks on N.P. Lemche, in *DBAT* 28 (1994, publ. 1995), should be understood as a cry of despair from a scholar who was left on the side-line as the scholarly world moved on, although he has certainly earned the right to be called one of the pioneers of the changes which have wrought havoc upon the scholarly consensus about the Old Testament as a history book. Cf. also T.L. Thompson, 'Offing the Establishment: DBAT 38 and the Politics of Radicalism', *Biblische Notizen* 79 (1995), pp. 71-87. I see no reason to comment further on this. My version of the history of recent research was published in 1994 in N.P. Lemche, 'Hvad er det vi har lavet, og hvor går vi hen?' ('What Have We Done and Where Are We Going?'), in N.P. Lemche and M. Müller (eds.), *Fra Dybet (Studies in Honour of John Strange) (Forum for Bibelsk Eksegese* 5; Copenhagen: Museum Tusculanum, 1994), pp. 130-43 (English translation to appear in T.L. Thompson and N.P. Lemche (eds.), *Changing Perspectives* (Copenhagen International Seminar; Sheffield: Sheffield Academic Press, forthcoming).

in his already-mentioned attack on Philip Davies, asked his audience to ignore his opponents and to put aside the production of the 'minimalists', although this may be seen as an implicit warning to the readership of the *Biblical Archaeology Review* of the *rabies theologiae* which Melanchton referred to hundreds of years ago.

7. *Conclusion*

After having worked our way through this highly interesting mono-graph, we cannot escape being a bit disappointed when approaching the conclusions to the book. Hardly anything new is said in this sec-tion; only a repetition of the main arguments of the book—originally presented in the introduction, that is, Israel's history is an imagined history, and in recent times the interest in this putative history has effectively blocked the way to any interest in the Western world in the history of the Palestinians, objectively the inhabitants of the landscape called Palestine.

I now come to the conclusion to this review which has generally been critical but positive. It had to be done! No doubt about it. Whitelam has written a very brave—but also a very politically correct—book, timely according with the establishment in Palestine of the first institu-tions of a Palestinian state. We are therefore entitled to ask Whitelam if he thinks that his book could have been written without the recent political changes in Israel/Palestine. I suppose that he will be the first to admit that he may have created a picture of, for example, Albrecht Alt in his own image. Alt was not able to foresee the establishment of an Arab Palestinian state because of the political developments in his own time. However, how different is this from a Keith Whitelam who is able to present a programme for the study of Palestinian history while at the same time being a witness to different political developments in Palestine?

The lasting value of this book is that it should open the eyes of the historians in order to make them see the past not only as interpreted by biblical writers but as modern historians using the crafts available to historical research. In this world of biblically-oriented scholarship, it is, however, also predictable that Whitelam will soon join Isaiah who was to preach to the Israelites 'so that they may not see with their eyes, nor listen with their ears, nor understand with their wits' (REB).

APPENDIX

History of Palestine or History of Syria

The following appendix is based on my lecture at the SBL International Meeting in Dublin. It contains some corrections and revisions in comparison with the published extended review of Keith W. Whitelam, *Inventing Ancient Israel*.[46]

Some people are not too clever. Most of the people taking part in this discussion today would have had a much easier career and far fewer problems if they had just decided to stay in the middle of the road instead of constantly looking for the extremes. Much of this is to be attributed to the aversive effects of the *'Doktorvater'*-institution, sometimes more directed towards the creation of clones of the *'Vater'* than of independent and critical minds. Few scholars have had the extraordinary luxury of a mentor who was in total disagreement with his or her own ideas although steadily loyal to the newcomer to the field. I belong among the lucky few, as my mentor always supported my doings. So if these notes should be dedicated to anybody, it is to my old teacher, Eduard Nielsen, who always taught me to be 100 per cent critical although he had at the time no idea of where this criticism would lead.

That was to be my good fortune. Other members of the panel have been less fortunate, although it seems an established fact that almost all members of the seminar have finally achieved tenured positions of the first rank. So maybe after all we did not get it all that wrong.

This being said, it is perhaps also typical of our group that we have never stopped being provocative, and deliberately so. Most, if not all, of us are constantly producing works which are considered to be on the edge of that kind of scholarship which is at the moment followed by the majority of scholars—some of it is even considered so dangerous that it cannot be included even in research libraries. I was thus informed only a couple of weeks ago in Jerusalem that my own books are not to be found in the library of the Albright Institute, as they are considered dangerous—I should very much like to know to whom?

On the contrary, most of what we have been writing should be considered rather conservative examples of an almost senseless continuation of an old paradigm which should be forgotten as soon as possible. To be more serious, Keith Whitelam has this year produced a handsome volume which will certainly be excluded from a number of libraries all over the world as being dangerous if not to ordinary readers then at least to the mental health of quite a number of scholars engaged in the study of ancient Israel—to use this tiresome and conventional term.

I therefore sincerely doubt that Keith Whitelam's new book, *Inventing Ancient Israel: The Silencing of Palestinian History*, will in the future find a home on the shelves of, for example, the Albright Institute—especially because of the way Keith

---

46. Whitelam, *Inventing Ancient Israel: The Silencing of Palestinian History* (London: Routledge, 1996).

Whitelam has handled Albright's literary heritage: in a most severe but probably not improper way.[47]

It can also safely be assumed that Whitelam's book will belong among those that everybody talks about but nobody (dares to) read. It will without doubt be ostracized as anti-Semitic, especially by people who have only seen popular reviews or have been told by other persons (who may never themselves have read it) that it is a piece of anti-Jewish propaganda.

But in answering such people the best way of countering their attacks would probably be to ask them first to read the book, as it is—though provocative—also a very correct book—perhaps even, as maintained by a student of mine, Tilde Binger, a bit tame.[48]

The subject of Whitelam's book , as probably well-known, is that the history of the ancient peoples of Palestine has been silenced in favour of an exclusive interest in one of Palestine's minor historical incidents: the incident of historical Israel, a comparatively short-lived political construction in central and northern Palestine in the ninth and eighth centuries. Scholars as well as laymen have over the last few generations steadily been paraphrasing the Old Testament's narrative about biblical Israel and have converted the story about this Israel into the history of Palestine in the so-called biblical times, whatever these were. In this way it has simply been overlooked that Israel was not the only historical state in existence in Palestine in the Iron Age, but we should also include the Philistine states in the south-western part of the country—states about whose existence we have just been reminded by the discovery a few weeks ago of a fragment of a monumental inscription from Ekron (Tel Miqne) containing the names of two kings of Ekron, Achish and Padi, formally only known from Assyrian inscriptions.[49]

Whitelam is not very specific as to the identity of his ancient Palestinians—he prefers to speak about the silencing of their history as such—the reason probably being that he has introduced a new entity to the historical scene, the ancient Palestinians, thus probably having invented a new people which may in fact never themselves have existed or recognized themselves to be Palestinians: the inhabitants of the strip of land otherwise in our tradition known as Canaan, the land of Israel, Palestine or the Holy Land, an entity which would certainly also have included the historical Israelites and Judaeans, alias the inhabitants of the two states of Israel and Judah.

Whitelam's enterprise is a very respectful one: to give back their history to the inhabitants of a certain country. I have few problems in lending my support to his project. What worries me, however, is the way it is done. It can easily be that political circumstances with a background in present political developments in Palestine/ Israel will only result in a repetition of the mistakes of past historical investigations,

47. Whitelam, *Inventing Ancient Israel*, pp. 79-90.

48. A review by T. Binger of Whitelam, *Inventing Ancient Israel*, will appear shortly in *Dansk Teologisk Tidsskrift*.

49. So far only announced in newspapers, as in the *Jerusalem Post*, in the summer of 1996. Padi and Achish (Ikausu) was formerly known from the annals of Sennacherib and Esarhaddon (*ANET*, pp. 287-88, 291).

that is, that scholars will in the future concentrate on a history of the Palestinian nation to such a degree and in such a way that it is at the same time forgotten that there never was a Palestinian nation, or rather that the Palestinian nation is the fruit in modern times of colonialism (including Zionism).

In my extended review of Whitelam's book I have included a short paragraph on ancient nomenclature. Israeli scholars especially have sometimes maintained that Palestine was not an ancient name of the land of Israel, whereas other scholars have been of the conviction that this is probably false, as the Assyrians named the area of the modern state of Israel including the occupied territories Palestine, and here they were later followed by Greek and Roman authors.

Strange as it sounds there may be no satisfying analysis available of the ancient names of this tiny piece of land. Was it in fact really called 'Palestine' in antiquity, for example, by its own inhabitants? I very much doubt it. In my book about the Canaanites[50] I made use of the emic/etic distinction as it has been applied by students of the concept of ethnicity between how people see themselves and how they are described by foreigners. In that volume the emic/etic distinction was used to explain the fact that there are no recordings from ancient times that the ancient Canaanites ever understood themselves to be Canaanites. Rather this was always a name which popped up when somebody in a more or less casual manner referred to the inhabitants of the south-western part of the Levant.[51]

If we, however, apply the same methodology to the use of the name of Palestine in ancient sources, we may very well end up with a similar situation, that it was only foreigners who named this territory Palestine, a habit perpetuated by the Christian tradition according to which the name of the country *is* Palestine, whereas only a fraction of the local inhabitants would have understood themselves to be Palestinians, that is the inhabitants of the coastal plain where the tradition of the ancient *Peleśet* may still have been around. Since the Assyrian line of attack normally went via the plains of Galilee over the pass at Megiddo and down into the coastal plain before they turned to the east and moved into the central hills, they would probably have cared very little about local political names and have used the term Palestine in a broader sense than the one current among the local inhabitants. Or to be accurate, they may have used the term in exactly the same sense as later Roman and Christian authors.

It could very well be the case that there never was one universally acknowledged name of the country which was accepted by all its inhabitants. I think that we can find evidence for this in the lack of any definite terminology which concerns the population of Palestine/Israel, and here Herodotus may provide us with a first-class piece of evidence. In his *History* Herodotus in fact mentions Palestine several times. I have listed them in my aforementioned review of Whitelam's book and shall not repeat

50. *The Canaanites and Their Land: The Tradition of the Canaanites* (JSOTSup, 110; Sheffield: Sheffield Academic Press, 1991), cf. esp. p. 51 n. 99.

51. In spite of N. Na'aman's seemingly devastating criticism of that book of mine (N. Na'aman, 'The Canaanites and their Land: A Rejoinder', *UF* 26 [1994, app. 1995], pp. 397-418), I will remain loyal to my ideas of ancient Canaan; see also my answer, 'Where Should we Look for Canaan? A Reply to Nadav Na'aman', *UF* 28 (forthcoming).

them here, but it is typical that Herodotus never talks about Palestine plainly. His Palestine is always considered to be a part of Syria; when he is more precise, for example, he speaks about Palestine as the name of the part of Syria which lies between the Phoenician cities and Egypt. In exactly the same manner he never speaks about Palestinians, but his Palestinians are Syrians living in the part of Syria called Palestine.

Although Herodotus may not be the best of all witnesses—it is unlikely that he ever visited the country—his idea of Palestine is, however, important as he may be reflecting the opinion of informed persons in Egypt (or in Mesopotamia if he ever visited that place) showing no idea about a 'nation' called Palestine or a national group of persons to be dubbed Palestinians. To this early classical author Palestine was simply a Syrian region, and it may be that he was in fact absolutely correct in maintaining this.

I cannot present anything here which resembles a definite answer to these questions. It would, however, be a nice topic for a PhD student to analyse the different ways of naming this territory and its inhabitants, not only in the Iron Age and in the Persian period, but in fact from the first references available in Near Eastern sources from ancient times. In this light scholars should not abstain from using the term 'Israel' when speaking about historical Israel, whatever it was—as in the inscriptions of Merneptah and of Mesha (leaving out at the moment the still unsettled problem about the genuineness of the Tel Dan inscription)[52] although it should at the same time be taken into consideration that the Assyrians almost entirely abstained from using the name of Israel. Without claiming completeness, a short review of the Assyrian references to Israel will show only a single reference to Ahab's Kingdom as *Sirlaa*, that is probably Israel.[53] Otherwise they consistently called the state of the kings of 'Israel' dating from Jehu and right down to the fall of Samaria either *Bit Ḥumriya* or *Samarina*, that is, Samaria. This should be compared to the places where they refer to the kingdom which had, as its capital, Jerusalem, as the Assyrians knew very well that the name of this state was *Jauda* or Judah,[54] not Jerusalem (by the neo-Babylonian chronicle called the city of Judah[55]). However, the historicity of the kingdom or state of Israel/*Bit Ḥumriya*/*Samaria* cannot be questioned, but it was certainly only one among the small states of the territory which in our tradition is called Palestine, and it is especially difficult to see from the Assyrian sources that this state should be considerably different from, say, Ashdod, Ashkelon or Gaza, all states mentioned by name in the annals of the Assyrian kings.

When we move back in time, the situation is not essentially different, although no reference is of course found to Israel's predating Mernephtah's inscription. In spite

52. Critical positions as to the genuineness of this inscription (by F.H. Cryer and G. Garbini) will be included in the volume on the Tel Dan Inscription, edited by F.H. Cryer (JSOTSup; Sheffield: Sheffield Academic Press, forthcoming).

53. In Shalmanesar III's famous monolith inscription (*ANET* 279-80).

54. In inscriptions from Tiglath-Pileser III down to Ashurbanipal. The habit was continued by the neo-Babylonians.

55. Cf. The Neo-Babylonian Chronicle B.M. 21946, rev. 12 in D.J. Wiseman (ed.), *Chronicles of Chaldean Kings (625–556 BC) in the British Museum* (London: The Trustees of the British Museum, 1956).

of Nadav Na'aman,[56] I have to say that there was no single name of the territory of Palestine/Israel in the Bronze Age which was in general and well-defined use. It is almost certain that the Canaanites did not know themselves to be Canaanites, and the name of Canaan was in this period used in a number of never well-defined meanings, thus sometimes embracing a landscape far bigger than anything attributed to it in the Old Testament. The Egyptians—the masters of this territory—in the Late Bronze period thus applied several names like *Canaan*, *Haru*, or *Djahi*—in the Middle Bronze period also *Retenu* and even more names. But nowhere is there an indication of a single name understood by the inhabitants of Palestine/Israel to be the name of their own country, not to mention a name which they saw as their own.

This is one part of the problem why a history of Israel taken in isolation is nonsense. Not because Whitelam is correct in maintaining that this history should be substituted by another history, the history of the Palestinians. It is not the history of the Palestinians which needs to be written but the history of all of the small sections of the country where no single section (such as 'Israel') is allowed to dominate the rest. The biblical evidence should be kept apart as this is not a direct testimony to the history of this territory in the Iron Age; it is rather a late reflection of the history of the territory which has transformed one component—Israel, in combination with Judah—into the single most important part of the country, although this was never the case except from, and only during, the incidence of the Omride dynasty in the mid ninth century BCE.

The second part of the problem is to see whether a history of this area seen as a whole should be isolated from its greater environment, that is, ancient Syria. As is well known, for example from the arrangements of the Persian provinces, the territory of Palestine/Israel was never an independent part. Although local governors are known, some of them even by name, they were not independent or even important civil servants of the Persian king like the satraps, and it is probably not without reason that Palestine was in general a part of the territory administered by the satrap of Syria. The Persians hardly saw Palestine as very different from Syria and certainly not as important enough to warrant an individual treatment. Rather it should be assumed that Palestine was a part of Syria—in fact one of Syria's minor regions, like Phoenicia to the north, or Damascus in the southern part of present day Syria—or even better: Syria can and should be divided into a number of subsections, following its natural geographical differences: the coast in the north including the territory of Late Bronze states like Ugarit, to the west of the *Gebel Ansariye*, next to it by the inner plain of Aleppo reaching down to and probably beyond Hamath, followed in the south by firstly the oasis of Damascus, and Transjordan, itself split into a number of subsections like the present *Aǧlun*, the territory around Amman, and the Plains of Moab. In the inner desert, Palmyre had its own history, and in the far east, Syria was bordering on Mesopotamian civilization as seen from the archives of the ancient cities of Mari and Emar. At the far western end, the territory of the present Palestine/Israel should at least be subdivided into three regions: Galilee, the Coastal Plain, and the Central Highland.

56.   Cf. n. 51 above.

Instead of considering such a regional history a reductionalist one, I would like to emphasize that it is in fact the only positive way to write a proper history of Israel— as finally seen in the right perspective. And the right perspective is all we should ask for.

SOME ASPECTS OF WORKING WITH THE TEXTUAL SOURCES[*]

Herbert Niehr

1. *Introduction*

The intention of this paper is to position the evaluation of textual sources within a greater and more comprehensive set of approaches necessary for reconstructing the history of Israel.

In writing a history of Israel different levels of approach have to be distinguished. The basic level can be termed *historical anthropology*. On this level we work without written evidence. The second level is made up by evaluating written *primary sources* from outside and inside Palestine. Archaeological evidence is also a *primary source*. The third level is given by the evaluation of biblical sources which have to be judged as *secondary* or even *tertiary sources*. The gap between these sources has to be taken seriously. Only then can attempts to bridge this gap be cautiously made. This work with the sources has to be followed by a trial to integrate the results into hypotheses.

2. *The Levels of Approach*

a. *Historical Anthropology*

By the term *historical anthropology* is meant all data delivered by climatology, geography, landscape formation, settlement archaeology, agriculture, sociology and economy. These data can be separately assembled for the central hills of Ephraim and Manasseh and for Judah.[1] Working within this level we get a picture of the *longue duree*

*   I am indebted to Lester Grabbe for improving my English style.
1.   R.B. Coote and K.W. Whitelam, 'The Emergence of Early Israel' (SWBA, 5; Sheffield: Almond Press, 1987), pp. 27-116; T. Thompson, *Early History of the Israelite People* (SHANE, 4; Leiden: Brill, 1992), pp. 215-412.

(Braudel), or in other words, we obtain a general frame which in the subsequent stages has to be filled with the events which have taken place within this frame.

b. *Primary Sources*

Generally a primary source can be defined as 'written at a time close to the event. It can be a report, a royal annal, a letter or an original story.'[2] Or to put it differently: primary sources are more or less contemporary or close to the events they narrate or testify.[3] It is useful to distinguish several classes of primary sources.

As regards the aim of writing a history of Israel it is important to see that primary sources are independent of the Old Testament. They did not undergo the censorship exercised by, for example, the Deuteronomistic theologians nor were they submitted to the process of canonization. That is why the clear distinction between primary and secondary sources has to be upheld.[4]

Written sources from outside Palestine. Data for constituting a history of Israel begin with the appearance of a Palestinian kingdom *bit ḥumri* in Assyrian inscriptions of the ninth century BCE and the mention of the Omrides and their kingdom in a Moabite source (about 850 BCE). The data given in these inscriptions are followed by the mention of Israelite and Judaean kings in Assyrian, Babylonian and Aramaic inscriptions. Not only kings but also events (battles, conquests, coalitions, tributes) are listed in these sources. There are even things reported in the sources which are not mentioned in the Old Testament, for example the battle of Qarqar and Ahab's participation in it (853

---

2.   G.W. Ahlström, 'The History of Ancient Palestine from the Palaeolithic Period to Alexander's Conquest' (JSOTSup, 146; Sheffield: Sheffield Academic Press, 1993), p. 21; cf. also *idem*, 'The Role of Archaeological and Literary Remains in Reconstructing Israel's History', in D.V. Edelman (ed.), *The Fabric of History* (JSOTSup, 127; Sheffield: Sheffield Academic Press, 1991), p. 117; J.M. Miller, 'Is it Possible to Write a History of Israel without Relying on the Hebrew Bible?', in Edelman (ed.), *The Fabric of History*, p. 94; E.A. Knauf, 'From History to Interpretation', in Edelman (ed.), *The Fabric of History*, p. 46.

3.   N.P. Lemche, 'On the Problems of Studying Israelite History', *Biblische Notizen* 23 (1984), p. 115.

4.   Contra I.W. Provan, 'Ideologies, Literary and Critical: Reflections on Recent Writing on the History of Israel', *JBL* 114 (1995), p. 598 with n. 61.

BCE) or the siege and conquest of Lachish (701 BCE). By reading these sources we get a very rough outline of Israel's and Judah's past.

There has been some discussion about the historical reliability of the Assyrian annals. Their reliability had been put into question because of the topoi, exaggerations, ideologies and propaganda contained in them. Nevertheless, the historical reliability of these sources has recently shown to be very high.[5] Further topics with special relevance for the histories of Israel and Judah which have also been investigated thoroughly are the western expansion of the neo-Assyrian Empire[6] and the tributes imposed.[7]

Written sources from inside Palestine. Further primary texts come from Israel and Judah themselves. This is the place for the evaluation of all kinds of epigraphical texts within the frame of historical dates obtained on the base of written sources from outside Palestine. In the case of epigraphical texts we are dealing with inscriptions on stone, metal, wood, leather and other materials and ostraca, seals and papyri.[8]

So far we have very careful analyses of writing techniques[9] and palaeographical development[10] of the Northwest Semitic scripts which are important for dating the primary written sources.

In this context the question of writing, scribes and scribal schools in Palestine deserves a special interest because the primary sources can be dated on palaeographic and archaeological evidence. The insights gained in this field are also influential for the political history of Judah

5.   Cf. W. Mayer, *Politik und Kriegskunst der Assyrer* (Abhandlungen zur Literatur Alt-Syrien-Palästinas und Mesopotamians, 9; Münster: Ugarit-Verlag, 1995), pp. 21-60.

6.   Cf. R. Lamprichs, *Die Westexpansion des neuassyrischen Reiches* (AOAT, 239; Neukirchen–Vluyn: Neukirchener Verlag, 1995).

7.   Cf. J. Bär, *Der assyrische Tribut und seine Darstellung* (AOAT, 243; Neukirchen–Vluyn: Neukirchener Verlag, 1996).

8.   Cf. the enumeration of the material in H. Weippert, *Palästina in vorhellensitischer Zeit* (Handbuch der Archäologie, II.1; Munich: C.H. Beck, 1988), pp. 578-87 and the edition of all epigraphical texts from the royal periods in Israel and Judah by J. Renz and W. Röllig, *Handbuch der althebräischen Epigraphik* (3 vols.; Darmstadt: Wissenschaftliche Buchgesellschaft, 1995–96).

9.   Cf. G. van der Kooij, *Early North-West Semitic Script Traditions* (Leiden: Brill, 1986).

10.   Cf. Renz and Röllig, *Handbuch der althebräischen Epigraphik*, II.1, pp. 95-208.

and Israel, including administrative considerations and also the dating of Old Testament texts.[11]

Archaeological evidence from Palestine. Archaeological evidence (e.g. buildings, artefacts) is also to be judged as a primary source, but compared to the written primary sources this evidence is a mute one so that deciphering these sources is still more open to misunderstanding than is the case with written sources.[12] But the deciphering and reading of archaeological sources can be learned[13] and important results have been achieved for the history of Israel and Judah,[14] especially for Jerusalem.[15] The special meaning of archaeology is that it shows us the everyday life of ancient people.[16]

This is also valid for the realm of iconography which in Palestine is mainly represented by seals. Their codes of understanding can be solved and thus much for the cultural and religious history can be learned from this kind of miniature art.[17]

c. *Secondary and Tertiary Sources*
A secondary source 'may be a copy of an original, an interpretive text, a rewriting, re-editing, distortion, falsification or the like.'[18] Because of its dating the Old Testament text falls into this category of secondary sources at least for the time of the kingdoms of Israel and Judah.

As concerns the Old Testament sources it has already been seen cor-

---

11. Cf. D.W. Jamieson-Drake, *Scribes and Schools in Monarchic Judah* (JSOTSup, 109; Sheffield: Sheffield Academic Press, 1991).

12. Ahlström, 'The Role of Archaeological and Literary Remains', p. 117.

13. Cf. Knauf, 'From History to Interpretation', pp. 28-41.

14. Cf. e.g. Weippert, *Palästina in vorhellensitischer Zeit*; H.-P. Kuhnen *Palästina in griechisch-römischer Zeit* (Handbuch der Archäologie, II.2; Munich: C.H. Beck, 1990).

15. Cf. K. Bieberstein and H. Bloedhorn, *Jerusalem. Grundzüge der Bauge-schichte vom Chalkolithikum bis zur Frühzeit der osmanischen Herrschaft I–III* (Beihefte zum Tübingen Atlas des Vorderen Orients, 100.1-3; Wiesbaden: L. Reichert, 1994).

16. Cf. M. Weippert, 'Geschichte Israels am Scheideweg', *TRu* 58 (1993), p. 84-85.

17. Cf. especially O. Keel, *Studien zu den Stempelsiegeln aus Palästina/Israel* (4 vols.; OBO 67, 88, 100, 135; Freiburg: Universitätsverlag; Göttingen: Vandenhoeck & Ruprecht, 1985–94).

18. Ahlström, 'The History of Ancient Palestine', p. 21; cf. also Knauf, 'From History to Interpretation', p. 46.

rectly that 'the Bible is presented from a Judahistic, Jerusalemite point of view. The historiography reflects the ideology of a certain group in Judah who believed that the kingdom of Israel should never have existed as a separate kingdom, because it was "sinful". Its cardinal sin was to have split the United Monarchy. At the same time this polemical attitude defends the political supremacy of the kingdom of Judah'.[19] This leads to the fact that our knowledge of the kingdom of Israel is even less than our knowledge of Judah. With respect to the history and the religion of Israel we have to reckon with an influential *damnatio memoriae*. This remark is valid, for example, for the existence of a Yahweh-temple in Samaria and for the historical roles of Omri and Ahab which cannot be fully recognized from the Old Testament alone because the roles of both of them are seriously minimized and thus distorted in the secondary sources.[20]

This does not exclude the possibility that Old Testament texts contain older materials, for example, from royal annals. But the existence of such older material in younger texts can only be reconstructed hypothetically. These hypotheses are open to debate as is shown by the example of the temple consecration prayer (1 Kgs 8.12-13) or the Cyrus edict (Ezra 1.2-4; 6.2-5). In both cases the historicity of the documents is highly debated and nowadays judged as unlikely. Even in those cases we judge more probable we have to admit that we 'simply do not have the documents; all we can do is in some cases reasonably assume that we may have copies of copies.'[21]

On the other hand the basic reliability of the royal successions and datings from Jeroboam to Hosea in Israel and from Azariah/Uzziah to Zedekiah in Judah, as verified by Assyrian and Babylonian primary sources, points to the existence of royal annals at the courts of Samaria and Jerusalem and their use by the Deuteronomistic Historian.[22]

An example of a tertiary source is that of the books of Chronicles which rework the Torah and the Deuteronomistic History during the second century BCE. It is not to be overlooked that the Old Testament

---

19. Ahlström, 'The Role of Archaeological and Literary Remains', pp. 129-30.

20. Cf. G.W. Ahlström, *Royal Administration and National Religion in Ancient Palestine* (SHANE, 1; Leiden: Brill, 1982), pp. 60-63; *idem*, 'The Role of Archaeological and Literary Remains', p. 131.

21. E.A. Knauf, 'King Solomon's Copper Supply', in E. Lipinski (ed.), *Phoenicia and the Bible* (Studia Phoenicia, 11; Leuven: Peeters Press, 1991), p. 47 n. 1.

22. Knauf, 'King Solomon's Copper Supply', p. 173.

can also serve as a primary source for the *histoire de la mentalité* of the time when it was written. This was already recognized by J. Wellhausen who wrote about the patriarchal narratives: 'Freilich über die Patriarchen ist hier kein historisches Wissen zu gewinnen, sondern nur über die Zeit, in welcher die Erzählungen über sie im israelitischen Volke entstanden'.[23]

As in the realm of epigraphic texts we have also to ask about the circles responsible for writing the Old Testament texts. Here it can only be mentioned that these circles of scribes and priests are not identical to 'Israel' as a whole.[24]

d. *The Gap Between Primary and Secondary Sources*
A difference has to be made between those secondary sources which are mainly fictitious and those which contain older data. In the early history of research, until the end of the last and the beginning of our century, all Old Testament texts from Genesis 1 to 2 Chronicles 36 were regarded as historical. Later on Old Testament scholars saw a frontier between the stories of the prehistory in Genesis 1–11, on one hand, and the history of the patriarchs from Genesis 11/12 onwards, on the other hand. But in the course of time this frontier moved beyond the patriarchal narratives, then beyond the exodus narrative or even beyond the times of Moses, Joshua and the judges. Others nowadays do not see any frontiers, declaring all texts from Genesis 1 to 2 Kings 24 as more or less historically unreliable. That is why it has correctly been stressed that there 'is no way in which history automatically reveals itself in a biblical text'.[25] The criterion to establish this frontier can only be an external one.

To my mind a frontier between unhistorical mythological narratives and historically reliable texts can only be seen between the narratives of Saul, David and Solomon, on the one side, and the history of the separated kingdoms on the other side. That is to say that we can start a critical reconstruction of the history of Israel only with the time of

---

23. J. Wellhausen, *Prolegomena zur Geschichte Israels* (Berlin: de Gruyter, 6th edn, 1981 [1927]), p. 316; ET *Prolegomena to the History of Israel* (trans. J.S. Black and A. Menzies; Edinburgh: Black, 1985), pp. 318-19: 'It is true, we attain to no historical knowledge of the patriarchs, but only of the time when the stories about them arose in the Israelite people'.

24. Cf. P.R. Davies, *In Search of 'Ancient Israel'* (JSOTSup, 148; Sheffield: Sheffield Academic Press, 1992), pp. 44-48, 94-112.

25. Davies, *In Search of 'Ancient Israel'*, p. 12.

Jeroboam and Omri. This is possible because we thus begin shortly before Omri, who founded the state of Israel mentioned in the Assyrian sources, and who is himself mentioned in other primary sources, that is, in the stela of Mesha. From Omri's time on we have primary written sources verifying at least some aspects of the secondary sources.[26] From the time before Omri we have a seal which perhaps mentions a servant of Jerobeam I.[27]

Furthermore, with Omri the lineage of the kings of Israel begins. The basic correctness of this lineage as concerns its succession and rough chronology is proved by primary evidence. In this case it is possible to bridge the gap between primary and secondary evidence.

At this point biblical data can be evaluated and integrated into the picture thus far achieved. In rough outline the biblical data can match the aforementioned data as concerns the lineage and successions of the kings from Omri to Hosea in Israel and from Azariah/Uzziah to Zedekiah in Judah.

But there can also be several contradictions between the data given in the primary sources, especially those from outside Palestine, and those in the secondary or even tertiary sources.

Further, the Old Testament also contains information which cannot (not yet?) be verified by external sources. That is why its historicity cannot be proven and must at least be left open to further debate unless its historicity is rejected for other reasons.

Biblical sources being judged as secondary or tertiary sources, at least for the kingdoms of Israel and Judah, cannot be taken at face value but should be examined critically in light of the criteria discussed in the preceding levels.

3. *Trying to Integrate the Sources*

The main task of the historian consists in working within these levels of evidence. This evaluation tends to give a connection of events indicated by and narrated in the primary and secondary sources as *history*.

26. Cf. Knauf, 'King Solomon's Copper Supply', pp. 172-80; M. Ottoson, 'Ideology, History and Archaeology in the Old Testament', *SJOT* 8 (1994), pp. 213-18.

27. Cf. L.G. Herr, *The Scripts of Ancient Northwest Semitic Seals* (HSM, 18; Missoula: Scholars Press, 1978), p. 82,1 who instead pleads for a date during the reign of Jerobeam II, but cf. now G.W. Ahlström, 'The Seal of Shemaᶜ', *SJOT* 7 (1993), pp. 208-215, with arguments in favour of the time of Jerobeam I.

That is to say, history is not in the sources but history is constituted by the work of the historian. This work is essentially a reconstructive one, a reconstruction achieved by hypotheses.[28] The plausibility of its results depends on what kind and what amount of sources the historian has at his disposal. Furthermore it also depends on the historian's reconstructive ideas and his ability at argumentation.

As concerns the evaluation of the sources, especially the secondary sources of the Old Testament a maximalist view 'which implies that everything in the sources that could not be proved wrong has to be accepted as historical',[29] thus relying heavily and uncritically on the Hebrew Bible, is to be distinguished from a minimalist view 'which means that everything which is not corroborated by evidence contemporary with the events to be reconstructed is dismissed',[30] which is in danger of being hypercritical. Both views seem to be radical and one-sided and call for finding a balance.

That those radical and irreconcilable extremes are on the market (the maximalist view still dominating) is due to the history of research in this realm.

The first stage of this history of research is given with uncritical summaries of what the Old Testament texts tell about the history of Israel. This naive and pre-critical approach consists in paraphrasing, harmonizing and combining the contents of the so-called historical books from Genesis to 2 Chronicles. All texts were taken at face value. This stage has not yet fully disappeared from modern books which often turn out to be rationalistic paraphrases of Old Testament narratives.

A second stage was inaugurated by J. Wellhausen's *Prolegomena*. Here we find a source critical approach which no longer takes the texts at face value but looks for tendencies in the texts. So in a revolutionary manner the Pentateuchal traditions of the sacred tent (P) were taken as exilic or post-exilic traditions reflecting the existence and the service of the Second Temple. It is important to state that Wellhausen developed his views on the basis of the Old Testament texts alone without drawing on external sources. Thus he tried to get a diachrony of

---

28. Cf. Knauf, 'From History to Interpretation', pp. 27-34; *idem*, 'The Cultural Impact of Secondary State Formation: The Cases of the Edomites and Moabites', in P. Bienkowski (ed.), *Early Edom and Moab* (Sheffield: J.R. Collins Publications, 1992), p. 47; Weippert, 'Geschichte Israels am Scheideweg', pp. 71-72.

29. Knauf, 'King Solomon's Copper Supply', p. 171.

30. Knauf, 'King Solomon's Copper Supply', p. 171.

Old Testament texts for his aim of establishing a religious history of Israel on this basis.[31]

Concomitantly to Wellhausen's work more and more ancient Oriental texts (Egyptian, Akkadian, Phoenician, Aramaic and later also Hittite) were published and threw light on Egypt, Mesopotamia, Syria-Palestine and Anatolia. It is interesting to know that Wellhausen himself refused to work with this external evidence because it would have changed his romantically-based picture of Israel's religious history.[32] This progress can be called the third stage of writing a history of Israel. From this stage on an integration of the history of Israel into the histories of the ancient Near East had to be undertaken. The difficulties associated with the attempt were demonstrated by the 'Babel-Bibel-Streit'.[33] This task given by the primary evidence has not yet been completed.

During the nineteenth century the scientific exploration of Palestine began, thus adding lots of topographical and archaeological insights to all reconstructive efforts.

A fourth stage is marked by a late dating of the Old Testament sources into mainly the exilic and postexilic times. The Old Testament is seen more and more as a secondary source the historical value of which is very much in debate. If we had no Old Testament text we would not be able to integrate the primary written and unwritten data into a history of Israel.[34] The Old Testament text is valuable and irreplaceable for an outline sketch of the history of Israel. Or in other words, the Old Testament 'primarily sets the parameters'[35] and 'when one combines artifactual and written evidence to produce a historical scenario, usually the written evidence takes precedence'.[36]

Finding this balance is a task to be undertaken ever anew. From the methodological point of view the difference between primary and secondary and even tertiary sources has first to be respected. Then all these texts adduced for reconstruction work are to be examined as concerns their literary genera, their *Sitz im Leben*, their intentions and

---

31. Cf. H.-J. Kraus, *Geschichte der historisch-kritischen Erforschung des Alten Testaments* (Neukirchen: Neukirchener Verlag, 3rd edn, 1982), pp. 257-58, 260-69.

32. Kraus, *Geschichte der historisch-kritischen Erforschung*, p. 298.

33. Cf. R.G. Lehmann, *Friedrich Delitzsch und der Babel-Bibel-Streit* (OBO, 133; Freiburg: Universitätsverlag; Göttingen: Vandenhoeck & Ruprecht, 1994).

34. Cf. Miller, 'Is it Possible to Write a History of Israel'.

35. Miller, 'Is it Possible to Write a History of Israel', p. 95; cf. also p. 99.

36. Miller, 'Is it Possible to Write a History of Israel', p. 99.

tendencies. Concerning the secondary evidence of the Old Testament sources the question whether these texts contain older material (e.g. annals, folk tales) has to be put. Last but not least, as it has already been underlined, secondary texts are sources for the time in which they have been written.

4. *Summary and Conclusion*

From the preceding paragraphs it follows that all kinds of written and unwritten sources have to be adduced and evaluated for establishing the goal of writing a history of Israel. The range of written sources goes from neo-Assyrian and neo-Babylonian inscriptions, Phoenician Moabite and Aramaic inscriptions to the Old Testament texts. But it also has to be stated that those sources are not on one and the same level. That is why they have to be evaluated according to their status as primary or secondary sources in their own right. Only in this case a *circulus vitiosus* of getting Old Testament texts 'proved' by archaeological findings and getting archaeological findings 'interpreted' by Old Testament texts can be avoided.

As a result of all this we can only achieve tentative sketches of a history of Israel and Judah which are always subject to a continuing process of alteration. In so far as more and more primary evidence will be detected and become available for scholarly evaluation, there will undoubtedly be a need to reduce the influence of the Old Testament texts and thus to change the hypotheses and paradigms by which we try to grasp the history of Israel and Judah.

That there will always be a subjective range of different opinions in this reconstructive work of history writing should be neither denied nor overlooked. The choice between those different opinions has to rely on the specific kind of method and argumentation which has been followed for establishing this opinion.

DEFINING HISTORY AND ETHNICITY IN THE SOUTH LEVANT

Thomas L. Thompson

I would like to begin my contribution by responding to two very recent popular publications which address themselves most centrally to the issue of ethnicity, biblical studies and history writing. The positions which they reflect are on one hand an interpretation of Palestine's archaeology in the context of an anachronistically projected biblical Israel, and on the other a rather explicit, polemically and apologetically motivated rejection of such a perspective. These two publications come to our question from quite conflicting methodological premises. William Dever's article in the recent *Biblical Archaeologist*[1] and Keith Whitelam's new book, *The Invention of Ancient Israel* published in 1996,[2] taken together, allow us a unique access to our meeting's

---

1. W.G. Dever, 'Ceramics, Ethnicity and the Question of Israel's Origins', *BA* 58 (1995), pp. 200-13. This article is closely related to a number of similar articles that Dever has written: W.G. Dever, 'How to Tell a Canaanite from an Israelite', in H. Shanks (ed.), *The Rise of Ancient Israel* (Washington: Biblical Archaeological Society, 1992), pp. 26-60; *idem*, 'Cultural Continuity, Ethnicity in the Archaeological Record and the Question of Israelite Origins', *Eretz Israel* 24 (1993), pp. *22-*33; *idem*, 'Will the Real Israel Stand Up? Archaeology and Israelite Historiography: Part I', *BASOR* 297 (1995), pp. 61-80, but it is in substantial disagreement with the position Dever takes in an earlier article—also written in reaction to this same study of Finkelstein—where he rejects the alleged ethnic significance of both the highland pottery as well as a number of technological characteristics of highland agriculture which he now is just as convinced offer us ethnic markers: W.G. Dever, 'Archaeological Data on the Israelite Settlement: A Review of Two Recent Works', *BASOR* 284 (1991), pp. 77-90, esp. p. 84. This earlier position of Dever is essentially in line with the positions put forward by M. and H. Weippert ('Die Vorgeschichte Israels in neuem Licht', *TRu* 56 (1991), pp. 341-90) and T.L. Thompson, *Early History of the Israelite People* (Leiden: Brill 1992), pp. 141-46), namely, that such pottery as well as the agricultural technologies and housing structures commonly associated with the central hills are responses to the demands of agriculture in the regions considered.

2. K.W. Whitelam, *The Invention of Ancient Israel: The Silencing of Palestinian*

questions about the Bible and its use for history writing considered with their political implications clearly explicit. It is my conviction that such strong political undertones dominate many reactions to recent developments in the history of the South Levant.

1. *Archaeology and Ethnicity*

Dever does not directly deal with Israel's origins in this article. He is rather discussing the use of ceramics to identify ethnicity, and thereby, to identify early Israel in the archaeological remains of Iron I. Although the association of Iron I with Israel's settlement is unsupported by any known extra-biblical evidence,[3] is against the biblical chronology and has come under substantial criticism recently,[4] Dever takes for granted that this period was in fact the historical context for Israel's origins. He does not tell us why. Nevertheless, however unargued the association may be between his ceramically based identification of ethnicity and Israel's origins, Dever correctly recognizes the necessity of establishing an Israelite unity (such as ethnicity) as a *sine qua non* of any understanding of Israelite origins.[5] If he can successfully argue that such a unity existed, he can thereby identify the existence of the biblical Israel he seeks in the context of the archaeological record, whence history for him might proceed. The implications of circularity in his covert argument, within the exclusive context of the Iron I highlands he insists upon, escape Dever. Nevertheless, his argument is clear: that if one would grant the assumption that Israel originated in the central hills during Iron I, Dever would be able to provide us with evidence.[6]

History (London: Routledge, 1996). Whitelam's book investigates a problem of scholarly limitations which Whitelam addressed earlier: *idem*, 'The Identity of Early Israel: The Realignment and Transformation of Late Bronze–Iron Age Palestine', *JSOT* 63 (1994), pp. 57-87.

3. Contra Ahlström and Edelman (G.W. Ahlström and D. Edelman, 'Merneptah's Israel', *JNES* 44 [1985], pp. 59-61), for whom the 'Israel' of the Merneptah stele— if it is to be associated with the later Iron Age state with its capital in Samaria— cannot be located in the central hills.

4. See P.R. Davies, *In Search of 'Ancient Israel'* (Sheffield: Sheffield Academic Press, 1992); T.L. Thompson, *The Early History of the Israelite People* (Leiden: Brill, 2nd edn, 1994).

5. Tacitly following the discussion in T.L. Thompson, *Early History*, pp. 27-28, 301-302, 353-54.

6. See on the question of this methodology, T.L. Thompson, 'William Dever

Dever's understanding of the archaeological remains in the central highlands during Iron I do not prevent him from criticizing Israel Finkelstein's previous identification of these same central hills with early Israel's origins. Finkelstein's problem in Dever's eyes—in spite of having already corrected this error several years ago—is that Finkelstein stated his assumption for this identification of the central hills with Israelite settlement explicitly.[7] Without directing himself to the discussion of this issue within historical research,[8] Dever contrasts his own understanding—and this must be described as a substantial paraphrase of Finkelstein—to Finkelstein's description.[9] In contrast to Finkelstein's study, Dever describes his own interpretation of this region's settlement as an 'archaeologically based' understanding of *Israel*'s origins. Dever does not justify his own focus on the central hills, nor does he clarify why his search for ethnicity renders Israel. What he does do is present an argument, which he claims to be based on a geographical association of pottery forms of the central hills, along with a much wider discussion of five commonly discussed characteristics of these settlements which he describes as ethnic markers.[10] The resulting whole is but a caricature of archaeologically based understanding, and this is disturbing to see in an article from a field archaeologist of such competence.

Since Dever's article proposes to be methodologically oriented—and the issues under dispute are certainly ones of method—it is necessary to recognize that Dever does not actually identify a *geographical* association of pottery forms in the central hills, nor does he clearly

---

and the Not So New Biblical Archaeology', in V. Fritz and P.R. Davies (eds.), *The Origins of the Ancient Israelite States* (JSOTSup, 228; Sheffield Academic Press, 1996), pp. 26-43.

7.   Most prominently in I. Finkelstein, *The Archaeology of the Israelite Settlement* (Jerusalem: Israel Exploration Society, 1988). Dever seems unaware that Finkelstein had since corrected his earlier error: so I. Finkelstein, 'The Emergence of Israel in Canaan: Consensus, Mainstream and Dispute', *SJOT* 5 (1991), pp. 47-59.

8.   See already on this issue: J.M. Miller, 'The Israelite Occupation of Canaan', in J.H. Hayes and J.M. Miller (eds.), *Israelite and Judaean History* (Philadelphia: Westminster, 1977), pp. 218-37, and N.P. Lemche, *Early Israel* (Leiden: Brill, 1985), p. 415, and rather comprehensively N.P. Lemche, *The Canaanites and Their Land* (Sheffield: Sheffield Academic Press, 1991). A discussion of this shift in scholarship can be found in Thompson, *Early History*, pp. 132-33.

9.   So I. Finkelstein, *Israelite Settlement*; see my *Early History*, pp. 221-39.

10.   W.G. Dever, 'Ceramics', p. 208.

define the boundaries of his central hills, in spite of the fact that this particular issue has been a central concern in discussions of both Israelite ethnicity and origins.[11] Is he speaking exclusively of the regions of Ephraim and Menasseh here, or does he include such biblically and geographically distinct regions as Benjamin, Issachar and Judah as well? While one can hardly consider the Galilee, the Shephelah, or the Gilead in these central hills, any interest in a biblically oriented 'Israelite' ethnicity must draw our attention to the settlement of these regions as well. Surely the implications for Dever's thesis are very great.[12] One is left to wonder whether Dever really has established a 'geographical association of pottery forms of the central hills.' He does not show that it is distinctive in itself or supportive of the historical and anthropological conclusions he draws. Dever seems unaware of the complexity of the question he addresses.[13]

a) Dever's first ethnic marker is that of settlement type and distri-

11. See T.L. Thompson, *Early History*, pp. 221-26, 239-44, 278-82, 288-92.

12. Here, I intentionally confine my geographical references to areas commonly associated with the Bible's ancient Israel. I have earlier discussed both some of the well-known differences between the pottery of Ephraim and Menasseh and those of the Galilee on the one hand and the many common features the hill country had with the lowlands: *Early History*, pp. 243-44, 251-52. Dever's claims for having established geographical associations of forms for Iron I ceramics are hardly to be credited.

13. One might consider here Y. Aharoni, *The Settlement of the Israelite Tribes in the Upper Galilee* (Hebrew University dissertation, 1957); *idem*, 'Nothing Early, Nothing Late: Rewriting Israel's Conquest', *BA* 39 (1976), pp. 55-76; M. Kochavi, *Judaea, Samaria and the Golan: Archaeological Survey 1967–1968* (Jerusalem: Israel Exploration Society, 1972); M. Liverani, 'Review of de Vaux L'Histoire d'Israel', *OrAnt* 15 (1976), p. 154; J.A. Callaway, 'New Evidence on the Conquest of Ai', *JBL* 87 (1968), pp. 312-20; *idem*, 'Excavating Ai: Et-Tell: 1964–1972', *BA* 39 (1976), pp. 18-30; Z. Zevit, 'Archaeology and Literary Stratigraphy in Joshua 7–8', *BASOR* 251 (1983), pp. 23-35; T.L. Thompson, *The Settlement of Palestine in the Bronze Age* (Beihefte zum Tübingen Atlas des Vorderen Orients, 28; Wiesbaden: Dr Reichert, 1979), *passim*; N.P. Lemche, *Early Israel* (Leiden: Brill, 1985), pp. 386-406; P. Beck and M. Kochavi, 'A Dated Assemblage of the Late Thirteenth Century from the Egyptian Residence at Aphek', *Tel Aviv* 12 (1985), pp. 34-35; I. Finkelstein, '*Isbet Sarta*: An Early Iron Age Site Near Rosh Ha'Ayin, Israel', *BARev* 299 (Jerusalem, 1986), esp. pp. 77-84; A. Zertal, *Arubbath, Hepher and the Third Solomonic District* (Tel Aviv dissertation, 1986); Thompson, *Early History*, pp. 221-39; G. Ahlström, *The Early History of Ancient Palestine from the Paleolithic Period to Alexander's Conquest* (Sheffield: Sheffield Academic Press, 1993), pp. 334-70.

bution. He neither distinguishes these nor discusses them in any detail, but, nevertheless, believes they are relatively unique to the central hills during Iron Age I.[14] He suggests this in spite of the fact that most of these sites have not been excavated. Moreover, yet many sites more—found in the lowlands, and hardly to be associated with the central hills—are of a comparable type.[15] I can think of no significant region in Palestine which does not know this type of site during the Iron I or early Iron II periods. Nor is the distribution—wholly comparable to that found among sites of the Galilee, the Acco and coastal plains as well as the valleys of the Jezreel and Beth Shan—characteristic of the central hill country sites so particular that Dever has warrant to use this characteristic as an ethnic marker.[16] What Dever describes here as an ethnic marker is characteristic of the whole of Syria's southern fringe.[17]

b) Dever takes the economy of the central hills as his second ethnic marker, describing this as based on small-scale terrace horticulture of olives and grapes (on the western slopes), on the dry-farming of cereals (in the intermontane valleys) and on stock-breeding (on the steppe and in marginal zones). Nevertheless, he describes this as a single form of agriculture—a subsistence one—and contrasts it to 'intensive agriculture, industry and trade'.[18] Dever describes this as 'subsistence'

14. For a convenient overview, cf. Kochavi, *Judaea, Samaria and the Golan*, and Finkelstein, *Israelite Settlement*. For a contrast with the Late Bronze Age, cf. Thompson, *The Settlement of Palestine*.

15. Here, I am thinking of such as *Tel Qiri* or *Tel Yin'am*, which I have discussed in *Early History*, pp. 251-54. For the critical archaeological literature, see M.L. Hunt, *The Iron Age Pottery of the Yoqneam Regional Project* (Berkeley dissertation, 1985); also A. Ben-Tor, 'Tel Qiri: A Look at Village Life', *BA* 42 (1979), pp. 105-13; H. Liebowitz, 'Excavations at Tel Yin'am: The 1976 and 1977 Seasons Preliminary Report', *BASOR* 243 (1981), pp. 79-94.

16. Of considerable importance for this issue is N. Zori, *An Archaeological Survey of the Beth Shan Valley* (Jerusalem: Israel Exploration Society, 1977); *idem*, *The Land of Issachar Archaeological Survey* (Jerusalem: Israel Exploration Society, 1977); see also, Thompson, *Early History*, pp. 239-50.

17. Zori, *Beth Shan Valley*: '. . . we see a shift from a few large urban centers to numerous small villages and hamlets in the hill country and adjacent steppe areas—the periphery or "highland frontier" of Canaan.'

18. Zori, *Beth Shan Valley*. For discussions of agriculture in the hill country of the Southern Levant, see G. Dalman, *Arbeit und Sitte in Palästina* (Gütersloh: Patmos, 1928–1942), *passim*; L.E. Stager, *Ancient Agriculture in the Judaean Desert* (Harvard dissertation, 1975); C.H.J. de Geus, *The Tribes of Israel* (Amsterdam:

farming as if the term referred to a quality of relative poverty or lacking surpluses, rather than as a term referring to a *type* of agriculture relating to self-subsistence understood in contrast to economies that are interdependent and market-based. One cannot reasonably think of these three geographically distinct agricultural strategies as a single form of agriculture nor as one that can survive without trade and intensive strategies, such as the use of supportive fertilizers, irrigation and terraces. Indeed, both terrace and irrigation based agriculture are by definition intensive![19] If the economy of the central hills is to be understood as contributing to the individuation factors of south Levantine peoples, the central hills could not thereby be defined as a single unit, but rather must be understood in varieties of polymorphic associations between the farmers of distinct regions.[20]

c) Dever's third ethnic marker is demographic: what he describes is a markedly rapid rise in the number of settlements in the central hills, which must be explained by immigration. Here, he is obviously referring to the regions of Ephraim and Menasseh—however much they differ from each other in this characteristic—rather than such regions as Judah or the Shephelah where such expansion in the numbers of settlement is both quantitatively and chronologically very different. His argument suffers somewhat from inattention to the archaeological evidence we have, as well as to its chronology. Not only are these sites very small, but a period of about two centuries, while perhaps sufficiently limited to suggest immigration from the lowlands and elsewhere,

Van Gorcum, 1976), pp. 133-60; T.L. Thompson, 'The Background of the Patriarchs: A Reply to William Dever and Malcolm Clark', *JSOT* 98 (1978), pp. 2-43; *idem, The Settlement of Palestine*, pp. 39-50; D.C. Hopkins, *The Highlands of Canaan* (SWBA, 3; Sheffield: Sheffield Academic Press, 1985); O. Borowski, *Agriculture in Iron Age Israel* (Winona Lake: Eisenbrauns, 1987); Finkelstein, *Israelite Settlement*; *idem*, 'The Emergence of the Monarchy in Israel: The Environmental and Socio-Economic Aspects', *JSOT* 44 (1989), pp. 43-74; Thompson, *Early History*, pp. 141-46; *idem*, 'Palestinian Pastoralism and Israel's Origins', *SJOT* 6 (1992), pp.1-13.

19. For my critique of Hopkins's concept of subsistence agriculture which Dever seems to be borrowing here, see my *Early History*, pp. 146-50.

20. See my 'The Background of the Patriarchs' for an earlier but still relevant critique of Dever's understanding of Palestine's economics and ethnography; also my 'Palestinian Pastoralism'. That Dever neglects to engage the discussion of the economy in the highlands is surprising since the cogency of his argument depends on his ability to identify and interpret the archaeological data.

is hardly sudden. Nor is it conducive to an argument for any single common origin which might have relevance to an argument concerning ethnicity. While Dever implies a contrast with the lowlands in his description, the exaggeration of this contrast is due largely to distance from the data on which his picture of the settlement history is based,[21] and on his perspective, particularly his nearly exclusive focus on the highlands. This has led him to ignore the Late Bronze region around Shechem as well as the coastal region at the end of the Late Bronze period and the lowlands generally in the early Iron Age for possible indigenous origins of his highland farmers.[22] As it is, one would hardly be contentious in suggesting that the shifts in Palestine's settlement patterns from late in the Late Bronze period to Iron II,[23] is associated with at least four distinct demographic factors: (1) immigration of new peoples from the Aegean, the Syrian and Anatolian coasts, and secondarily from Egypt;[24] (2) the indigenous population of Palestine radically changing its pattern of settlement and economic strategies, following an economically necessary shift in subsistence patterns;[25] (3) the sedentarization of pastorally oriented nomadic groups of the highland and steppe regions;[26] and (4) an increase of the indigenous

21. The archaeological evidence requiring a shift in this perspective is already clear in N. Zori's Beth Shan survey published in 1962. Dever's failure to access archaeological evidence relating to surveys in Israel and Palestine is regrettable given his question which relates primarily to such evidence. All claims to the contrary, Dever assumes a biblicized interpretation of only secondary archaeological literature throughout his discussion.

22. E.F. Campbell, 'The Shechem Area Survey', *BASOR* 190 (1968), pp. 19-41. That much of the central highlands was lacking a sedentary population during the Late Bronze Age has been well known since the publication of Kochavi's West Bank surveys (*Judaea, Samaria and the Golan*) and was understood to clearly define the central highlands in Thompson, *The Settlement of Palestine, passim*. For a geographically less-limited perspective of this settlement expansion and its background, see Thompson, *Early History*, pp. 205-13 and 215-21 and especially pp. 250-60.

23. This is a shift that can hardly be restricted to Iron I, nor one which can find its teleological denouement in the bible stories of the United Monarchy as Dever implicitly does. Iron I is only part of a transition period throughout Palestine. See, on this, Thompson, *Early History*, pp. 301-34.

24. The most critically acute treatment of this issue today is Ahlström's *Early History of Ancient Palestine*, pp. 282-333.

25. Here, Thompson, 'Palestinian Pastoralism'.

26. This is particularly interesting in regard to the end of Iron I and early Iron II in Judah. Cf. Thompson, *Early History*, pp. 278-92.

population through a possible rise in birth and survival rates in what appears to be a period of general peace and prosperity.[27]

d) Dever's functional argument for an ethnic marker, defined by farm and village layout, has much to say for itself, particularly as he does not see it as confined to the central hills. Nevertheless as this characteristic is a functional one, it does relate both to where the structures and settlements are built and to the manner of life which took place in them. Such a characteristic certainly would have an honorable place on any ethnograph's shopping list. However, lacking exclusivity or confirmation through close correspondence with other comparable 'ethnic markers', one must ask whether it is in fact ethnicity which is marked by such functionally determined remnants of Palestine's population, rather than much more immediate aspects of society such as economic form, geographic diffusion and quite specific historical architectural inspirations. That such a quality as ethnicity in fact existed at this early period is an assumption that does not easily arise from any analysis except one originating in the Bible.

e) Dever's fifth and final 'ethnic marker' is also the weakest: technological change: specifically, such technological developments as terraces, silos and cisterns which he sees as contrasting with the agricultural technologies of the Late Bronze lowland settlements. This argument is extraordinary. Dever argues that these technological changes are (in combination) innovative in hill country agriculture, and thus exemplify a specific new ethnic entity as the explanatory cause of such a common denominator.

This ethnic entity he identifies—and yet at this crucial juncture of his discussion without argument—with the 'Israel' of the Merneptah stele. He states that 'simple logic' requires us to identify the 'facts' of the implications of his ethnic markers with that of the Merneptah stele. This effort of Dever to identify his archaeological descriptions with inscriptional data which belongs to historical events of another period and region parallels biblical archaeological efforts to identify the Iron I and early Iron II cultures of Palestine's coastal region as ethnically identifiable with the biblical Philistines.[28] It is also strikingly similar

---

27. See, Ahlström, *Early History of Ancient Palestine*, pp. 334-70. That peace and prosperity led to an increase of population is, however, a very questionable assumption.

28. See T. Dothan, *The Philistines and Their Material Culture* (New Haven:

to his own early efforts to identify pottery with ethnicity; namely that of Palestine's Early Bronze IV period—long associated by biblical archaeology with the patriarchal narratives—with what Dever understood to have been ethnic "Amorites" immigrating into Palestine from Mesopotamia.[29]

Apart from his insufficiently argued association[30] of the hill country settlers with the group called 'Israel' which was briefly mentioned in a thirteenth-century Egyptian campaign inscription, Dever's archaeologically based arguments for ethnicity have five additional failings: (1) The agricultual techniques he discusses are not limited to the central hill country of Ephraim and Menasseh. Comparable techniques of agriculture, water supply and food storage can be found throughout the Mediterranean world. (2) The specific techniques of each of these developments vary considerably within the central hills themselves. For example, terracing differs according to construction, solar exposure, association with water resources, crops supported and topographical locations. These differences often have a chronological factor. Cisterns vary from rock cut, slaked-lime and terracotta, and there are profound differences between the pottery forms of the cisterns of the Ephraim hills and those found in the Galilee. Comparable differences exist in grain storage facilities. (3) These techniques have a much wider chronological range than that which Dever considers. (4) In spite of Borowski's efforts to portray the Iron I highland settlers as inventors of new techniques[31], there is nothing particularly unique about the historical association of these Iron I sites and such technology. (5) Dever's contrast of such highland agricultural technologies with the farming techniques of the lowlands—and indeed a lowland agriculture of an earlier period—is inappropriate. Which one of us can imagine terraces

Yale University Press, 1982) but also Ahlström, *Early History of Ancient Palestine*, pp. 282-333.

29. W.G. Dever, *The Pottery of Palestine in the EB IV/ MB I Period, c. 2150–1850 BC* (Harvard dissertation, 1966). For a review of Dever's thesis see T.L. Thompson, *The Historicity of the Patriarchal Narratives* (BZAW, 133; Berlin: de Gruyter, 1974), pp. 144-71. Dever still maintains this 'ethnic' identification in his effort to establish the Middle Bronze II period as the time of the patriarchs: cf. W.G. Dever, 'The People of Palestine in the Middle Bronze Period', *HTR* 64 (1971), pp. 197-226; *idem*, 'The Patriarchal Traditions', in Hayes and Miller (eds.), *Israelite and Judaean History*, pp. 102-20.

30. Following Ahlström and Edelman, 'Merneptain's Israel'.

31. Borowski, *Agriculture in Iron Age Israel*, pp. 163-64.

along the *Nahal Yarqon*,[32] or cisterns in the plains of the *Nahal Qishon* and underground storage facilities along the lower reaches of the Nahal Halazon? One need only look at a topographically sensitive map to discover that such technologies are reflective not of ethnicity but of ancient agriculture's adaptation to its environment.[33]

In spite of the biblical orientation of Dever's questions regarding ethnicity, his historical misunderstanding and methodological failure are essentially the result of the mode of his archaeological interpretation which is transparently based on his commitment to find a harmony between archaeologically derived socio-cultural scenarios and his reading of the Bible. Ethnicity, however, is an interpretative historiographical fiction: a concept construing human relationships, before it is a term (however conducive) to descriptions based on material remains. Ethnicity deals with intentional and functional structures of relationships between societies: distinguishing them and discretely identifying them. The physical effects of such collective decisions are often arbitrary and are, indeed, always accidental. Simply put: once ethnicity is identified, we can describe it, but we can not conclude that it exists until we first have knowledge of its presence. Ethnicity is hardly a common aspect of human existence at this very early period. Whatever we might assert to be 'markers' of an unknown ethnicity, such factors as Dever has pointed to are distinguishable material aspects of human existence. As such they tend to coalesce on the basis of their functional—not their ideological—relevance. Dever nowhere defines or describes ethnicity. What he describes from the archaeological record are regionally identifiable correlationships: clusters of material goods. Such clusters can *a priori* be expected to reflect similarities in the material lives of people who in fact lived in the same and neighbouring towns and villages, in the same valleys and along the same hillsides: both in the same geographical subregions and in close neighbouring regions and subregions. Marked by a variety of forms of contiguity as they are, such clusters identify and distinguish regions on the basis of their economy. This affects (and is also affected by) their language, their systems of belief and their customs.

32. We cannot expect them in the central hill country's *Biq'at ha-Netofa* either.
33. For example, Map of Israel, 1 : 100,000 (Carta, Jerusalem, 1996) sheet Nos. 14-15; 16; 22 and 41. D. Edelman, in a forthcoming article on ethnicity, also expresses scepticism concerning the validity of Dever's ethnic markers (Edelman presented her views to our Copenhagen senior seminar in January 1996).

Of course there are differences between highlanders and lowland farmers, between the mixed populations of the coastal areas and the more homogenous mixtures of inland valleys, between the Mediterranean farmers of the agricultural zones and the hunters and shepherds of the steppelands, between the relatively dense population of the north and the scattered settlers of the marginal lands of the south, between the transient shepherds of the Dead Sea region and the *Araba* and the village boy engaged to watch the animals of his neighbours. There is a great deal of difference between the highland olive grower and the fishermen of the coast. These are not ethnically marked distinctions, but quite ordinary classifications of demographic and economic aspects of the population of a complex region that every archaeologist must consider in dealing with historical interpretation. Ethnicity should be left to the historiographical anachronisms of texts, not potsherds.

In the macro-structures discernible in the archaeological remains of the southern Levant, variable economies have created potentially distinctive differentiations in the settlements of the desert, of the steppe, of the highlands and of the agricultural valleys. Comparable distinctions can be found to distinguish settlements related to overland trade from those which support Mediterranean shipping; such, as we might expect, distinguish Gaza from Tyre. It is in this context, I think, that Herodotus's observations which my colleague Lemche cites in a recent article,[34] become particularly apt. Herodotus—the greatest of the early Greek ethnographers, if not the father of history—speaks of the region of Palestine as a subregion of Syria, and he speaks of the people of this region as southern Syrians.

And indeed they are! The larger *ethnos* is, of course, that of the Semites, which can be identified through linguistic associations from the third millennium, which in Palestine at least, can be given geographic location from at least the fourth millennium and can be given characteristic description of the basis of hundreds of material details reflecting their way of life.[35] The Semites are a large and very complex group. They can be further distinguished linguistically and on the

34. N.P. Lemche, 'Clio is Also Among the Muses! K.W. Whitelam and the History of Palestine: A Review and a Commentary', *SJOT* 10 (1996), pp. 88-114; here, pp. 98-99; reprinted in the present volume, pp. 124-51, above.

35. Very useful in this respect is the survey by R. de Miroschedji, *L'époque pré-urbaine en Palestine* (Cahiers de la révue biblique, 13; Paris: Garibalda, 1971); see also Thompson, *Historicity*, pp. 89-117 and *idem*, *Early History*, pp. 171-214.

basis of material, cultural and intellectual traditions between the Mesopotamian world, that of Syria and—in the course of the Bronze Age—Arabia. In Syria, we might comparably distinguish Palestine (along with the southern and increasingly marginal Syrian fringe) as an identifiable cultural region, extending (depending on the period of consideration) from *Jebel Bishri* to the Central Negev highlands. In changing shifts of economic strategies, the population has frequently adapted itself to the stresses and opportunities of climatic, historical and political change: change which also has affected the geographical boundaries of this region's sedentary character. The Syrian heartland, of course, lies in the great cities of the north, while the population of the Southeast and the South survive in forms of comparatively impoverished farmers and a variety of transient pastoralists and hunters, periodically associating themselves with overland trade and the mining industry of the desert.

Dealing with specific sites, Acco and Tell Keisan may be described as essentially Phoenician in character, while Dan and Hazor belong more to the Syrian heartland than to Palestine, just as Gaza and Ashqelon reflect the outreach of Egypt. Most of the rest—except in the very best of times, only too often defined by foreign domination—is witness to a scattering of small towns without a centre: to scrub-farmers, living in small clusters of villages and hamlets in the region's few fertile areas where water is available. The topography of the region is so radically divisive that one small subregion often quickly differentiates itself from its neighbours in unique cultural clusters embracing only a few hundreds of people. This multi-regional Palestine, with variations surpassing Joseph's coat, is what modern ethnographers should be exploring in this generation's effort to create an independent history of the South Levant. Reading the whole of the region's history through biblical lenses is no longer appropriate.

On the other hand, Dever's analysis, based as it is on the assumption that people are to be distinguished by the pottery they use, may be able to identify the biblical peoples such as the Philistines, Israelites and Canaanites. But those are peoples writ large in tradition for purposes fictional. Dever's analysis neglects the historical world of the South Levant, and its remains in the archaeological record, which is much more complex. According to Greek tradition members of an *ethnos* share a common context, culture and history. They understand themselves to have a common blood, language, religion and land. In dealing with the secondary quality of Palestine's culture on one hand and the very complex differentiation of its topography on the other, both of which prevented it from ever becoming a significant entity or a serious player in the politics of this part of Asia, archaeological description must learn to avoid distinction blurring harmonies. Archaeology offers us one of our best tools for encouraging the many different regions of the South Levant to speak with their own voice rather than with that anachronistic one of the long-since discredited forms of 'biblical archaeology'.

2. *Palestinian Ethnicity*

This discretion in archaeological description—allowing for the many different cultures of the region to find their appropriate place in history—is exactly Keith Whitelam's proposal. This new book might well serve as a useful methodological prolegomena to a history of Palestine.[36] Whitelam's book is a brilliant polemic on behalf of a history of Palestine that has exposed many of the motives affecting our long concentration on the history of Israel and preventing a clear and balanced regionally based history. In this I am afraid he attacks all of us here, and too often his attack is justified—and very important.

Unlike Dever's inappropriate personal assaults,[37] coupled with the neglect of historical topics of substance about which there is disagreement, Whitelam's essay implicitly challenges a central development of my book: namely, that transition in which I move from a discussion of archaeological sources relating to a complex pattern of regional settlement, limiting both Israel and Judah's historical role to their respective regions, to a discussion of Assyrian, Babylonian and Persian deportation practices.[38] Here the book's real strengths get lost in my efforts to create what was after all hardly history, critically speaking, but rather just another rationalistic paraphrase for biblical

---

36. Whitelam, *The Invention of Ancient Israel.* While my discussion here might be understood as a response to Whitelam's perceptive review of my *Early History* (K.W. Whitelam, 'New Deuteronomistic Heroes and Villains: A Response to T.L. Thompson', *SJOT* 9 [1995], pp. 97-118), section 3 below is written in partial response both to Whitelam's *The Invention of Ancient Israel*, and to his excellently comprehensive *JSOT* article, 'The Identity of Early Israel'.

37. Dever, 'Cultural Continuity' and 'Will the Real Israel Stand Up?'

38. *Early History*, pp. 301-39 and 339-51 respectively.

Israel.[39] And, as soon as I enter this world of the Bible, the rest of my Palestine disappears and my Persian and Hellenistic periods know only the exciting world of story. In this, Whitelam rightly judges this effort, to create a region-wide historiography independent of the biblical tradition's perspective, to fail, and become but a history of Israel destroying the history of Palestine.

Of course, Whitelam's references to the population of ancient Palestine as 'Palestinians' is hardly to be accepted as a reference to any historically existent ethnicity. It is at best a term of convenience referring to the peoples of this region. This strategically brings us to a necessary observation—which is, I think, Whitelam's intention. Not only is the history of Israel (and Judah for that matter) not biblical history, but the Israel of history is a small part of the much greater history of Palestine, as are also the separate and distinct histories of Judah, the Jezreel, the Gilead, the Galilee, the Negev, the Shefelah, the Jordan valley, Phoenicia, etc.[40] These hidden histories have long been lost by the habits of our field. We usually do all right with the Stone Age, but we do have Emmanuel Anati's *Palestine Before the Hebrews*, and the Bronze Age only too often finds its description in terms of a trajectory aimed at earliest Israel.[41] The past twenty years, which has seen the

39. My colleagues in Copenhagen allow only a remnant of this historiographic scenario to survive: namely my *a quo* dating in the Persian period for the theoretically earliest possible context for the development of the biblical (in contrast to historical) concept of Israel. This is fully in accordance with *Early History*, p. 356 n. 10.

This tendency in my book to integrate and use biblical scenarios historically, implicitly contradicting the historiographical principles to which the book is dedicated and as a whole does establish, has also been noticed and appropriately criticized in the excellent review written by Marit Skjeggestad in the *Norsk Teologisk Tidsskrift* of 1994.

40. A historical methodology which attempts to develop a history of Palestine independent of biblical traditions is more successfully developed in the preliminary proposal of T.L. Thompson, F.J. Goncalvez and J.M. Van Cangh, *Toponomie palestinienne: Plaine de St Jean d'Acre et corridor de Jérusalem* (Publications de l'institut orientaliste de Louvain, 37; Louvain La Neuve: Peeters, 1988).

41. This was of course central to earlier works such as W.F. Albright, *From the Stone Age to Christianity* (Garden City, NY: Anchor, 1957) and is implicit in the common Israeli designation of the Bronze Age with the biblical term 'Canaanite'. My own studies for the *Tübingen Atlas* (*The Settlement of Palestine in the Bronze Age* [Wiesbaden: Dr Reichert, 1979]), and Helga Weippert's *Palästina in vorhellenistischer Zeit* (Munich: Mohr, 1988), as well as N.P. Lemche's *Die Vorgeschichte Israels: Von den Anfangen bis zum Ausgang des 13. Jahrhunderts V. Chr.* (Biblische

biblical history of Israel deconstructed step by step from a history of the Patriarchal Period in 1974 and 1975 to that of an historical exile in more recent times, has been a willing prisoner of what I find it useful to think of as a 'watershed' mentality. As soon as we can find something historical, then we stop being critical regarding all subsequent periods. We can accept the most rigorous of methodologies for all Bible stories that come before the watershed, but thereafter we quickly resort to the fundamentalism of our childhood.

This is a problem endemic to the question of historicity. It is a wonderful tool to draw out aspects of literary creation, but, unfortunately, it is only convincing when the conclusion is negative. It is not a tool to use to build up a body of evidence. I cannot imagine what a biblical text would look like that was judged to be 'historically wholly reliable'. One of the problems with dealing with the historical reflections of texts in the world of such ancient history is that we can only critically determine degrees of unreliability. The razor's edge of the question of historicity identifies fiction, not history. Nevertheless, in spite of being trained to use this tool critically and with historical acumen, most people in our field who claim to talk about the 'history of Israel' are really offering us one or other variety of a biblical paraphrase: without any redeeming quality. It is a serious error: this attention to biblical views of the past; or for that matter such views as those of Josephus. We all know that the real world which such so-called 'historiographies' reflect is that of their author's; and they are never any better than that. If we want to develop methodologically sound and critical history, we need to deal with texts in terms of what they imply, not of what they say. They are not the writings of colleagues, but remnants from the past. As such, they are data, not evidence.

If we see our goal as one of reconstructing the past, we are pursuing an impossible dream. We are trying to represent a past reality that does not and cannot exist. Archaeological materials and texts, however—both as remnants of the past—do exist. What I understand as a pivotal distinction between contemporary historiography in our field and that of a generation ago is that when we write history today, we do not create scenarios in fancy, but first of all we attempt to explain,

Enzyklopädie, 1; Stuttgart: Kohlhammer, 1996), in spite of its title avoid, I believe, the bias Whitelam describes. Indeed, the entire *Tübinger Atlas des vorderen Orient* project has, with only a few exceptions such as the maps relating to Iron Age Palestine, rather successfully avoided this biblicistic, and indeed anachronistic distortion.

understand and describe these fragments of the past, and in doing so interpret them as evidence for understanding what is still part of our world, namely its past. History is interpretation of data within the contemporary world of historical scholarship. As such, it is a fragmented, not a reconstructed past, that we need to describe.

I find the old-style abusive questions (such as what must have or what probably happened, about what might be reasonable to believe if our imagination—and our logic—were infinite?) very deceptive, however seductive, because, lacking warrant, they always go beyond our evidence. These are rather anti-histories. They become particularly pernicious when they form the foundations for increasingly speculative scenarios. From such nonsense we have created the Amorite migrations, the amphictyony and the peasant rebellion hypothesis, and have tempted three generations of archaeologists to treasure hunt. I do not know whether we can always avoid such monsters—I have not done so—but we should and can avoid encouraging them, or worse, writing them into our methodology.

In attempting to respond to the issues proposed by Lester Grabbe, Whitelam's challenge has been very much on my mind and I find myself reflecting on the techniques and strategies which I have actually used, as much as on those critical principles I only tell myself I should use. In writing ancient history, data derived from archaeological field work, and from the application of the data of geology and geography renders extensive information that helps to create a useful and chronologically sensitive perspective on the historical periods in which we are engaged. My own focus—which, of course, is shared by many—has concentrated on issues of correspondences: first as related to such material data, and then on such correspondences that are found between such information and the implications of our textual remains, both contemporary and traditional, rendering judgments of similarity and difference along a potentially infinite spectrum of comparable data and correspondences. I think this 'spectrum method' with which Cryer, Lemche and I have been working, shows some promise in dealing with both large quantities of data and data of great variety. It allows us to systematize and question our assumptions about the accidental quality of our comparative data, supporting our ability to deal with a considerable number of known and possible variables—both material and literary—as we focus on those aspects of our data that correspond typologically, chronologically and geographically. Both the quality and the character of our history depends on our sources from any given period. Methodology must follow the association of evidence with the questions we ask.

The history we create will vary greatly from period to period depending on the data available. In the Late Bronze Age, literary texts might easily dominate, particularly—as Lemche has shown us—as our questions direct us toward intellectual history.[42] For social, and especially for cultural and economic history, material remains—not just archaeologically excavated materials but also those drawn from geography, climate studies and soils research—will provide us with indispensable primary evidence. If we are dealing with the Hellenistic or Graeco-Roman periods, biblical texts, intertestamental literature and the scrolls from the Dead Sea may become paramount for understanding the ancient literary and intellectual world, for which these written materials will provide us with our primary sources.

Except very rarely, I doubt that we have yet the ability to argue in any convincing way that such texts and traditions contain any materials that are themselves earlier than the Persian period. It will be difficult enough to show that they contain data even that early. It is only when we have independent historical knowledge from these earlier periods that we come to see how the biblical tradition has been able to turn such materials to its own quite distinctive purpose.

In dealing with biblical traditions as sources for history, we must remember that any history of the South Levant we choose to write—even a history of that portion of it which was ancient Israel or ancient Judah—will not render us a context for understanding or interpreting the Bible, however much our training in German form criticism's search for its ever chimerical *Sitz im Leben* tells us that we need it. Not only is the Bible not written from the perspective of ancient Israel, but even the New Israel—which *is* the Bible's perspective—does not have any such historical context except within the literature in which it exists. Only texts have contexts.[43]

---

42. Lemche, *Die Vorgeschichte Israels*, pp. 151-207.

43. This is my primary reason for distancing myself from Lemche's effort to identify the Bible as a Hellenistic tradition: N.P. Lemche, 'The Old Testament—A Hellenistic Book?', *SJOT* 7 (1993), pp. 163-93. On the other hand, Lemche's chronology is sound because the earliest texts we have that clearly give evidence for the existence of biblical books as Hellenistic, and a dating from the second century BCE

3. *Summary and Prospects for the Bible and History*

The Persian period does not provide us with an historical context for the Bible's formation but only an *a quo* potential for that process, and, as in the Elephantine texts, it provides us with some of our earliest sources for a history of Judaism. Neither Ezra–Nehemiah, 1–2 Maccabees nor Josephus are safe foundations for a critical history when they lack independent corroboration. The historicity of such Hellenistic and Graeco-Roman historiographies should now be the focus of further deconstruction. Neither the extent of influence and power asserted for these alleged Judaisms nor the coherence of such a society that is implied by these traditions is supportable. We need to understand not only ancient Israel and Judah, but also the Judaism of Yehud, of Jerusalem and of Roman Palestine reflected in these three different traditions, as discrete issues both within a much more variant regional history of the South Levant and within the greater context of this region, its politics and religions as aspects of the history of Greater Syria.[44]

It is within this context; namely the history of Syria, that the regional histories which Whitelam and I have been arguing for as the focus of a more archaeologically based historiography can be pursued. The methodological separation of the perception of the past rendered in traditional texts from an understanding of the past based on more archaeologically derived sources and on traditional texts only as reflecting the historical world of their composition is a necessary first premise for critical historiography.

Whitelam is right that the quite explicit presuppositions (and abiding preoccupation of research) regarding ethnography, is a serious problem. As the biblical eponymous *topos* of the *benei Israel*, or as Jeremiah's typological identification of Israel with Jerusalem, had been central in the formation of the Bible's Jewish voice—that voice we might call a voice of the New Israel or of the New Jerusalem—the scholarly association of such early Jewish voices with both Judah as a geographical concept and with an historical Jerusalem, is tendentious,

to the second century AD stands as a solidly conservative point of departure from evidence.

44. As Herodotus, for example, understood this region. See Lemche, 'Clio Is Also among the Muses'.

albeit this is a tendentiousness that has its roots in the efforts of much biblical and related literature to centre holy Zion at Judaism's ontological, if not historical, core. Seeing the Bible as a product of Judaea, however, or even perceiving biblical texts as Jewish, in the sense of a product reflective of an existent religion that we might call 'Jewish' is, perhaps, more anachronistic than we are prepared to admit. It does exclude, however, nearly every critical possibility of understanding the historical context of the Bible's formation.

It is this thesis that Keith Whitelam's new book rightly nails firmly to the church door.[45] Of course, Palestinians were not an ancient ethnic entity in the South Levant. They are not—that is not yet—an ethnic entity today. Many are the descendants of early Christians and Jews, and of the many other religious groups of the Graeco-Roman and Byzantine South Levantine population. In a similar vein, many Jews of Israel today are descendants of the nearly thoroughly hellenized Graeco-Roman diaspora, only some of whom had originated in Palestine. Both nations today are in the process of developing competing ethnicities under the tendentious banners of exilic returnees and *'am ha-'aretz*. As historians we need to be aware of this. Central to this conflict is the exclusive, but ultimately sectarian claim to legitimacy of the theologically defined 'New Israel' of the biblical paradigm.

This is not an historical perspective. If we are about writing history for this southern fringe of Syria we are going to get only very meagre help from such anachronisms. Contrary to the impression left by Whitelam, a regionally based history began some time ago. Think of the studies of Manfred Weippert, Axel Knauf and Uli Hübner.[46] The geographical and regional basis for this kind of study has now clearly been established by the *Tübinger Atlas*, and might soon be further supported by an exciting new CD-Rom 'interactive atlas' being planned by Cynthia Edenberg of Tel Aviv's Open University. While Whitelam is correct that critical independence quickly breaks down as soon as we enter biblical periods (nowhere is this more clearly seen than in

---

45. Whitelam, *The Invention of 'Ancient Israel'*.

46. M. Weippert, *Edom: Studien und Materialien zur Geschichte der Edomiter auf Grund schriftlicher und archäologischer Quellen* (Tübingen dissertation, 1971); E.A. Knauf, *Ismael: Untersuchungen zur Geschichte Palästinas und Nordarabiens im 1sten Jahrtausend vChr.* (ADPV; Wiesbaden: Harrasowitz, 2nd edn, 1989); U. Hübner, *Die Kultur und Religion eines transjordanischen Volkes im 1sten Jahrtausends* (Heidelberg dissertation, 1991).

moving from chapters 11 to 12 in Ahlström's *History of Palestine*), the problem is only a temporary one of a new approach. We have already identified 'ancient Israel' as a literary construct,[47] and are in the course of identifying ancient Judaism as a religious one.[48]

Regional histories have also been well begun in Western Palestine. Historical Israel belongs to the ninth–eighth century and to the central hills south of the Jezreel. Judah finds its home in the eighth–sixth centuries and can be related to Jerusalem in the seventh–sixth centuries. The geographical extent of these patronage states, comparable to such as Ammon, Moab and Edom, hardly extended beyond the highlands. The Iron Age histories of the Syrian cities of Hazor and Dan, as that of Hamath now needs to be written. We also have a history of the Jezreel and Beth Shan to write, of the Galilee and of Transjordan's Gilead.

In the Persian period we have the imperial province of Jehud, but that was no more reflective of a people than other Persian provinces. This is no less true of Samaria/Sebaste. Any constructs of ethnic or cultural unity must at least begin with evidence, and here, the texts from Elephantine may prove more important than anachronistic biblical ones. The modernist historian's *hubris* that anachronisms can be removed rendering critical history is nonsense: Samaria should be the test case for this issue.

Rather than substituting the history of the South Levant during the Hellenistic period with a paraphrase of First or Second Maccabees, we need to think more about Philistia, Phoenicia and the Decapolis, about the towns of the lowland and of the coast. We must especially think of Beth Shan and the towns of the Jezreel, and we must not forget the Galilee. We might also think of Judaism in the Graeco-Roman period more as an intellectual and philosophical movement of Hellenism itself rather than so conveniently as a reactionary religious movement of Palestine's least Hellenized 'Jews'. Was the temple an expression of Judah's religious coherence or was it rather the remnant of one of the factions of Jerusalem's political aspirations? If kingship continued to be an epitomizing factor of patronage, what was the significant factor

47. Davies, *In Search of 'Ancient Israel'*.
48. J. Neusner, 'Was Rabbinic Judaism Really Ethnic?', *CBQ* 57 (1995), pp. 281-305. Until the fourth–fifth centuries Judaism was a philosophy not a religion. Israel is a counterpart of the church or to the nation of Islam, not to Albanians, Italians or Algerians.

of Idumaean power in Judaea: especially regarding their relationship to Jerusalem's temple?

From another perspective, we must ask how it is that Galileans and Samaritans are Jews? What does it mean that in the Persian period soldiers in Elephantine are Jews? Where did they come from? Or is it a term that distinguishes their religious association with a cult of Yahweh? Were there scholars in Alexandria who were Jews? Where did they come from? Were other adherents of Yahwism called Jews: such as those from Tiberias, Acco and Hamath? What did it mean to be a Jew in Palestine—or in the diaspora—of the Roman empire? Why is it that the rabbinic traditions of the Talmud—arguably reflecting traditions of the second to fourth centuries—seem to know so little of the immense world of the Jewish diaspora: that was wholly Hellenized and Greek speaking? And how was this international culture—so well reflected in the Septuagint and in the pseudepigraphic traditions—eventually lost to the Jewish world?

And, lest we be distracted by this question, what were the non-rabbinic components of the complex region of the Syrian fringe in the Graeco-Roman period? Are we to understand them as non-Jewish, anachronistically identifying Judaism as a product of the Mishnaic rabbis? And, if not, is Judaism itself a meaningful term to be used in the South Levant in the Hellenistic and early Graeco-Roman periods?—for can it refer to anything else than generally religious aspects found among the indigenous population of Palestine, which—lacking any necessary or recognized centre—lacked also any universally distinguishing feature? For this period, we might define Judaism as any religious aspect acculturated by the indigenous population of Syria's southern fringe. And if so, what lost historical societies does the Bible give voice to?

If we will have a critical history, we must deal with the anachronisms we have created. Are the biblical books, themselves, a product of ancient Judaism? Is the continuity between the Bible and Judaism reflective of a chronologically linear development, or is it an aspect of rationalistic anachronism, ideologically motivated: a continuity asserted—like that of Christianity's claim of the *New Testament* and the *Septuaginta*—by theological necessity? I do not think any of us would deny that the Bible was a central creative force in Judaism's formation. The self-identity which is expressed through biblical texts is that of the *benei Israel*: a sectarian perception expressive of the true

Israel: a radical alternative to the historical Israel's lost past. This is not simply a self-identity of rabbinic tradition, but one which is known also to have been shared at least by Judaeans, Galileans, Idumaeans and Samaritans of the Graeco-Roman peoples of Palestine (sometimes otherwise described in terms of the philosophical schools of Pharisees, Sadducees and Essenes), as well as by a wide range of groups inside and outside of Palestine, among whom were groups who later understood themselves as Christians and who polemically identified the Judaism of the rabbis with the biblical metaphor of old; that is, false, Israel.

Historically, the Bible and the books which make it up are products of the south Levant's worldview: their tradents were those who emerged in the course of the first or perhaps better early second century CE as Samaritans, Jews and Christians; they were both Greeks and Hebrews; both indigenous and people of the diaspora. While all would identify their own heritage with the land of the Jews', this was a religious assertion of faith, not a statement of historical fact. Their associations to Judaism were created in Egypt, in Babylon, and in all of the great cities of the Graeco-Roman world.

Texts do not give direct evidence for the construction of a history of any world asserted by their authors, but rather for a history and perspective of the author's world, implied in the texts' projections. That world is rather Graeco-Roman than Lemche's Hellenistic. Lemche's Hellenistic dating, like my Persian period scenario before him, provides only an *a quo* chronology. We should be dating not traditions but the historical contexts of *texts*. These are first known from Qumran in the second century, BCE, in contexts which clearly show that the formation of biblical books is still in process: hence my chronology of 165 BCE to 135 CE. We must also date specific entities and concepts. No Bible existed in the Hellenistic period, only some very specific texts. The analysis and interpretation of these texts is our primary historical source for understanding Hellenism in Asia. The intellectual worlds of the Old and New Testament text traditions hold a common perception, distinguishable at most as older and younger contemporary witnesses of a common tradition. Old Israel is the lost Israel: the human Israel of an unknown past. The Bible's world has rather the voice of a new Israel.

REFLECTIONS ON THE DISCUSSION

Lester L. Grabbe

One of the main purposes of the Seminar was to come to understand one another—to see where we actually agree and where we really differ. What soon became clear is that some disagreements were matters of words only, of misunderstandings arising from ways of expressing ourselves. Two issues illustrate this.

Several of us have suggested that the principle of probability is an important factor in evaluating data and sources. This was objected to on the grounds that probability is impossible to determine in the period of history with which we are dealing. The difference was one of definition: 'probability' as a general term meaning the degree to which something is likely to happen based on common experience, and 'probability' in the narrower statistical sense which presupposes sufficient data to make the question statistically significant. There is agreement that statistical probability is usually ruled out because of lack of data, but most are comfortable with a more general or common-sense use of the term. (Bob Becking's use of a ten-point scale was not discussed, however, and it remains to be seen how useful other members of the Seminar find it.)

A second example concerns the term 'reconstruction'. Again, this is a widely used expression, though there was some objection to the idea and even to the use of the term. On the other hand, most of us in the Seminar use 'reconstruction' without a second thought but with the specific meaning of a theoretical construct. In other words, a reconstruction is simply a way of making sense of the data, is always tentative, and is in the nature of a hypothesis to be tested. If it becomes enshrined as 'fact', methodology has already been violated. Further discussion clarified that there was no opposition to the use of 'reconstruction' in the sense of drawing up a hypothesis to be tested.

We all agreed that history writing—whatever form that history takes—should have the goal of covering all the region and the peoples in it, whether one uses the term Palestine, Syria, the Levant, or whatever. This would not prevent a partial history from being written (e.g. a history of Edom), and an interest specifically in Israel or Judah is understandable. But to treat a history of one particular 'nation' as *the* history is mistaken, especially if that history accepts only a chauvinistic ideology which treats others inhabitants of the region as inferior, insignificant, non-existent, or even as worthy only of annihilation. To canalize all our activity through a particular view of 'ancient Israel', as is so frequently done through 'biblical history', 'biblical archaeology', 'biblical geography', etc., is simply to write bogus history (to steal a term from Robert Carroll). To write a 'history of Israel' as the history of an *ethnic* entity is simply too question-begging, as Keith Whitelam has demonstrated.[1] Even using 'Israel' as a *political* term has its problems (unless perhaps it is confined to a specific kingdom controlled from Samaria, as known from the Assyrian inscriptions).

It is important to recognize that *not one* member of the Seminar denies the existence of the 'kingdom of Israel'—alongside the 'kingdom of Judah'—in the early first millennium BCE (cf. especially Davies and Lemche). That such entities existed is well known from Assyrian inscriptions, though it should be noted that 'Israel' (or what seems to be the Assyrian equivalent of 'Israel') as the name of the northern kingdom occurs in only one inscription (Lemche). Rather, Seminar members object to two common assumptions: (a) that the *literary* construct of 'biblical Israel' can be immediately translated into historical terms, and (b) that 'Israel' should dominate and canalize study of the region in antiquity. The biblical picture of a large Israelite empire is to be treated with great scepticism. 'Israel' and 'Judah' were probably only minor 'states' in Syria (depending on how one defines 'state' and which specific period is being discussed).

There was strong agreement that the implications of postmodernism for the historical question need to be accepted (cf. especially Carroll and Barstad). Yet accepting the impact of postmodernism need not require us (contrary to some postmodernists) to abandon the historical task (Barstad). Indeed, as historians we still remain positivists to some extent (Barstad, Niehr, Grabbe). The question of whether we are ready to accept a genuine paradigm shift, however, is an acute one since even the more radical of the 'minimalists' are still really in the old

---

1. K.W. Whitelam, *The Invention of Ancient Israel: The Silencing of Palestinian History* (London: Routledge, 1996).

mould (Barstad). To me it is not clear what such a paradigm shift would involve, but however positivist our goal, postmodernist study shows the difficulty in reaching it.

This leads on to the question of how one might approach the practical task of writing a history of the Palestine/Syria in the late second and early first millennia BCE. Should one abandon the narrative format (Thompson)? Will our history really consist of a series of debates? To some extent, I have already taken such an approach in my history of Second Temple Judaea because it has seemed to me that a historical narrative is not possible for large sections of the Second Temple period.[2] On the other hand, the proposal that narrative history is the way forward (Barstad, Davies) seems to go in quite a different direction. The implications of this suggestion were not worked out in detail, so I for one would be curious to know what such a history would look like.

One point emerging in the discussion is that members of the group have different ideas of what constitutes a history. For some, it seems to mean a connected narrative based on primary evidence. If this is the criterion, we should probably give up the task right now. However, my paper argued that history can be applied even to the bare outline of a pre-historic society based almost entirely on archaeology. If that possibility is accepted, then history could take various forms. One of these forms might be a series of arguments (Thompson). On the other hand, I personally think there can be a good deal of value in a history which includes imaginative reconstruction, as long as the basis is clearly indicated and the hypothetical nature of the reconstruction is always kept in mind. Writing history is an art, not a science, and the evaluation of evidence is always something of a juggling act (Grabbe, Barstad, Becking).

It was my desire not to let the problem of the biblical text dominate discussing the question of whether a history of ancient Israel could be written. There is a danger that a fixation with the biblical text can blind us to clearer issues about historical methodology. That is, we should be able to come to some theoretical position about writing such a history, even if we leave the Old Testament text out of the equation. Nevertheless, we kept coming back to it, almost like a moth drawn to a candle. I think there were at least two reasons for this: first, the

2. L.L. Grabbe, *Judaism from Cyrus to Hadrian* (2 vols.; Minneapolis: Fortress Press, 1992).

biblical text has been widely used—and abused—in writing history, so it must be dealt with, if only to show the inappropriate use of it as a source; secondly, the Old Testament text is the most extensive collection of data which claims to represent ancient Israel, and questions of whether and how it can be used must be addressed.

My main fear, however, is that even in our debate, 'history of Israel' will wrongly be equated with 'history according to the Hebrew text', as it has so often been in influential recent histories of ancient Israel. Thus, Robert Carroll seems to reject any history of Israel as 'bogus history' because of the problematic nature of the biblical text. Most of us would agree with this if such a history is basically only a paraphase of the biblical text. But some of us who would argue that we can and must use the biblical text would also argue that it must be used very carefully and critically (Niehr, Becking, Grabbe).

Perhaps one of the problems with dealing with the biblical text is that it is not demonstrably straight fiction. There is clear evidence that the writer(s) of 2 Kings knew something about the names and relative sequence and even the rough chronology of most of the Israelite and Judaean kings from Ahab to Zedekiah (Grabbe, Niehr, Barstad). What the source of this information was can be guessed at, though at present we do not really know. But the presence of such data may seem to contradict the view that the biblical text contains no data demonstrably earlier than the Persian period (Thompson); however, Thompson's point is that the data in a Persian period document give a Persian period perspective. For example, external data demonstrate that an Ahab lived, but many of the details of the biblical text are not confirmed; indeed, in some cases they are refuted by the Assyrian texts. The question of how to evaluate what seem to be early data or memory in a later document needs much more discussion before it will be clear how far apart our positions really are.

The problem, then, is not whether the authors knew something about Israel and Judah's past but how much they knew and how usable is the information imbedded in what is plainly an ideological work (Carroll). How much really does finding a seal with the name 'Berekyahu b. Neriyahu' prove about the stories in Jeremiah? One could even argue that the seal actually contradicts the book of Jeremiah, for why would a major official in the bureaucracy hire himself out as a mere amanuensis to a controversial prophet? In other words, the author of Jeremiah may have simply appropriated a famous name while creating a fictional narrative, much as is done by thousands of fiction writers in our own time. (Does the mention of Winston Churchill and genuine events of World War II authenticate the contents of all the hundreds of thrillers which contain these data?) In fact, there are recent rumours that this seal is a fake. If so, one wonders whether the motive for making the counterfeit was merely financial or, more cynically, ideological.

It seems that we can proceed in one of four different ways (though each of these can be further nuanced; each represents only one point on what is in fact a continuous scale):

1. Assume no history is possible and give up the historical task. Despite some statements which might seem to take that position (e.g., Carroll), no one has in fact chosen this alternative.

2. Ignore the biblical text as a whole and write any history entirely on archaeology and other primary evidence. This is the true 'minimalist' position and is one way to go. The difficulty is that the interpretative framework still depends heavily, if indirectly, on data from the Bible at certain points. Also, many would argue that since the biblical narrative is not entirely fiction, it would be foolish to dismiss it as a source of potential value. In reality, none of the Seminar has chosen this route.

3. Give priority to the primary data but make use of the biblical text as a secondary source, allowing it to contribute to the historical task but cautiously and critically.

    The views of Seminar members almost all seem to fall somewhere in (3) or perhaps between (2) and (3), in so far as such a crude scale can describe actual positions. It should be noted that if one takes a spectrum of views from all over biblical scholarship, though, these positions all fall toward the 'minimalist' end of the spectrum. It is clear that all members of the Seminar in Dublin rejected

4. The 'maximalist' position, if by this is meant the position of accepting the biblical account except where it can be shown to be wrong.

The ideological and secondary nature of the biblical text is recognized in every case, though it is handled in a different way as far as the extent to which it is allowed to influence the historical reconstruction. The disagreements were about how to deal with this text which all members of the Seminar accept as problematic. Indeed, one of the problems with establishing a dialogue seems to be that the 'minimalist' and 'maximalist' positions depend on such a different conceptualization that dialogue is difficult, if not impossible. In other words, one could argue that positions (2) and (3) are points on a spectrum, but positions (1) and (4) really represent something completely different and even outside the spectrum. Position (1) rejects the historical task, plainly, but in fact so does (4) because it treats the biblical text differently from other historical sources.

Some members of the Seminar have raised objections to the use of the terms 'maximalist' and 'minimalist' as inaccurate and distorting. Philip Davies has recently noted that these can become labels to dismiss one's opponent without really engaging the arguments.[3] All members of the Seminar are interested in using the maximum amount of usable data; the issue is what is the legitimate maximum. 'Minimalist' might imply looking for as little as possible, which is not the case at all.

One of the observers raised the question of whether one should not use a forensic model as the appropriate model for doing history. He went on to suggest that, on this analogy, the biblical text should be judged 'innocent until proved guilty'. Some of us may well feel that a forensic model could be useful in some aspects of dealing with history. However, it needs to be recognized that the adversarial system of the Anglo-Saxon judicial tradition, so well known in Britain and North America, is only one model. The inquisitorial system is widely used on the Continent, and some would argue that it is a better model. In any case, where the forensic model is misused is in suggesting that the biblical text is being treated as a defendent 'on trial' and should thus be 'presumed innocent'. If there is any analogy here, the biblical text is a 'witness' and should be thoroughly cross examined to test its trustworthiness. No historian can take the view that sources are to be treated 'innocent until proved guilty'. It is not a question of either innocence or guilt, since both terms are inappropriate in the historiographical context; it is a question of critical analysis which makes considered judgments about the trustworthiness of the source.

It seems clear that the question of the biblical text will continue to dominate many future discussions.

3. 'Introduction', in V. Fritz and P.R. Davies (eds), *The Origins of the Ancient Israelite States* (JSOTSup, 228; Sheffield: Sheffield Academic Press, 1996), especially pp. 11-14.

Some statements in the papers may suggest that the place of archaeological data is differently evaluated by various members of the Seminar, but this is not yet clear. Both Carroll and Barstad seem to say that archaeological data are not ultimately any more reliable than textual. This is certainly evident in blatant cases of circularity in which the archaeology is interpreted by the biblical text. But while all Seminar members recognize the subjectivity of any interpretation, the artefactual data are contemporary sources—'primary sources' (Niehr). Views on the relationship between the archaeological and the textual will be further clarified, one hopes, in future discussions.

The differences of approach are well illustrated in comparing the papers of Carroll, Barstad and Thompson, all of whose conclusions about the nature of the biblical text would probably be fairly similar. Thompson sees the biblical text as a late ideological work, to be viewed with suspicion as a source of historical data for an earlier time, with primacy given to archaeology, geography, geology, etc. Carroll sees the biblical text as an ideological entity and thus bogus for historical purposes, but he finds archaeology also problematic. Barstad sees the biblical text similarly as an ideological construct, containing much fiction. Yet the recent return to narrative history recognizes that historical truth can be gleaned from a text (e.g. the Deuteronomistic History) which is a mixture of history and fiction. It is not a case of 'true' or 'false' but of different degrees of truth and falsity.

Most of our interchange concerned the First Temple period, when it focused on a particular period of history. This was partly because this is where the controversy has developed in recent years. It seems to me, however, that an investigation of the Second Temple period could be a useful way of getting a clearer perspective on the problems with the First Temple. As I said in my paper, I do not believe the basic epistomological problems relating to writing history differ from one period to another. Everything in the past is past. Yesterday is no more directly accessible to us than four thousand years ago. In each case, we must rely on sources which are subjected to critical scrutiny. The difference between historical periods lies in the nature and the abundance of the sources. This fact means, naturally, that the actual practice of reconstructing and writing history will vary according to the nature of the evidence (cf. Thompson), and the end result is likely to be more tentative or less tentative, depending on the sources. The Second Temple period has a number of problems parallel to those of the First Temple period, but because the biblical text is not involved for much of the time, it may help us to approach the question more neutrally.

Thomas Thompson asks a number of questions about the Second Temple period with his usual acute perception, especially the latter part of this period which he sees as the primary context of the biblical text. Those of us who specialize in this period (e.g. Davies, Grabbe) would thoroughly agree, for example, that Judaism was an entity well integrated into the process of Hellenization.[4] Some of us are also on record as rejecting the existence of a 'normative Judaism' before 70 CE.[5] Unfortunately, there seems to be a recent counter movement back toward the idea of a Pharisee-dominated Judaism, so vigilance in this quarter is by no means unwarranted.[6]

One of the outcomes emerging starkly from the discussion is the need to focus on specific areas, topics or problems. It was far too easy to go round in circles and to talk past one another. For this reason, it was decided that the next meeting will concentrate on the subject of 'the exile'. A number of other topics or foci are potential subjects for future meetings.

A few hours of discussion are hardly going to resolve some major and long-term problems, and it is not at all surprising that there was still a considerable difference of approach on a number of issues. Yet it seemed evident to me that there was movement, that overall our positions had shifted somewhat closer even if we still differ considerably in some areas. This was encouraging, because it was clear (and will be clear to anyone who reads the papers in this volume) that we did not all start from the same perspective by any means. We still have a long way to go before understanding each other, much less coming to a common agreement. Indeed, I expect that in the end we shall all

---

4. See Grabbe, *Judaism from Cyrus to Hadrian*, chapter 3, for a survey of relevant literature and discussion of the issues involved. The question is complex and is still too often answered simplistically in some widely used treatments.

5. I said so twenty years ago ('Orthodoxy in First Century Judaism: What Are the Issues?', *JSJ* 8 (1977), pp. 149-53, but I was only following my elders and betters. We are all indebted to Morton Smith's seminal article, 'Palestinian Judaism in the First Century', in M. Davis (ed.), *Israel: Its Role in Civilization* (New York: Harper, 1956), pp. 67-81. For an extensive discussion, see chapter 8 of my *Judaism from Cyrus to Hadrian*.

6. See the arguments and references in my '4QMMT and Second Temple Judaism', in F. García Martínez (ed.), *Legal Texts and Legal Issues: Second Meeting of the IOQS, Cambridge 1995* (Leiden: Brill, in press).

have differences on various issues, but we do not yet know to what extent we agree or disagree on many points, and only a good deal of further discussion will clarify the situation. What is encouraging to me, though, is that we were able to sit down together and debate the issues from different perspectives in a reasonable atmosphere and feel that we were not just wasting our time.

The most successful outcome of our first meeting, in my opinion, is that we agreed to meet again next year and that there was still considerable enthusiasm for doing so.

INDEXES

INDEX OF REFERENCES

INDEX OF AUTHORS

JOURNAL FOR THE STUDY OF THE OLD TESTAMENT
SUPPLEMENT SERIES